DAVID D. LEWIS

Computational Morphology

ACL–MIT Press Series in Natural Language Processing
Aravind K. Joshi, Karen Sparck Jones, and Mark Y. Liberman, editors

Speaking: From Intention to Articulation
Willem Levelt

Plan Recognition in Natural Language Dialogue
Sandra Carberry

Cognitive Models of Speech Processing: Psycholinguistic and Computational Perspectives
edited by Gerry T. M. Altmann

Computational Morphology: Practical Mechanisms for the English Lexicon
Graeme D. Ritchie, Graham J. Russell, Alan W. Black, and Stephen G. Pulman

Computational Morphology

Practical Mechanisms for the English Lexicon

Graeme D. Ritchie
Department of Artificial Intelligence, University of Edinburgh

Graham J. Russell
Institut Dalle Molle pour les études sémantiques et cognitives (ISSCO), University of Geneva

Alan W. Black
Department of Artificial Intelligence, University of Edinburgh

Stephen G. Pulman
Computer Laboratory, University of Cambridge, and SRI International Cambridge Computer Science Research Centre

A Bradford Book
The MIT Press
Cambridge, Massachusetts
London, England

This book was printed and bound in the United States of America.

Library of Congress Cataloging-in-Publication Data

Computational morphology: practical mechanisms for the English lexicon / Graeme D. Ritchie . . . [et al.].
p. cm—(ACL-MIT Press series in natural-language processing)
"A Bradford book."
Includes bibliographical references and index.
ISBN 0-262-18146-0
1. Grammar, Comparative and general—Morphology—Data processing, 2. Lexicology—Data processing, 3. English language—Morphology—Data processing. I. Ritchie, Graeme D. II. Series.
P241.C65 1992
415'.0724—dc20 91-810
CIP

Contents

Preface

The work described in this text was carried out at the Universities of Edinburgh and Cambridge between 1984 and 1987, with funding from the UK Science and Engineering Research Council and the Alvey Directorate (grant no. GR/C/79114 (IKBS 008), "A Dictionary and Morphological Analyser for English Language Processing Systems"). This was one of three closely related projects (all supported by SERC/Alvey) which came to be known as the "Alvey Natural Language Tools Projects" — Henry Thompson and John Phillips (University of Edinburgh) implemented a feature-grammar parser, and Ted Briscoe, Claire Grover (University of Lancaster), Bran Boguraev and John Carroll (University of Cambridge) devised a large grammar of English sentences, together with a software support system for testing and experimenting with grammars. We are indebted to these colleagues for discussions, arguments, and ideas, and for generally contributing to a combined framework which allowed various issues in computational linguistics to be investigated in a particularly thorough fashion. Thanks are also due to Dr Karen Sparck Jones, who, as coordinator of natural language research within the Alvey Programme, played an important role in initiating and linking the three projects.

We would also like to thank various people who provided assistance or advice in the course of the work — Kimmo Koskenniemi, for detailed technical discussions; Robert Rae, for arranging distribution of our software; Henry Thompson, Jo Calder, Robert Dale, Greg Michaelson, and an anonymous referee for giving us valuable comments on the draft of this book. Some of the work reported in Chapter 8 was supported by the CEC (DGXIII/Eurotra) under a contract to SRI International, Cambridge.

AWB would like to thank the Department of General Linguistics at the University of Helsinki for acting as hosts for a visit in 1987, and the Centre for the New Oxford English Dictionary, Waterloo, Canada, for providing a fellowship which allowed him to visit the Centre and carry out useful experiments with a large lexicon.

The software and data files (which contain the linguistic data and rules) for the full set of Alvey Natural Language Tools running under Common Lisp is available in computer readable form. At the time of writing, copies have been supplied to about fifty institutions throughout the world. Details of the distributed system can be obtained from:

The Software Secretary,
Artificial Intelligence Applications Institution,
University of Edinburgh,
80 South Bridge,
Edinburgh EH1 1HN.
email: aiai@ed.ac.uk

GDR, GJR, AWB, SGP
April 1991.

1 Introduction

1.1 The need for a computational lexicon

Within computational linguistics, there is an active and growing interest in designing computer interfaces which will allow the user to interact with systems such as databases or teaching systems in natural languages such as English, instead of stylised formal languages such as those traditionally used to interrogate databases. The problem of getting a computer program to "understand" English sentences and phrases is not just a (very difficult) problem in advanced automation — it also raises most of the essential theoretical problems of linguistics in a very immediate way, and hence is of interest to those carrying out fundamental research into the nature of language, as well as to those with particular applications in mind.

Although it would be a great over-simplification to suggest that a consensus has formed over the architecture of such *natural language front ends* (NLFEs), it is fair to say that most practical systems assume that there is some module which acts as a store of information about words of the language. This component, usually called the *dictionary* or *lexicon* is used directly by a sentence processing component, usually called a *parser* or *analyser*. Even models which are not generally concerned with computational or processing issues (typically those developed within theoretical linguistics) include some similar proposal in their decomposition of the grammatical and semantic mechanisms. In such non-processing models, the lexicon is usually related to some abstract sentence grammar, rather than to a program which analyses sentences.

We are consciously ignoring here the particular issues involved in speech processing, since that raises problems of segmentation, phonetics and phonology which are beyond our present remit; it will be assumed that sentences are in a machine-readable form, using normal orthography, punctuation and spacing. Loosely speaking, this means that we shall be dealing with separate "words" as this notion is commonly understood, rather than unsegmented streams of phonetic data. Our theoretical mechanism makes no particular use of the concept of a word, but we shall continue to employ that term for informal expository purposes.

We shall be examining the nature of this lexical component, from both a practical and a theoretical standpoint. Among the questions we shall be considering are:

- What information must the dictionary provide to the sentence-level component, whether that component is viewed as a grammar or as a parsing program?
- How can this information be computed for a given word, in a manner which is both general and relatively efficient?
- How can such information be specified in a perspicuous and economical way by the designer of the dictionary?
- What formal notations (such as rules) are suitable for controlling these various computations and specifications, subject to the dual goals of ease of use and computational practicality?

Although we shall have as our guiding aim the need to construct a practical computational lexicon which could be used realistically and flexibly within a NLFE, we shall also take account of general theoretical issues, so that the proposals we make should be of relevance to non-computational linguistics. This slightly hybrid methodology results in certain guidelines:

- Linguistic descriptions should be stated as abstract rules, not directly as program.
- We should be very careful in deciding which concepts are inherent in the software (our equivalent of the linguist's "universal") and which are merely part of our description of English linguistic phenomena.
- Linguistic descriptions should, as far as possible, meet the standards of elegance and generality normally sought within theoretical linguistics.
- Since the software is intended for a variety of users, facilities should be flexible enough to allow reasonable experimentation with other linguistic descriptions.
- Where possible, definitions should be declarative.
- Rule formalisms and other devices should be defined precisely, not just used as informal expository notations (notice that defining something precisely is *not* the same as defining it *declaratively*).

- All definitions of formalisms should be amenable to realistic (i.e. relatively efficient) implementation.

There is of course a certain amount of conflict between these aims, and it is necessary to make compromises. However, the commitment to providing a general purpose tool which is moderately efficient will override, in some cases, the aims of declarativeness or complete linguistic elegance.

This research involved the implementation of a medium-sized computational lexicon for English, and most of our discussion in later chapters will be centred on that experimental system, and we shall wherever possible use examples from that work.

First, however, we shall give an introductory review, couched in very general informal terms, of the issues involved, before proceeding to discuss, in later chapters, the particular solutions that we believe to be appropriate.

1.2 What is the lexicon?

If we assume that a NLFE takes in sentences in the form of a sequence of separate typewritten words, from which it has to compute a meaning and subsequently a response, then the role of the lexicon is to associate linguistic information with words of the language. The information associated with a word is called its *lexical entry.* Many words are ambiguous, in the sense that they have more than one meaning, or more than one set of grammatical properties, so the lexicon must have the facility either to associate several lexical entries with a word, or to include several options within a single entry. Most work in theoretical linguistics, even when discussing lexically relevant issues such as word structure, makes very few substantive or detailed proposals regarding the way in which the content of a lexical entry is specified, or the way in which the association between word and entry is defined. Practical implementations often rely on fairly ad hoc mechanisms, sometimes blurring important theoretical distinctions.

Once we have developed our various linguistic representations in later chapters, we shall be able to give a more precise definition of what we postulate as the basic contents of a lexical entry. For the moment, it is enough to indicate in general terms the four linguistically relevant fields or components of each of our entries:

1. Citation field. This is a sequence of characters in a pre-defined *lexical alphabet.* It could include non-English alphabetic symbols; for example, we use the plus sign "`+`" to mark most affixes. Since blank spaces are permitted, phrases such as "`New York`" or "`by and large`" could be included as single items.
2. Syntactic features. This is a set of morpho-syntactic properties associated with the phrase, word or part word for which this is the entry.
3. Phonological field. This is a representation of the pronunciation of the phrase, word or part word represented in the entry. As we are not exploring phonetic or phonological issues, we shall have nothing further to say about this field, but it is included for completeness.
4. Semantic field. This is an expression in whatever semantic representation language is chosen by the lexicon writer. As with the phonological field, we are, in this work, not concerned with the content of this field, but it was included to allow others to experiment and for compatibility with linguistic practice.

Some of the issues we shall be examining are concerned with the construction of the lexical entries (e.g. how to make it simpler for the user to insert information into the lexicon) and some are concerned with the look-up process (i.e. how to organise the computation of the lexical entries for a particular word). As we shall see, it is not always obvious which questions relate to which of these two issues.

1.3 Morphology

It is clear that the words of a language are not totally separate items without any similarities between them or regularities within their structure. It has been traditional within linguistics to describe the regularities in the structure of words by postulating that a single word can be viewed as made up of one or more smaller units, called *morphemes.* These are traditionally classed into two kinds — *free morphemes* are able to act as words in isolation (e.g. `think`, `permanent`, `local`); and *bound morphemes* can operate only as parts of other words (e.g. `ise`, `ing`, `re`). In English, the latter usually take the form of *affixes*; those which come at the end of the word are called *suffixes*, those coming at the front are called *prefixes*. The morpheme (often a free morpheme) which forms the central part of the word, roughly speaking, is often called the *stem*. A word can be made up of one or more morphemes, e.g.

`think`	stem `think`
`rethink`	prefix `re`, stem `think`
`localise`	stem `local`, suffix `ise`
`denationalise`	prefix `de`, stem `nation`, suffixes `al`, `ise`

The study of word structure is referred to as *morphology*, and this is often subdivided into two kinds — *inflectional morphology* and *derivational morphology*.

Inflectional morphology is typified in English by the adding of endings to verb stems to form various parts of the verb (`like + s` → `likes`), or the adding of endings to form plural nouns (`dog + s` → `dogs`). Inflectional morphology has certain characteristics:

1. Systematic: adding a particular affix to a stem has the same grammatical or semantic effect for all stems; for example, making a noun plural.
2. Productive: new additions to the language automatically conform to the rules for affixation; for example, a new verb will acquire all possible forms (past tense, progressive form, etc.) immediately.
3. Preservation of category: the broad grammatical category of the word is not altered by the inflection process — verbs remain verbs, nouns remain nouns.

Derivational morphology can be thought of as the formation of new words from existing stems, such as `national` from `nation + al`, or `localise` from `local + ise`. It typically has the following characteristics:

1. Unsystematic: adding the same affix to two different stems may have radically different semantic effects; for example, compare `criticise` and `localise`. It could be argued that idiosyncratic examples (e.g. `criticise`) should not be viewed as morphological formations, but should be seen as single morphemes which accidentally look like non-atomic forms; see point (2) below.

2. Partly productive: it would be misleading to say that new words in the language automatically undergo derivational morphological processes. For example, when the verb `gazump` came into British English (around 1970), it did not automatically give rise to `gazumpment` or `gazumpation`). However, new morphological forms are often created (e.g. `Thatcherisation`) which demonstrate that these internal patterns are not merely historical relics — they reflect rules of formation which native speakers can use today.
3. Category alteration: the words created by affixation may differ in category from that of the stem; for example, `national` is an adjective formed from a noun, `localise` is a verb formed from an adjective. The category may in some cases be unaltered — `communism` is a noun formed from a noun.

Morphology is of practical relevance to constructing and using a dictionary in a NLFE, for the following reasons:

1. Smaller dictionaries: if there is no need to store every form of a regular verb because the various forms can be computed by rule, the dictionary may be smaller; for a language like Spanish, this would be a large saving.
2. Ease of entering data: the user need not enter every possible form of a word, only the stem.
3. Neologisms: the system will be able to recognise words formed by derivational morphology, even if they have not been seen before; for example, `reprogrammability`.
4. Look-up: it may be possible to have a simpler or faster look up process based on the morphological analysis of the input word. (This is far from certain — sophisticated morphological analysis may not be worthwhile for simple applications.)

If a system is to operate by using morphological analysis as part of its look-up process for input words, two of the most crucial issues to be considered are — the segmentation into morphemes, and the computation of the grammatical characteristics of the overall word.

1.4 Segmentation and orthography

If a lexical access mechanism operates by morphological analysis, it will almost certainly have to segment the sequence of characters in the word into morphemes. This is not a trivial task. Although certain simple cases look straightforward:

`looking` → `look + ing`
`rethink` → `re + think`

the segmentation cannot be done simply by spotting a familiar affix and detaching it — consider

`*thing` → `th + ing`
`*read` → `re + ad`

More complex words would confuse such a naive algorithm even more — `assassination` contains `a` (three times), `s` (four times), `as`, `ass`, (twice each), `sin`, `in`, `nation`, `at`, `ion` (the word, not the suffix), and `on`, none of which are relevant to the morphological decomposition (`assassin + ate + ion`).

A further complication for the segmentation process is the fact that minor alterations in spelling (which may be reflected in the pronunciation) often occur at the boundaries between morphemes. For example:

`loved` → `love + ed` [extra `e`]
`churches` → `church + s` [deleted `e`]
`flies` → `fly + s` [`i` to `y`, delete `e`]

Such phenomena have been called *graphotactic*, or *morphographemic*[1] (there is already a linguistic term *morphophonemic* to refer to phonological variations related to grammatical structure). Although these effects are systematic enough to merit rules, there is no standard descriptive technique which could be incorporated into a segmentation process. However, we have developed a workable system based on recent work by Koskenniemi [Kosk83a, Kosk83b, Kosk84], the details of which will be explained in Chapter 2.

1 Martin Kay is sometimes credited with inventing this term.

1.5 Word structure

If we suppose that we have a way of correctly segmenting a word into morphemes, including the readjustment of the spelling into some standard form for the stem and the affix(es), there is then the question of combining the grammatical information about each morpheme into a composite label for the whole word. From a linguistic point of view, there is also the issue of *morphotactics* — which morphemes are allowed to combine with each other to form valid words? Again, there is no standard method for describing such regularities. Whatever system is used, it should take into account certain aspects of the way English words operate:

1. Each affix can be attached only to stems (or partial words) of a particular category.
2. The broad grammatical category of the whole word may be the same as the stem (e.g. `likes` is a verb) or may depend on the affixes (e.g. `nationalise`)
3. Both the stem and the affix may contribute information to the overall details for the word; for example, the fact that `inserts` is a transitive verb (i.e. a verb which takes an object) comes from the stem, while the fact that it is third person singular comes from the affix.

Hence, some simple form of compositional rule is needed to specify the possible morpheme combinations and what the results of the combinations are. This is directly analogous to the question of constituent structure in the grammatical analysis of sentences, and the solution we shall be proposing in Chapter 3 depends directly on this parallel — we use a feature grammar roughly of the sort proposed by Gazdar et al. [Gazd85b] to characterise word structures. (See also [Bear86] for similar proposals.)

1.6 The unit of storage

The notion of morphological analysis raises the question of what the units stored in the lexicon should be — complete words, or individual morphemes? In fact, if complete words are to be stored, then there is no point in performing morphological analysis as part of the look-up process — all that is needed is a vast table, and the various advantages listed earlier are then lost. While this would be acceptable for a very small system, it seems unattractive for a system with a larger vocabulary.

One could also consider storing phrases (cf. [Beck75]) but that is not an easy option, as further issues then arise. For example, there is the need to consider the words within the phrase as well as treating the phrase as a fixed idiom (`kick the bucket` could be an idiomatic phrase meaning `die`, or could be a literal phrase meaning `strike the pail with a foot`), and coping with inflections inside a phrase (`kick`*ed* `the bucket`). Moreover, items which behave like single words can also be split up in a sentence (`please log off` vs. `please log me off`). In general, the problems involved in a serious treatment of phrasal items are beyond the scope of this work, although we do allow for the very limited case of a completely fixed sequence of words such as `by and large` appearing in the lexicon (see Chapter 6 for further discussion).

1.7 Lexical redundancy

There are many regularities and recurring patterns in the information stored in the lexical entries, quite apart from the regularities in the shape of the words (as discussed above). Many entries are very similar, and many entries contain information which is predictable from other data in the lexicon. This leads to the notion of having *lexical redundancy rules* of various kinds, which express these regularities and which allow a reduced amount of information to be held explicitly within the lexicon. This has the advantages of permitting a smaller dictionary and making it easier to enter data, since only minimal entries need be provided by the user, with the rest being computed by the system.

Various sorts of regularities may occur, depending on the grammatical theory adopted and the overall design of the dictionary:

1. Predictable information: within a single lexical entry, some of the grammatical information may be predictable from other markings there. For example, if verbs in English are subclassified into *auxiliaries* (`can`, `do`, `be`) and *main verbs* (`take`, `derive`), then the entry for `do` need only be marked as `auxiliary` — the fact that it is a `verb` is computable by a rule which embodies the classification of

verbs.

2. Default markings: for certain grammatical possibilities, there may be one value which is the "normal" or "assumed" value. For example, it might be possible to assume that all verbs in the dictionary are main verbs unless marked as auxiliaries, thus saving the need to explicitly label virtually every verb as `main`. That is, lexical entries could be left partly unspecified, with *default rules* to fill in the blank values. Notice that this is subtly different from (1) above — *predictable* information is where one aspect of the entry helps to fix another aspect quite unequivocally; a *default* rule does not affect all entries, only those entries in which there is no information to the contrary.

3. Consistency checks: it may be possible to state rules about the possible shapes of lexical entries, and to have the system check the data provided by the user to see if there are any contradictions or linguistically incorrect markings.

4. Related entries: the presence of certain entries in the dictionary may indicate that there must also be other entries with some systematic relationship to them. For example, for some transitive verbs (i.e. verbs which take a direct object, like `see` or `calculate`) there is a corresponding intransitive verb (i.e. one which takes no object). The intransitive entries can be inserted by rule (unless the transitivity information is being held within a single entry for the verb, in which case this falls under case (1) above). To take another example, for most regular transitive verbs there is a corresponding "passive" form:

`Mary beats John`	[ACTIVE FORM – direct object]
`John is beaten by Mary`	[PASSIVE FORM – phrase with `by`]

   It might be possible to incorporate this into the dictionary by having the passive forms of verbs inserted automatically for transitive verbs (except any explicitly marked as exceptions).

The dictionary system we shall propose contains all of these forms of lexical rules (see Chapter 5).

1.8 Preprocessing and look-up

As mentioned earlier, there are two important processing stages in the use of a dictionary — construction (i.e. building the lexical entries) and use (i.e. looking up words). For some of the rule mechanisms discussed above, particularly those concerned with lexical redundancy, it is not at once obvious which of these processes they affect. One possible approach is to have a significant preprocessing stage, during which lexical rules operate to expand the data supplied by the user, thus constructing a much larger and fully specified dictionary. The look-up process then uses morphological analysis, but not lexical redundancy, in its computation. In such a scheme, the only practical advantage gained from the lexical redundancy rules is the reduction of labour on the part of the person who constructs the dictionary — the space required is not reduced. Nevertheless, there are still the theoretical advantages that the lexicon as written by the linguist is more compact and elegant, and that linguistic regularities in the lexicon are explicitly stated.

This is the approach which we have adopted in the system which we shall be outlining in later chapters.

1.9 What this book is about

This book is *not* a general review of computational work on morphology; rather, it describes an integrated approach to some of these issues, which is both theoretically sound and computationally practical. Our methodology in investigating the various questions outlined earlier has been to develop linguistic formalisms of various kinds, suitable for stating precise and elegant descriptions of morphological phenomena, and to devise a significant description of English using these notations. (The English description is compatible with a broad coverage English sentence grammar written by Boguraev, Briscoe, Carroll and Grover [Grov89], but we shall not be describing that grammar here.)

We have implemented some fairly general software modules (mainly interpreters and compilers) which manipulate rules and lexical entries written in our notation. These modules are implemented as a set of Common Lisp programs which allow the user to specify lexical entries in a relatively brief form, to have these entries fleshed out using lexical redundancy rules, and then to use the resulting lexicon to look up individual words in a way which is specified by linguistic rules of morphological structure. That is, the whole system has its behaviour controlled by rules written in linguistic formalisms which have a meaning independent of this particular implementation.

This book is split into eight chapters and various appendices. Chapters 2 to 5 give a description of the theoretical components (and their related formalisms) that we propose for the lexicon. Chapter 2 describes the history and motivation for our mechanism for segmenting words into morphemes. Chapter 3 describes the rule formalisms for defining the internal structure and properties of words. Chapter 4 discusses how various linguistic generalisations can be extracted from the word structure rules and phrased as more abstract *feature passing conventions.* Chapter 5 defines some fairly basic (but very general) notions of lexical redundancy rules which can be used to expand a basic lexicon into a richer set of lexical entries.

Chapter 6 gives a description of a significant subset of English morphology using the formalisms described in Chapters 2 to 5, Chapter 7 gives details of a computer system which implements these formalisms, and finally Chapter 8 discusses some of the limitations of our proposals, and some ways in which these could be remedied, taking account of some more recent research.

The appendices include more detailed information about the formal definitions of the various notations, and a description of the English lexicon.

2 Morphographemics

As indicated in Chapter 1, there is a need for a mechanism to segment words into their component morphemes, taking into account any orthographic variations which occur between the *surface form* (the word as normally printed) and the *lexical form* (the standardised spellings of the various morphemes). To be more precise, this issue can be broken down into several questions:

- How can segmentation be specified?
- How can spelling changes be specified?
- How can the solutions to these problems be integrated with the specification of the set of morphemes in the language (the lexicon)?
- How can these mechanisms be integrated with a way of specifying the valid combinations of morphemes in the language (morphotactics)?
- What is a practical computational interpretation of these specifications?

In this chapter, we shall outline an integrated set of solutions to these questions, by presenting a formalism, a procedural interpretation for that formalism, and conventions which relate these mechanisms to a lexicon of morphemes and to a formal statement of morphotactic rules. As our solution is essentially adopted from work by others, this chapter is almost entirely concerned that earlier research, as well as some subsequent work. In the earlier sections of this chapter, the emphasis will be on the question of specifying spelling changes in a computationally interpretable way, but we shall refer to the other aspects later on.

2.1 Generative phonology

In the field of formal, or semi-formal, linguistics, particularly Chomskian generative linguistics, there has been very little consideration of rules which describe orthographic representations of words — the emphasis has been on spoken language, so that rules define phonological and phonetic variation, rather than accidents of spelling. The typical, and perhaps definitive, work on generative phonology of the 1960s was [Chom68], which explored many aspects of the formalisation of phonological description using detailed evidence from English phonology. Within this general paradigm, individual phonological/phonetic segments were represented as sets of values for *distinctive features*. For example, the sound normally written as "p" could have been written as:

```
[- vocalic, + consonantal, - high, - back,
 - low, + anterior, - coronal, - voice, -continuant,
 - nasal, - strident]
```

where each named feature (e.g. `vocalic`) is allowed two possible values (+ or -) and not all features within the system need to appear explicitly in the representation of a segment; i.e. the feature sets can be underspecified. The advantages of this notation, particularly the use of underspecification, were outlined in [Hall62].

Phonological rules were generally written in the form

```
S  ->  P / Q __ R : C
```

meaning "the segment S is re-written as the segment P when in the context of segments (or sequences of segments) Q and R, providing condition C holds", where either Q or R or C might well be null. For example [Chom68, p.349]:

```
[ - voc, + son]  ->  [- voice] / ___ [- voice, - cons]
```

represents the rule that nonstrident continuants (such as `f` or `v`) are devoiced before voiceless vowels.

Occasionally the portions S and P would contain more than one segment, in which case a notation like that often used for syntactic transformations was used; for example:

```
Structural Description:
     [+voc, -cons]  [-cons]  [+voc, -cons]
           1           2           3

Structural Change:
       1 2 3  ->  2 1 3   ; except when 2 = 3 = [a]
```

The assumed arrangement was that there was an underlying sequence of phonological segments, each segment being represented as a set of values for one or more distinctive features, and that rules operated to transform this underlying form (which was closely related to the grammatical and morphological descriptive levels of the abstract linguistic model) into a fully specified surface form (which was intended to be compatible with the phonetic description of the language). The representational vocabularies at the two levels (underlying and surface) were the same — sets of distinctive feature distinctive features values — which meant that it was quite possible for one rule to operate on a sequence which had been produced by the operation of another rule.

Various questions arise about the applicability of rules to sequences. For example, consider the situation in which rules $R1$ and $R2$ are applicable to some sequence S, but the operation of either of the rules will produce a sequence which is not a suitable input to the other rule. What is the appropriate interpretation in such a case? This led to the issue of rule ordering — were rules to be given some sort of priority or ordering, so that rules earlier in the ordering were applied first? Or should a phonological grammar simply be an unordered set of rules, which were defined as applying whenever they matched the sequence of segments under consideration? The evidence which was brought to bear on such questions included the consequences of allowing rules to *feed* or *bleed* each other. A rule $R1$ was said to *feed* a rule $R2$ if the application of $R1$ would produce a sequence to which $R2$ would then apply, although the original input to $R1$ would not have been a possible input to $R2$ if left unchanged. Similarly, $R1$ was said to *bleed* $R2$ if the operation of $R1$ transformed a possible input to $R2$ into a sequence which could not then have $R2$ applied to it. Although some of these questions were discussed in the generative literature, there were a number of different proposals as to how best to resolve them, none of which were wholly successful. It must be emphasised that none of these mechanisms was intended as a potential computational device. The aim was to provide an elegant declarative statement of the relationship between underlying and surface forms. Although there was a notion of rules transforming sequences of segments, and the application of one rule following another, this was merely an abstract way of characterising that relationship. Chomsky and Halle's definitions were more explicit than most proposals within generative linguistics, but they did not explore all the formal characteristics of their mechanisms.

2.2 Formalising phonological rules

Johnson [John72] examined in detail some of the formal issues that are involved in the sort of phonological descriptive system that Chomsky and Halle were proposing. He considered three sorts of rule, which he termed *iterative*, *simultaneous* and *linear*, and showed how these rules, when fully defined, were equivalent in expressive power to various sorts of transducers. (He also tentatively outlined a further form which he called *linear iterative*, but did not advocate the use of rules of this kind.)

Johnson accepted the overall generative framework in which sequences of sets of distinctive features were mapped into other sequences by the rule application which matched both the portion being transformed and the surrounding context. His rules, like those of Chomsky and Halle, had a left-hand side describing a segment to be rewritten, and a right-hand side describing the context *and* the rewritten form.

An *iterative rule* seemed to capture one of the ideas that generative phonology had considered, in which a rule was applied to its own output as many times as it matched the sequence of segments, ceasing to apply only when the rule no longer matched. (For simplicity, we shall assume for the moment that all rules are what Johnson called *elementary rules* — that is, they contain no abbreviatory devices, only complete phonological feature specifications.)

A *simultaneous rule* mapped a sequence S into a sequence S' if and only if S and S' could be partitioned into (possibly empty) subsequences $P_1, \ldots, P_n$ and $P'_1, \ldots, P'_n$ respectively such that the even-numbered pairs (P_i, P'_i) were valid applications of the rule (i.e. P_i was mapped into P'_i by the rule) and the odd-numbered pairs were such that the rule did not apply to P_i and $P_i = P'_i$. In defining the applications of the rule, any contextual portions were matched against the original sequence S (or $P_1, \ldots, P_n$), not the corresponding parts of S'. Since we are considering elementary (fully specified) rules, "matching" was essentially ordinary equality — the use of more complex matching is embodied in the conventions for expanding rule schemata (see below) into elementary rules. (These are merely outlines of Johnson's much more detailed and precise definitions.)

Linear rules were subdivided into two varieties — *left linear* and *right linear*. A right linear rule could be thought of as scanning the initial sequence from left to right, rewriting each portion of the sequence that matched its conditions. A sequence S was mapped into a sequence S' if there were partitions $P_1, \ldots, P_n$ of S and $P'_1, \ldots, P'_n$ of S' such that all the odd-numbered pairs (P_i, P'_i) result from an application of the rule, with the left-context part matching $P'_1, \ldots, P'_{i-1}$ (i.e. the already transformed material) and the right-context part matching $P_{i+1}, \ldots, P_n$ (i.e. the remaining part of the original sequence). Moreover, the even-numbered pairs should be such that $P_i = P'_i$ and no application of the rule (with left and right contexts matching as described) could re-write any portion of P_i. That is, the even-numbered elements of the partition were unaffected areas which the rule did not alter. A left linear rule was exactly comparable, but scanned the sequence from the right to the left.

Johnson rejected the use of iterative rules (which were essentially what Chomsky and Halle had been proposing) on the grounds of excessive power, since an arbitrary rewriting system (a Chomsky type 0 grammar) can be simulated by a finite sequence of such rules, with or without the use of simultaneous rules; however, a system using simultaneous rules alone is equivalent to a finite transducer (see below), which is a weaker and hence linguistically more acceptable device. Linear rules are of a similar power to simultaneous rules, and, on the basis of some phonological evidence, Johnson speculated that it would be feasible to rely solely on linear rules (right and left).

Generative phonology, like the rest of generative linguistics, had always used various abbreviatory notations and conventions to allow families of related rules to be compressed into a single, more elegant statement of the linguistic regularities. Johnson also formalised this aspect of phonological rules, by defining a rule to be a schema representing a set of elementary (unabbreviated) rules, and by providing recursive definitions of what it meant for a schema to subsume (i.e. include within its interpretation) a particular elementary rule. That is, Johnson did not use schemata merely to conflate expressions denoting sequences of phonological segments, but added to the basic vocabulary the symbols `->`, `/`, and `___` (i.e. the punctuation used in the statement of rules) and allowed a rule to be, in general, a schema which represented a set of elementary rules. The definitions of rule application summarised earlier were then generalised to such composite rules, by stipulating that a rule schema applied to a sequence if and only if one of the elementary rules it represented applied to that sequence. The devices which he allowed for the construction of rules included:

- concatenation
- disjunction
- conjunction
- iteration (zero or more occurrences of an item)
- variables ranging over distinctive feature values
- variables ranging over single phonological segments
- appending of Boolean conditions to a schema

Although this repertoire appears very powerful, and certainly facilitates the succinct expression of linguistic generalisations, it is important to notice that, because there is a finite vocabulary of distinctive features within the system, and a finite set of values for these features, any schema not involving the iteration symbol could in principle be rewritten as a finite set of elementary rules, even if it contained variables or attached conditions. (It is not entirely clear what effect the inclusion of conditions has, as Johnson does not go into much detail about this aspect.) Thus this notational system amounts to a way of specifying regular sets of elementary rules, where the traditional definition of a regular set over a given alphabet A is as follows:

> The empty set is a regular set; the set containing just the empty string is a regular set; for any element $a \in A$, $\{a\}$ is a regular set; if P and Q are regular sets, so are the sets $\{x.y \mid x \in P, y \in Q\}$ (i.e. the concatenation of elements), the union of P and Q, and the set of indefinitely many concatenations of an element of P (cf. [Aho72, p. 103]).

As the schematising devices include conjunction, an entire phonological grammar can be written as a single rule schema, providing that all the rules in the grammar are all of the same sort — iterative, simultaneous, right linear or left linear — since the mode of application of a rule is defined to be the same throughout all the elementary rules subsumed by a schema. It is not wholly clear how Johnson envisaged a grammar defining the well-formedness of a sequence in the case where this conflation into a single rule is not feasible.

2.3 Transducers

Johnson also explored the question of what class of string-processing automaton would be equivalent in power to each sort of rule. Since the rules do not merely accept or reject strings (i.e. define membership of some string-language), but transform strings into other strings, the appropriate kind of device is not a recognising automaton but a *transducer*; that is, an automaton with *input* and *output*. The normal definition of a *finite state transducer* is as follows (based on the definition in [Aho72, p. 224] of a *finite transducer*):

> A finite (state) transducer consists of a finite set of states (one of which is designated an initial state, and some of which are designated as final states), a finite set of input symbols, a finite set of output symbols, and a transition mapping which indicates, for each pair of a state and an input symbol, a successor state and a sequence of zero or more elements of the output alphabet.

The informal interpretation of these definitions is that if a scanner started at one end of an input string and in the initial state of the transducer, it could generate an output string by following transitions which were indicated for the current input symbol, and outputting the output symbol(s) for that transition. If this process caused the scanner to be in a final state of the transducer when the input string was exhausted, then a successful generation would have occurred. It is fairly normal to assume that each transition specifies exactly one output symbol, rather than a string.

One alternative interpretation that is sometimes given for such a transducer is as a *two-tape recogniser*. That is, it is viewed as a fairly simple generalisation of a traditional finite state automaton in which two input strings are scanned, and a transition may be taken only if both the input symbol and the other ("output") symbol associated with it match the current symbols in the corresponding input strings.

A transducer is normally referred to as *deterministic* if, in any state, the input symbol currently being scanned uniquely determines which transition to take. Notice that the question of whether a transducer is deterministic or not depends on the exact interpretation adopted. If each transition is assumed to be defined by just one input symbol, and produces as a result an output symbol (i.e. the transducer scans just one string and creates another output string), then determinism has to be defined in terms of the single input symbol uniquely determining the choice of transition. On the other hand, if the transducer is taken to be simply a two-tape recogniser, then it will be deterministic if the *two* symbols for each transition, taken together, uniquely determine the choice of the next state. Consequently, a non-deterministic two-tape recogniser would be amenable to the standard algorithm for determinising a finite state automaton [Hopc79], and so an equivalent deterministic recogniser could always be constructed. However, for a *genuine* transducer (i.e. one which produces output in response to input), such determinisation may not be possible (cf. [Bart87, Section 5.6.4]).

Johnson made a distinction between a *right transducer* (which is a deterministic finite state transducer which scans the input string from left to right), and a *left transducer*, which scans deterministically from right to left.[1] Johnson showed that a single (simultaneous or linear) rule schema can be simulated by a pair $(M1, M2)$ where $M1$ is a left transducer, $M2$ is a right transducer, and the output of $M1$ supplies the input to $M2$.

Some years later, but apparently independently, Kay and Kaplan (in widely cited but notoriously unpublished work) investigated the relationship between phonological rules and finite state transducers, with a more direct interest in the computational ramifications of such a representation. They were particularly interested in the use of established finite state techniques to compile a phonological grammar automatically into a set of finite state transducers, and to combine this set of transducers serially into one single (probably very large) transducer. Not only did this approach provide a well-defined theoretical framework in which the properties of rules could be explored, it held out the hope that there would be an efficient implementation of the rules, since finite state machines are efficiently implementable. Kay and Kaplan did not use pairs of left and right transducers, but relied upon conventional finite state transducers as defined above (they were not adopting Johnson's

---

1 There is great scope for terminological confusion here. Johnson also introduced a further kind of device, due to Schutzenberger[Schu61], and called it a *finite transducer*, but that is *not* what Aho and Ullman [Aho72] define as a "finite transducer". As noted earlier, the latter has since come to be called a "finite state transducer". Schutzenberger had shown that a pair of left and right transducers, such as Johnson uses, is equivalent to a single (Schutzenberger-style) "finite transducer".

particular formalisation of phonological rules). We shall return to this strand of work in Section 2.8.1 below.

2.4 The two-level model

Following on from Kay and Kaplan's work, Koskenniemi ([Kosk83a, Kosk83b, Kosk84]) proposed a scheme with the fundamental restriction that all rules referred to the same *two* levels (the lexical and the surface), thus eliminating the possibility that a rule could operate on the output of another rule — no *feeding* or *bleeding*, as described in Section 2.1 above, would be possible. The symbols at these levels were atomic items representing either *phonemes* or typewritten characters; that is, Koskenniemi had moved away from using matrices of phonological features to describe segments. The rules were presented in two possible forms — as a high-level rule notation and as finite state transducers.[2] Although the rule notation was intended to supply the definitive linguistic statement of the rules, it was (in the original implementation) not actually used to compute relationships between surface and lexical forms. In principle, two-level rules were to be compiled into the finite state transducer form, which supplied a precise semantics and a route to computational implementation. This compilation was left unspecified in Koskenniemi's earlier work, and the actual rules were written directly as transducers, with the high-level rules supplying a semi-formal notation in which the content of the transducers could more clearly be explained (possibly approximately). This slightly unsatisfactory situation was remedied when Koskenniemi [Kosk85] refined the high-level rule notation and outlined a procedure for compilation to transducers; it is this later work that our mechanism uses.

2.5 The transducer version

As mentioned above, Koskenniemi's rules were regarded as operating on two sequences of symbols (or two *tapes*, to use the terminology of automata theory), one representing the characters in the lexical representation of one or more morphemes and the other representing the characters in the surface form. For example, if we assume that the

2 A good exposition of the latter representation can be found in [Antw90].

English word `moved` is to be analysed as `move` and `+ed`, where `+` is an arbitrary symbol used by the lexicon writer to mark certain affixes, then the rules should specify that the combination

```
m  o  v  e  +  e  d
m  o  v  e  0  0  d
```

is allowable. Here, `0` is a special null symbol which has been necessary because there are fewer symbols in the surface form than in the corresponding lexical form, and the rules deal in terms of *symbol-pairs* — ordered pairs of one lexical character and one surface character, such as

```
m
m
```

or

```
+
0
```

For textual convenience, we shall write these pairs separated by a colon — `m:m`, `+:0`, etc., with the *lexical* symbol first. The transducers define acceptable sequences of these symbol-pairs. The usual way of depicting a finite automaton using a table of transitions can be adapted to transducers, by using symbol-pairs in place of single elements of the alphabet. The columns of the table are labelled with symbol-pairs, the rows are labelled with state-identifiers (integers are used here), and the entries in the table indicate the state to be entered on encountering each symbol-pair. If no state is indicated, then the automaton or transducer *blocks* in that situation — it fails to accept the sequence of symbol-pairs.

A transducer which represents the above phenomenon might be as follows:

	v:v	e:e	+:0	e:0
1	2	1	–	–
2	2	3	–	–
3	2	1	4	–
4	1	1	–	1

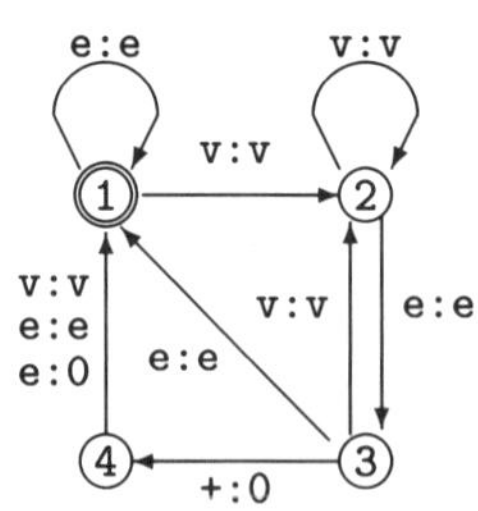

This very crude transducer (in which state 1 is both initial and final) will accept the sequence of pairs `+:0` and `e:0` if and only if they follow in sequence after `v:v` and `e:e`, and will reject them (i.e. the transducer will block) if they are encountered in any other context. This illustrative transducer has various deficiencies, one of which is that it will block if it encounters any symbol-pairs which are not explicitly listed, such as `m:m` or `d:d`. What is needed is a simple way to specify how the device should operate for "all other symbol-pairs". Koskenniemi introduced certain notational conventions to make it easier to write such transducers. A set of symbols (e.g. {`a, e, i, o, u`}) could be represented by a single mnemonic, and the special symbol = could match any actual symbol, subject to the provision that within any given state, the arc labels were to be interpreted in order from the most specific to the most general. Thus arcs marked with = were interpreted as denoting only those symbol-pairs which were not already described by some more specific arc from the same state.[3]

The interpretation of these abbreviatory notations was also subject to the convention that any abbreviated symbol-pair (that is pairs containing sets, such as `=:a` or `Vowel:Vowel`) could denote only those *concrete pairs* (i.e. unabbreviated pairs of actual characters) which appeared somewhere in the set of rules or in a supplementary list of pairs provided by the grammar writer. Thus the pair `=:a` would not necessarily match any lexical character whatsoever paired with the letter `a` — it would match only those symbol-pairs which had `a` as the surface part and appeared explicitly elsewhere.

Karttunen and Wittenburg [Kart83b] offer the following transducer to describe the effect that a lexical `n` must correspond to a surface `m` if and only if it is followed by a pair whose surface symbol is in the set `B` = {`b, p`} (as in `impossible` matching `in possible`):

3 This broad outline (which is all that is given in the papers cited) is not wholly precise, since it does not define formally the notion of "more specific", and it is not obvious what the interpretation of a set of arcs is when two of them (e.g. `a:=` and `=:a`) appear to be equally specific. Reape and Thompson [Reap88] propose a formalisation of the transducer model in which the linguist specifies an ordering on the arcs, and this ordering must not put arcs which are clearly less specific ahead of more specific ones.

Figure 2.1
A finite state transducer

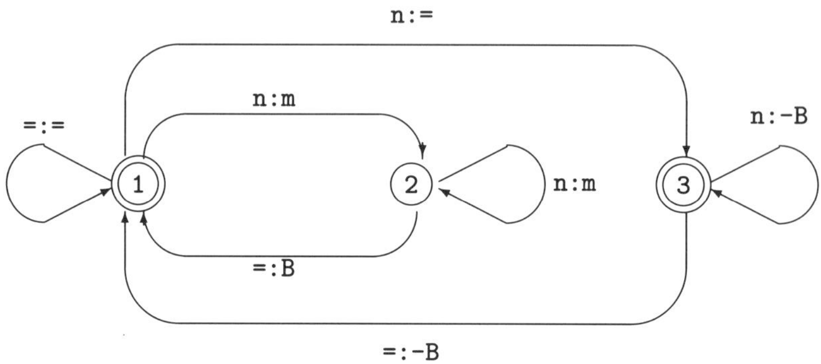

	n:m	=:B	n:=	n:-B	=:-B	=:=
1:	2	1	3	1	1	1
2.	2	1	-	-	-	-
3:	-	-	-	3	1	-

where -B indicates the set complement of the set B, final states are marked with a ":", and non-final states with a ".", after the state number. This can be represented by the traditional diagram, shown in Figure 2.1. In this transducer, the initial state (1) can act as an "idle" state, in which any pairs which do not match the two specific arcs (n.= and n.m) can be accepted without any effect. Only when a potentially relevant symbol-pair (something with n on the lexical side) is encountered does the transducer move into a state which is more selective about subsequent pairs. Both states 1 and 3 are marked as *final*, so a sequence of symbol-pairs which leaves the transducer in 1 or 3 is acceptable; whereas state 2, representing the first part of the phenomenon in question, can cause blocking if the stipulated configuration is not completed. (As Karttunen [Kart83a] points out, there are more entries in the transition table than there are arcs in the diagram, as the interpretation of the diagram depends on the principle that less specific arcs match only items which would not match more specific arcs from the same state.)

Kay and Kaplan had proposed a representation of phonological (or orthographic) variation as finite state transducers, with the transduc-

Figure 2.2
Scanning of transducers: cascading (left) and parallel (right)

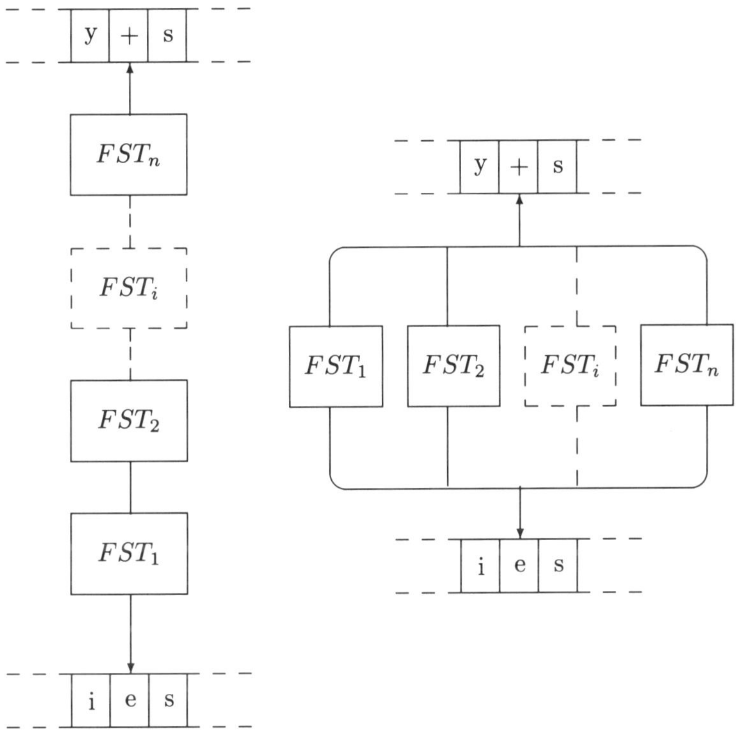

ers being arranged sequentially, in the sense that the output of one transducer would form the input to the next (an arrangement sometimes known as *cascading*). Koskenniemi's innovation was to arrange the transducers to act *in parallel*, in the sense that they all scanned the surface and lexical forms simultaneously, and a particular combination of surface and lexical form would be classed as well-formed by the set of transducers if and only if *all* the transducers accepted the combination — if a single transducer blocked, then the combination was deemed invalid (see Figure 2.2).

This emphasises the importance of the =:= arc in the initial state of the transducer given above — each transducer should accept any pairs about which it has no particular constraints. All the transducers proceed in step — as the scan of the lexical tape and the surface tape steps forward by one position, all the transducers process the new symbol. The null symbol `0` is allowed to appear in symbol-pairs on arcs in the transducers, and can be thought of as matching without the corresponding tape being advanced; however, if this is done, *all* the transducers must accept that postulation of an abstract null symbol (and non-movement of the head) at that point — it is not valid for some of the transducers to be processing some non-null symbol from a tape at the same time as others are deemed to be scanning a null symbol.

2.6 The two-level rule notation

Koskenniemi's high-level rules[4] can be viewed as constraints specifying which sequences of symbol-pairs are or are not valid, by supplying contexts (sequences of symbol-pairs) within which a particular symbol-pair might or must occur. For example, the rather trivial rule

```
e:0  =>  v:v  ___  +:0
```

would specify that the pair `e:0` could occur only if it were surrounded by `v:v` on the left and `+:0` on the right. There are three types of rule, but they all have the same overall form — a single symbol-pair whose behaviour is being specified, followed by an operator (`=>`, `<=` or `<=>`), a left context, a punctuation to indicate where the symbol-pair appears relative to the context (we have used "`___`" here), and a right context; in BNF,

```
<rule>  ::=  <symbol-pair>  <operator>
             <left context> ___ <right context>
```

where `<left context>` and `<right context>` denote sets of sequences of symbol-pairs. The three types of rule are as follows:

Context Restriction Rule (operator =>) : states that the specified `<symbol-pair>` can occur only in the given contexts.

Surface Coercion Rule (operator <=) : states that if the contexts occur, and the lexical symbol is as given in the `<symbol-pair>`,

4 There are various differences in notation or interpretation between Koskenniemi's 1983 and 1985 rules. Any information given here which is not otherwise qualified applies to both versions.

then the surface symbol must be the `<symbol-pair>` specified in the rule.[5]

Composite Rule (operator <=>) : a rule of this sort is an abbreviation of two separate rules (a Context Restriction Rule and a Surface Coercion Rule) made up of exactly the same symbol-pair, left context and right context.

The interpretation of a set of rules was as follows. For a sequence of symbol-pairs to be acceptable, if any symbol-pair in it was the subject of one or more Context Restriction Rules, then at least one of these rules must apply to the surrounding sequence (i.e. the contexts must match); if the surrounding contexts of any symbol-pair matched the context parts of any Surface Coercion Rule, then the symbol-pair must obey that rule. That is, in a rule set (a morphographemic grammar), the Context Restriction Rules for a particular symbol-pair were deemed to be a *disjunction* of constraints, and the Surface Coercion Rules were a *conjunction* of constraints (see Appendix F.4 for a precise definition).

In specifying symbol-pairs in rules, whether in the pair being restricted or within the contexts, various convenient abbreviations were available. Just as in the transducer version, symbols denoting sets of characters could be used instead of individual characters, thereby making it easier to state rules which referred to "all vowels" or other classes. This once again had the proviso that such abbreviations did not refer to all possible pairs, but only to *feasible pairs*; that is, those concrete pairs which appeared somewhere in the rules or in a supplementary list stated along with the rules. Since the rules were no longer in the form of transducers, it was no longer possible to define the "wild-card" symbol to mean "anything not already covered by arcs from the current state", but the = symbol was defined to mean "any symbol including the null symbol", and the rule writer could achieve more specific effects by defining various symbols to denote abstract sets which could match some particular range of symbols. (In the 1983 version, the set complement and set difference symbols could also be used to create new set expressions from the symbols which denoted sets of characters, and the empty set (not to be confused with the null symbol) could be used to indicate that a

5 In the 1983 version, the interpretation of a Surface Coercion Rule was that the whole symbol-pair must be as given in the rule, but the surface part of the symbol-pair could be a mnemonic for a *set* of symbols.

particular character could not match anything in a particular context.) Variables (not to be confused with sets) were also available for conflating rules which were very similar. A variable was declared locally within a rule as ranging over some set of symbols, and then the rule in which that variable appeared was taken to be a schema representing one rule for each of those values. Variables differed from sets in that all the occurrences of a variable within a rule had to be instantiated to the same value, whereas set mnemonics, which were declared globally, stood for any member of the set whatsoever, even if occurring more than once in a rule.

In specifying contexts (left and right), it was possible to supply more complex expressions than just sequences of symbol-pairs. Essentially, regular expressions of symbol-pairs were allowed (*regular pair expressions* as Koskenniemi called them), since notation was available to state alternation (disjunction), optionality, and the occurrence of zero or more instances (Kleene star). Also, *identity pairs*, in which lexical and surface characters were identical, could be written using just the single character; i.e. `a` would be an abbreviation for `a:a`.

Hence rules such as the following (from the work of Karttunen and Wittenburg [Kart83b]) could be framed:

```
+:e  <=>  { { c | s ( h ) } | S  | y:i } ___ s
```

where `S` is the set consisting of `z` and `x`, parentheses enclose optional elements, and braces enclose alternatives, separated internally by vertical bars. This rule says, informally, that a lexical `+` corresponds to a surface `e` when it follows either `c`, `s`, `sh`, `z`, `x` or `y` realised as an `i`, and is followed by `s` (this rule is merely illustrative, and does not give a correct description of English orthography). A slightly more complicated example, also from Karttunen and Wittenburg, is the gemination (consonant doubling) rule:

```
+:CL  <=> {' | # } C* V CL ___ V
```

where `CL` is defined to be a variable ranging over {`b, d, f, g, l, m, n, p, r, s, t`}, `C` is the set of consonants, `V` denotes the vowels {`a, e, i, o, u`}, and `'` and `#` are lexical markings for stress and word boundaries (presumably corresponding to surface null symbols).

The corresponding rules from our own description of English[6] are:

6 See Appendix D for more examples, and for justification.

```
+:e <=> { < s:s h:h > S:S y:i } --- s:s
    or  < c:c h:h > --- s:s
    or  < =:C { =:o =:u } > --- s:s

+:X => <{ < q:q u:u > C:C } V:V =:X> --- { =:V2 =:a }
    where X in { b d f g m p s t z }

+:Y => < C:C V:V =:Y > --- =:V2
    or < C:C V:V =:Y > --- < =:a =:NN >
    where Y in { n l r }
```

Notice that a *disjunction* of possible contexts is allowed in a rule, and the **where** clause declares a *variable* (as described earlier) for this rule.

We have already discussed the use of the null symbol to allow some abstract character (e.g. +) to correspond to nothing at all on the surface. This device (a linguistically motivated symbol at the lexical level which has no realisation on the surface) is so useful that, in the 1983 version, Koskenniemi proposed a convention that any number of such pairs could occur in a sequence of pairs without it affecting the matching of the sequence to the contexts of the rules. That is, it was not necessary to mention explicitly in the rules all possible pairs consisting of a *lexical feature* and the null symbol, since these were allowed to occur freely. This proposal, which could have unpleasant computational consequences, was dropped from later versions. The early version also included a few other notations and conventions to collapse sets of similar rules into textually smaller units. These included allowing rules with the same symbol-pair to be conflated and allowing rules with the same contexts to be conflated.

It should be emphasised that in the original (1983) outline of the two-level morphographemic formalism, there was not a fully defined procedure for interpreting the notation; that is, there was not even an approximate algorithm for using a set of rules to match a surface and lexical sequence, or to compile the rules into transducers. Some of the conventions proposed by Koskenniemi were extremely powerful, but this was not a serious problem since the notation was interpreted by humans rather than machines, so issues of decidability or tractability did not arise. Although Koskenniemi [Kosk83b] developed a treatment of Finnish morphology, and [Dalr83] contains various illustrative two-level grammars, the grammars which were actually computer-tested were written directly in the form of transducers (as in Section 2.5 above), and the rules in the form described above were used solely for expository purposes (i.e. there were essentially two formalisms in use, with an assumption that they were equivalent). In 1985, Koskenniemi discarded a few of the notational devices, and settled on a notation for which a compilation into transducers was definable, and it is a minor variant of that later formalism which we have implemented (see Chapter 7).

2.7 The lexicon and word grammar interface

The mechanisms described so far have provided a way of relating one sequence of symbols to another sequence, with the relationship being looked upon either as a matching process (two-tape recognition) or a transformation (generation of one sequence from another). There has been no difference between the roles played by the two sequences, and no explicit indication of how these rules might achieve the practical task of segmenting a word into a set of lexical forms which appear in a dictionary. In practice, it is quite straightforward to use these rules for segmentation and lexical look-up.

The first convention that is needed is quite simple — the sequence of lexical forms (the second "tape") is regarded as being supplied by any valid concatenation of lexical forms. That is, the set of lexical entries implicitly defines an infinite set of tapes of indefinite length, formed by any concatenation of lexical forms. The interpreter for the two-level rules (whether written as transducers or in the form of rules) must have this convention built in to it.

In [Kosk83b] and [Kart83b] the interface to the lexicon is slightly more complicated, since they build the morphotactic information into that interface, in the following way. A lexical entry (for a single morpheme) contains one or more *continuation classes* which indicate what categories of morpheme might follow it within a valid word; for example, a noun stem is marked as allowing a noun suffix as a possible continuation. The morphemes are not held in a single, uniform dictionary, but in a set of sublexicons, where each lexicon corresponds to some single morphotactic class. Hence, when the look-up process has found a particular morpheme (say, a noun stem) by matching entries in the noun stem sublexicon, the indication that a noun suffix is a possible continuation will cause the look-up process to continue scanning in the noun suffix sublexicon as it matches the input word from left to right. This can be rephrased in a more declarative way by stating that an input string S corresponds to a sequence of lexical forms $L_1, \ldots, L_n$ if S matches $L_1, \ldots, L_n$ (the concatenation of the forms) according to the morphographemic rules, and for each i between 1 and $n-1$, L_{i+1} is in a continuation classescontinuation class of L_i.

In the overall system we describe in this book, we have not used cross-linked sublexicons in this way, since it builds a particular form of (finite state) morphotactics into the method of lexicon access, rather than allowing more general rules to express such regularities. If using cross-linked lexicons, the choice of valid sublexicon to use after a morpheme L_i depends only on the lexical entry for that morpheme, and does not depend on morphemes preceding L_i in the sequence, nor on the overall syntactic category of combinations of morphemes. For example, if we decompose `renationalise`, the internal structure might be:

```
[ re [  [   [ nation ]  al ]  ise ]  ]
V    V  ADJ N         N    ADJ     V  V
```

This leads to the complication that the prefix `re` would normally require a continuation class of verbs, but is immediately followed by a noun, `nation`.

We have avoided this problem by having a separate level of morphotactic description (see Chapters 3 and 4), which allows much richer statements to be made about morpheme combinations and the overall morphosyntactic properties of combinations. In our system, the morphographemic component (i.e. the collection of two-level rules) need only segment and label the morphemes, without indicating any grouping. Hence we do not need to have several sublexicons — all morphemes are entered into a single lexicon. It might appear that this loses some scope for optimising the look-up process, since using linked sublexicons narrows down the search slightly, in that the scanner will not consider all possible morphemes when some particular subclass (e.g. a noun suffix) is predictable. There is indeed such a trade off. The use of linked sublexicons depends on that mechanism to embody all morphotactic statements, with a concomitant loss of expressive ability; the use of a separate stratum of morphotactics and single lexicon is wholly general, but may lose a certain amount of efficiency. However, some of the efficiency could be regained by having some arrangement of sublexicons, but with a subtler way of guiding the search than the continuation classes used by Koskenniemi. For example, it might be feasible to separate morphemes into possible word-initial forms, possible non-initial forms, etc., or (depending on the complexity of the autonomous morphotactic level) compute possible continuation classes from the separate morphotactic rules, either dynamically (during look-up) or statically (comparable to the parsing techniques outlined for context free grammars in [Aho72]). Some of these options were explored in our implementation — see Chapter 7.

Notice that there is no special symbol indicating a morpheme boundary or word boundary (whether or not linked sublexicons are used). Although the writer of the two-level rules will probably find it useful to insert certain special symbols (e.g. the + used in the example in Section 2.5 above), these have no particular significance within the definition of the rule formalism, and rules must be written to define how they relate to other symbols. The boundaries between morphemes are implicit in the successful match between the surface form (via the two-level rules) and the concatenated sequence of lexical forms.

It is also important to note the status of *null* symbols, usually written as 0 in two-level rules. The two-level notation itself has no special notion of a null symbol — the rules (whether written as transducers or in high-level notation) are stated in terms of symbol-pairs, and the null symbol may appear in all the positions that an ordinary alphabet symbol can. Where the special interpretation of the null symbol arises is in the interface between the two-level rules and the actual surface string, or between the rules and the lexical forms. The entire mapping between surface string and lexical forms can be viewed as having three stages, the middle one being the mediation by the two-level rules between two symbol sequences of identical length (see Figure 2.3).

That is, the relationship between the lexical forms and the lexical tape is by concatenation, and possibly insertion of null symbols; the relationship between the two equal length tapes is by the rules; and the relationship between the surface tape and the surface string is by removal of explicit nulls.

In actual implementations, these conventions are usually built into the spelling rule handler, so that the creation of lexical and surface tapes embodies these assumptions, and the actual two-level rules are then

Figure 2.3
Lexical and surface tapes and forms

LEXICAL FORM:	*move*				*+ed*		
LEXICAL TAPE:	m	o	v	e	+	e	d
SURFACE TAPE:	m	o	v	0	0	e	d
SURFACE FORM:	*moved*						

faced with a simpler matching problem. The formalisation in Appendix F makes these notions fully precise.

In processing terms, the interface between the morphotactic *word grammar* (Chapter 3) and the two-level morphographemic rules is that the word grammar analyser calls the two-level rule analyser as necessary to supply the next morpheme in the left-to-right scan (see Chapter 7 for fuller details).

2.8 Formal issues

2.8.1 Regular relations

Karttunen et al. [Kart87] describe another implementation of a compiler for two-level rules (see Section 7.3.5 for more details). The emphasis in their version is on the relationship between the context descriptions in two-level rules and regular languages of symbol-pairs. As Koskenniemi [Kosk83b] commented, the context expressions in the rules can be seen as characterising regular sets of sequences of pairs. Karttunen et al. develop this further, using the various properties of regular sets to define a general compilation method, based on the systematic creation and manipulation of finite state transducers. Their system allows the compiler to check automatically for clashes between rules of the sort described in [Blac87]. Although this results in a computationally intensive compilation process, it automates much of the debugging of the two-level grammar that might otherwise require intricate investigation by the grammar writer.

Kaplan [Kapl88] generalised some of this work further, by formalising the algebraic manipulations of regular sets of pairs, which he called *regular relations*. His formal definition is exactly analogous to that of a regular set (or regular language):

> The empty set is a regular relation.
> The set consisting of a single ordered pair of symbols, either of which may be empty, is a regular relation;
> If R_1 and R_2 are regular relation, so are $R_1 \cup R_2$, $R_1 R_2$, and R_1^* (i.e. the union of the two sets, the set consisting of concatenations of elements from the two sets, and the set consisting of zero or more concatenations of elements from a set).

Regular relations can then be described using regular expressions over symbol-pairs, much as in Section 2.6 above. Kaplan observed that every regular relation is accepted by some finite state transducer, and that every finite state transducer accepts some regular relation. The only difference between this formalisation and the regular pair expressions discussed earlier is that a special empty symbol is allowed, which means that a regular relation can associate strings of *unequal* lengths together. In their associated transducer form, the empty symbol corresponds to no symbol being scanned or no symbol being output.

Kaplan stated various results about regular relations, regular languages, and their combinations. In particular, if R_1, R_2 are regular relations, and L_1, L_2 are regular languages, then the following are regular relations:

> $R_1 \circ R_2$ (the composition of the relations);
> $L_1 \times L_2$ (the direct product of the sets);
> $Id(L_1)$ (the relation in which each element is paired with itself);
> R_1^{-1} (the inverse relation).

and

$$Dom(R_1) \text{ (the set of sequences of first elements of pairs in } R_1)$$

is a regular language.

Kaplan pointed out that intersection and complementation do *not* in general yield regular relations if empty symbols are involved, but will do where all the symbols are non-empty. He also developed more subtle results about combinations of regular relations and languages, including the result that an operator IF can be defined which forms a regular relation from two such relations:

$$IF(R_1, R_2) =_{def} \{xy \mid \text{if } y \in R_2, \text{ then } x \in R_1 \}$$

With these algebraic devices, he expressed the meaning of Koskenniemi's rule notation as regular expressions. These re-expressions describe the basic rule mechanism which operates on equal length sequences of symbols, so once again we leave aside the notion of genuine *empty* or *null* symbols. The rule

```
a:b  => LC ___ RC
```

defines a regular relation which can be expressed as:

$$IF(\pi^* LC, \mathtt{a:b}\pi^*) \cap IF((\pi^* \mathtt{a:b})', (RC\,\pi^*)')$$

where π is the set of all possible symbol-pairs (and hence π^* is the set of all possible symbol-pair sequences), and the prime denotes complementation with respect to π^*.

Similarly,

```
a:b <= LC ___ RC
```

defines the relation:

$$(\pi^* LC(Id(Dom(\mathtt{a:b})) \circ \pi^* \sim \{\mathtt{a:b}\})RC\,\pi^*)'$$

where "$\sim$" denotes set difference. (Both these expressions need to be made more complicated to allow for sets of context-pairs in rules, but there is no difficulty in principle.) A sequence of symbol-pairs is then well-formed if and only if it is in the intersection of all the regular relations corresponding to its rules[7]. Kaplan also showed how the systematic

7 Strictly, this last intersection is correct only if there is no symbol-pair which is on the left hand side of more than one Context Restriction Rule, but any two-level grammar can be formulated in this way — see [Ritc90].

deletion/insertion of null symbols (which is necessary to characterise the entire mapping — see Figure 2.3) can also be stated as a regular relation.

2.8.2 Generative power

As observed in Section 2.4 above, the historical development of two-level rules has led to the situation where there are in fact two distinct formalisms in use within the computational linguistics community — high-level rules (compiled into some arrangement of transducers) and parallel intersections of finite state transducers, written in a directly interpretable form. Although the assumption was made at first that these mechanisms were equivalent, this is far from obvious. Kaplan's work (Section 2.8.1 above) has justified the practical arrangement whereby high-level rules are compiled into arrangements of transducers, and proves that any statements which can be written in the rule notation can be re-phrased somehow in a configuration of transducers. It does not, however, demonstrate the reverse — that any arrangement of transducers, including arbitrary parallel intersection, can be simulated in the rule notation.

The rule notation, as formalised in Appendix F (a set of definitions which are an accurate reflection of Koskenniemi's original interpretation) is in fact a weaker mechanism, in the sense that there are regular sets of sequences of symbol-pairs (in Kaplan's terms, equal length regular relations) which cannot be characterised by two-level grammars. Ritchie [Ritc89, Ritc90] proves the following result which establishes this:

> Let G be a two-level morphological grammar, and suppose that E_1, E_2, E_3, E_4 are symbol-pair sequences such that E_2 is in $L(G)$, E_3 is in $L(G)$, and $E_1E_2E_3E_4$ is in $L(G)$. Then E_2E_3 is in $L(G)$.

This shows that all sets of symbol-pair sequences generated by two-level grammars have a particular property. However, not all regular sets of symbol-pair sequences have this property, since the regular set of symbol-pairs defined by

```
b:b ∨ (a:a b:b)*
```

contains `b:b` and `a:a b:b` as well as `a:a b:b a:a b:b` but does not contain `b:b a:a b:b`. Hence, not all regular sets of symbol-pairs (equal length regular relations) can be generated by two-level rules. Since Kaplan has shown that regular relations and transducers are equivalent, this shows that some transducer-generated sequences cannot be described by two-level rules. This proves that the two formalisms are indeed distinct, and results about one cannot always be carried over directly to the other. Note that this comparison involves simply the central phase of surface-to-lexicon correspondence, in which rules match symbol strings of equal length, without empty symbols.

2.8.3 Computational complexity

Although the two-level rule formalism, in any of the variants outlined earlier, seems fairly simple, and the possibility of re-expressing the rules as finite state transducers conveys the impression that the underlying processing model is essentially very efficient, Barton [Bart86] has challenged this superficial appearance of efficiency. Barton argues that although there has been no suggestion that the linguistic problem of morphographemic matching is inherently computationally complex (in the way that certain classic matching and searching problems in artificial intelligence are), the definition of the two-level formalism allows the statement of exponentially difficult problems; more precisely, the problem of recognising an arbitrary string using two-level rules and a given lexicon is NP-hard, and NP-complete if no null symbols are allowed [Gare79].

Barton's analysis is phrased in terms of the parallel transducer representation of two-level rules (rather than considering the higher-level rule formalism), so the possibility has to be considered that it is some aspect of the transducer mechanism which introduces the complexity. This is, in principle, not a mathematically absurd possibility, particularly in view of the generative power discrepancies mentioned in Section 2.8.2 above — it is easy to imagine a situation whereby some restricted formalism (e.g. a context free grammar) is compiled, for practical purposes, into a "program" for a very general "machine" (e.g. a Lisp program). A complexity analysis of the more general machine would not necessarily be a faithful analysis of the original formalism (even though the compilation process was completely correct). However, defenders of two-level morphology who wish to claim that the fundamental operations in their formalism (recognition and generation) do not lead to computationally intractable problems cannot resort to this escape route. Our definitions, as given in Appendix F, give rise to a very similar analysis, but with no explicit mention of transducers (see Appendix G).

Barton et al. [Bart87] also show that the transducer model with nulls is PSPACE-hard, a higher level of complexity than NP-hardness. However, their analysis is very much dependent upon the ability to construct parallel intersections of arbitrary transducers, and so does not carry over directly to the weaker formalism under consideration here.

This still leaves open the theoretical question (upon which Barton speculates) of whether such a simple phenomenon (morphographemic analysis of real natural language) really needs such an intractable mechanism, and how the mechanism could be restricted to something less complex but still empirically adequate. Koskenniemi and Church [Kosk88] argue that linguistic phenomena do not in general exhibit the kind of phenomena that lead to high levels of computational effort.

2.8.4 Decidability

The question of whether two strings of equal length (i.e. with no notion of *nulls*) are generated by a two-level grammar is decidable. Extending this to simple lexical segmentation is also decidable, providing there are no wholly null lexical items.

Once genuine null symbols are allowed, or (equivalently) we consider the entire process in which explicit nulls are deleted (as would be the case in a real system), this certainty is lost, since the general mechanism allows arbitrary sequences of nulls to appear between symbols. In practice, this has never been a problem, since (as Barton et al.(op.cit) observe), if there is a further constraint that no lexical form can correspond to a completely null surface sequence, the problem remains decidable.

2.9 Summary

We have given a brief outline of one strand of development of the use of finite state devices, and related formalisms, in morphological processing. There are two slightly different two-level formalisms under consideration here, with slightly different generative power but both (in the general case) giving rise to a recognition problem of exponential computational complexity. Our implementation (Chapter 7) incorporates most of the facilities of the two-level rule model, with a few minor limitations.

These rules fulfil one part of our requirements for a complete lexical look-up system — they can segment an input string into separate lexical forms, thereby looking up these forms in a basic morpheme lexicon so that their lexical entries are available.

3 Word Structure Rules

The rules described in Chapter 2 are primarily concerned with defining the relationship between the superficial orthography of words and an underlying abstract form which the linguist posits as part of the lexicon. Those rules also lend themselves very naturally to the task of segmenting a surface string into a sequence of lexical forms (morphemes). Hence two of the requirements discussed in Chapter 1 can be met by using the two-level morphographemic model — initial segmentation of the input into morphemes, and allowing for orthographic variation. The next requirement is for some suitable means of specifying which morphemes can or cannot combine with each other, and what sort of item (morpheme or word) they form when they have combined. That is, we can now assume the existence of some mechanism for segmenting the input into morphemes, and go on to explore the question of imposing structure upon such a sequence of morphemes. This chapter outlines the mechanism we adopted to specify such information in a computationally usable form.

3.1 Context free rules

Viewed abstractly, the question of how to stipulate the allowable combinations of a sequence of items, and to assign labels or categories to various sorts of sequence, is a familiar one. In constructing simple grammars for sentences, the traditional *context free grammar* allows the formal specification of exactly this kind of information. As a first suggestion, therefore, we might try to characterise sequences of morphemes using simple context free rules such as:

Word → Stem Suffix
Word → Prefix Stem

These rules could be informally glossed as "a Word can be formed from a Stem followed by a Suffix" and "a Word can be formed from a Prefix followed by a Stem." Of course, this grammar is much too simple even for the linguistic regularities in English — words may contain both prefixes and suffixes, so perhaps a more adequate grammar might include recursion:

Word → Word Suffix
Word → Prefix Word

It soon becomes apparent that much more refinement is required to achieve linguistic adequacy. Some words cannot take any form of suffix (e.g. `of`, `opens`), and words which take suffixes generally take particular classes of suffix, not just any one (e.g. `dull` can take `ness`, but `arrive` cannot). This seems to require more detailed rules, such as:

Word → Wholeword
Word → Verb
Word → Noun
Verb → Verb Verbsuffix
Noun → Noun Nounsuffix
Verb → Verbprefix Verb
Noun → Nounprefix Verb

At this point, matters can be seen to be rather awkward. This set of rules is increasingly inelegant, even though it is still not adequate to describe the data. What is happening here is a familiar phenomenon from research into syntax. A simple context free grammar uses a single symbol to represent all the information about a particular item, and so a great many symbols and many very similar rules are necessary to state the linguistic facts. Elegance is lost, and it is difficult to state general patterns. (This problem — the lack of flexibility of single symbols in rules — was discussed in generative phonology by Halle [Hall62], and in transformational grammar by Chomsky [Chom65]).

3.2 Features and categories

A very influential remedy to the inelegance and verbosity of pure context free grammars has, at the sentence level, been the development of *feature grammars* or *unification grammars* (of which there are many variants — see [Shie86] for a good introduction), in which linguistic items are labelled not with single symbols but with complex entities, usually called *categories*. A *category* consists of an unordered set of *feature specifications*, where each feature specification consists of an ordered pair of a *feature name* and a *feature value* (Appendix F gives precise definitions of all the formal concepts in this section). For example,

```
{(V, +), (N, -), (PLU, +)}
```

(using conventional set theoretic notation for the moment) would be a category containing three feature specifications, which have the feature names `V`, `N` and `PLU`, and the feature values `+`, `-` and `+`, respectively. (Informally, this would be a description of a plural verb — see Section 6.9.1.) No two feature specifications which are elements of a category may contain the same feature name, so that a category can be viewed as a (partial) function from feature names to feature values, but not a more general relation between names and values. For example,

```
{(V, +), (V, -)}
```

would not be a properly formed category. Feature names are normally atomic symbols, as in the above example, but feature values may (in many systems) be allowed to be structures of some sort; in particular, they may be categories, so that the definition of a category is recursive. For example, if we wanted the feature `AGR` ("agreement") to take as its value an entire category describing the type of constituent needed, then

```
{(V, +),  (N , -), (PLU, +),
     (AGR, {(N, +), (V, -), (PLU, +)})}
```

would describe a plural verb which required for agreement a plural noun.

The advantage of using structured labels like this is that similarities between items can be represented very directly — two similar but not identical constituents may have category labels which are largely the same, with perhaps one or two elements (feature specifications) differing. Moreover, linguistic rules can take advantage of this using a convention of *underspecification* of categories. In a pure context free grammar with simple atomic symbols, the applicability of a rule to a set of labels is defined very directly using identity of labels — that is, a rule such as

NounPhrase → Article Noun

is applicable to two adjacent constituents if and only if they are labelled "Article" and "Noun". There is no question of "degrees of similarity" of labels, or of a rule "matching" constituents in any way other than identity. However, in a feature grammar, there is the possibility of having partial categories within rules, and defining the applicability of a rule in terms of matching these underspecified categories against the categories of constituents. For example, a rule such as

$$\{(\texttt{V, +})\} \rightarrow \{(\texttt{V, +}), (\texttt{Stem, +})\}\ \{(\texttt{V, +}), (\texttt{Stem, -})\}$$

can be interpreted as meaning

> any item whose label contains the feature specifications (V, +) and (Stem, +) (plus possibly others) can combine with an item whose label contains the feature specifications (V, +) and (Stem, -) (plus possibly others) to form an item whose category contains {(V, +)} as a subset.

That is, each category in a rule is deemed to apply to any constituent whose label is a superset of that category.

3.2.1 Notation for categories

Before we show how this mechanism can be applied, very naturally, to morphological description, let us introduce some simplifications of the notation. So far, the expressions we have used in examples are in traditional set theory notation as borrowed from mathematics. It is commonplace to write categories in a more Lisp-based notation, in which a single type of bracket is used to group the information. For example, a category containing four features (named N, V, PLU and BAR) with the values +, -, + and 0 respectively (i.e. the label of a plural noun in our description of English — see Chapter 6) can simply be represented as:

```
((N +) (V -) (PLU +) (BAR 0))
```

This can be thought of as the basic, or canonical, notation for categories. In this notation, the hypothetical rule given above might be written as:

((V +)) → ((V +) (Stem +)) ((V +) (Stem -))

We also make use of a notational variant influenced by linguistic work such as Generalised Phrase Structure Grammar [Gazd85b]. In this, a category can be written as a *feature bundle* in which the feature specifications are separated by commas, and the whole category is enclosed in square brackets. For example, the category given above could also be written as

```
[N +, V -, PLU +, BAR 0]
```

These are purely notational trimmings, and do not affect the essential meaning of a category as an (unordered) set of ordered pairs. (See [Gazd88] for a further discussion of the notion of a "category".)

It should also be noted that in later discussions, when we wish to describe an individual feature specification, in isolation from any category, we shall usually use the Lisp-style notation (e.g. `(V +)`).

3.2.2 Extension and variables

We can now make more precise the definition of "matching" one category against another. As observed earlier, in allowing a category such as `((V +))` to stand for, or match against, any category which contains those features, a notion very similar to the set theoretic notion of *superset* is being used. One of the ways in which the relation is not exactly the traditional superset relationship relates to features whose values are *variables*. It is normal practice in feature grammars to allow the linguist more control over the matching of categories, by permitting the inclusion of named *variables* as feature values. Each variable is then deemed to stand for any valid value of that feature; moreover, each occurrence of a particular variable within a given category, or within a given rule, is deemed to stand for the same value. Hence, if we assume that `ALPHA` is a variable, the category

```
( (V ALPHA) (N ALPHA) )
```

describes (or matches) all categories in which the values of the N feature and the `V` feature are the same. Similarly, if `BETA` is a variable, the rule

```
( (V +) (Aux BETA) ) →
        ( (V +) (Stem +) (Aux BETA) )
        ( (V +) (Stem -) )
```

imposes the constraint that the value of the feature `Aux` in the first item in the concatenation must be the same as the `Aux` value in the combined structure. Any suitable convention can be adopted to define what counts as a variable — for example, stipulating that all variable names must commence with a particular character, or declaring an explicit list of variable names as part of the grammar. The use of variables means that the notion of "matching" between categories must be refined slightly. The modified form of "superset" used is called *extension*:

A category A is an *extension* of a category B iff:

1. Every feature f which occurs in B also occurs in A, and either

   (a) f has the same non-variable atomic value in both A and B; or

   (b) f has a variable value in B.

2. Wherever two features f_1, f_2 in B have the same variable as their value, then the values of f_1 and f_2 in A are the same.

This means that

```
((N +) (V +))
```

would be an extension of

```
((N ALPHA) (V ALPHA))
```

(where `ALPHA` is a variable), but

```
((N +) (V -))
```

would not be.

The above definition does not cater for the use of non-atomic feature values (i.e. having whole categories embedded as the value of features). To allow such recursive categories, the definition would have to be extended to:[1]

A category A is an *extension* of a category B iff:

1. Every feature f which occurs in B also occurs in A, and either

   (a) f has the same non-variable atomic value in both A and B; or

   (b) f has a variable value in B; or

   (c) f has a category as its value in both A and B, and the value in A is an extension of the value in B.

2. Wherever two features f_1, f_2 in B have the same variable as their value, then the values of f_1 and f_2 in A are the same.

This fuller definition allows

```
((V +)  (AGR ((N +) (Num Sing))) )
```

1 See Appendix F for full precise definitions of these concepts and others in this chapter.

to be an extension of

```
((V +)  (AGR ((N +))) )
```

In this way we can define a relation *is an extension of* between categories which is reflexive (any category is an extension of itself), antisymmetric (if two categories are extensions of each other, they are identical[2]) and transitive (if A is an extension of B and B is an extension of C, then A is an extension of C). The simplest category is the empty category (the empty set of feature specifications), and every properly constructed category is an extension of it[3].

We can then define the application of a rule such as those exemplified above as follows:

A rule

$$A \rightarrow B_1\ B_2 \cdots B_n$$

states that n entities labelled with categories $C_1, \cdots, C_n$ may be concatenated to form an entity labelled D providing that:

1. For $1 \leq i \leq n$, C_i is an extension of B_i
2. D is an extension of A
3. If X is a variable and a feature specification $(f\, X)$ occurs in one of $A, B_1, \cdots, B_n$, and the value of f in the corresponding category (i.e. from $D, C_1, \cdots, C_n$) is k (where k may be a variable, an atomic symbol or a category), then if the feature value X occurs anywhere else in $A, B_1, \cdots, B_n$ in a feature specification $(f'\ X)$, then the corresponding category in $D, C_1, \cdots, C_n$, must contain the specification $(f'\ k)$. (This last requirement is rather cumbersome to state semi-formally, but it essentially means "variables must always match consistently throughout a rule".)

---

2 Strictly, they are identical up to the systematic renaming of variables within a category; even this caveat could be eliminated by using a more abstract (but probably less perspicuous) notion of "variable" which was independent of the names used. See Appendix F for a more precise treatment.

3 Mathematically-minded readers will note that this means that categories form a *meet semi-lattice* under the partial ordering "is extension of" [Macl67]. It can be made into a full lattice by adding an abstract entity which is not a valid category, but which contains every possible feature specification, so that it is an extension of every valid category. We will not explore such formal avenues here.

This apparatus is quite powerful (see [Ritc85]), since it allows a rule to express very general constraints between parts of category labels on linguistic items. For example, a verb phrase rule could stipulate that a (transitive) verb takes a complement whose exact type depends on the value of the verb's SUBCAT feature:

```
( (CAT VP) ) →
        ( (CAT V) (SUBCAT ?X) )
        ( (CAT ?X) )
```

3.2.3 Unification

The above definitions are concerned wholly with giving a declarative statement of when a combination of items is licensed by a rule (or more generally, when a linguistic statement is applicable to a set of categories). In a computational system which actually manipulates representations of linguistic category structures, it is often necessary to match categories against each other, or compute categories which meet certain requirements involving extension. The abstract operation of *unification* is directly useful when defining processing mechanisms for categories, as follows:

If A and B are two categories (as defined earlier), then the unification of A and B (sometimes written $A \sqcup B$) is the smallest category C (if any) which is an extension of A and is an extension of B; if no such category exists, the unification of A and B is undefined[4].

For example, the unification of

```
((V +))
```

and

```
((N -))
```

is

```
((V +) (N -))
```

and the unification of

```
((V ALPHA) (AGR ((N +))))
```

4 Readers who took an interest in the observation in an earlier footnote about lattice structures will note that unification is the *join* operation for that lattice.

and

```
((V +)  (AGR ((V +))))
```

is

```
((V +) (AGR ((N +) (V +))))
```

The notion of *smallest category* may seem rather vague, but it can easily be made precise. The requirement in the definition above is that there must be no category D (not equal to C) which is an extension of A and B, and such that C is an extension of D.

Historically, the meaning of rules involving features has often been discussed using the notion of *unification*, but *extension* is the essential idea, and unification is relevant only when considering (as a parser often does) the question — "what category would be an extension of these two categories, but would not contain any extra information that is not in these categories?"

3.3 The word structure formalism

Having introduced the basic concepts of feature based grammar rules, we can now outline the details of the formalism which we use for describing word structure. The assumption is that the morphographemic rules (see Chapter 2) have segmented the input into a sequence of morphemes, each of which has one or more lexical entries associated with it. Each lexical entry contains, as one of its fields, a syntactic category of the sort described above (i.e. an unordered set of feature specifications). We shall ignore for the purposes of this discussion the question of there being multiple segmentations of the input string; this is just one further source of ambiguity which a processing system as a whole has to cope with, but it does not directly affect the abstract definition of the word structure level of description.

As well as a set of *rules*, of the general feature-based variety outlined in Section 3.2 above, the word structure grammar consists of a set of *declarations* which assign particular significance to particular symbols; for example, stating which symbols are to count as variables in rules. The presence of these declarations (exactly analogous to declarations in a programming language such as Pascal) has two motivations — it renders the linguistic description more explicit, by forcing the linguist to state exactly what is intended; for computational purposes, it simplifies (or in some cases, makes possible) the implementation.

3.3.1 Aliases

Since categories can often be cumbersome when written out in full, it is convenient to have some abbreviatory conventions for commonly occurring categories. An *alias* is an abbreviation which allows an atomic name to be associated with a category (or part of a category), and hence can be used to express more succinctly that category or its extensions. For example, the aliases `Noun` and `Verb` might be declared as:

```
Alias  Noun = ((N +) (V -))
Alias  Verb = ((V +) (N -))
Alias  -V   = ((V -))
Alias  -N   = ((N -))
```

With the above alias declarations, the category

```
[N +, V -]
```

could also be written simply as

```
Noun
```

Also, an alias can be followed by a *feature bundle* (in the sense of Section 3.2.1) to specify it further. For example, the category given earlier for "plural noun" could be written either as:

```
[N +, V -, PLU +, BAR 0]
```

or as

```
Noun[PLU +, BAR 0]
```

(See Appendix A for full details of the formal syntax of the grammatical notation.)

Either category notation may used in declaring aliases; for example:

```
Alias  Prep = [V -, N -]
```

Also, aliases may be declared in terms of aliases (but recursion is not allowed in the definition of aliases).

3.3.2 Feature definitions

All features used in the word grammar (and lexical entries) must be included in the declarations. There are two types of features, *atomic-valued* and *category-valued*. Atomic-valued features must be declared with an explicit list of possible atomic feature values. Category-valued features can take any valid category as their value, and are declared using the keyword `category` (or `CAT`), e.g.

```
Feature  N    {+,-}
Feature  BAR  {-1,0,1,2}
Feature  AGR  category
```

This defines `N` to be an atomic-valued feature whose only allowable values are `+` and `-`, `BAR` to be an atomic-valued feature with the possible values given, and `AGR` to be a category-valued feature. No feature can have a range which is a mixture of atomic values and categories, and no details can be given of the exact values which a category-valued feature can take. (The association of a range with a feature can be thought of as analogous to associating a type with a variable in a programming language like Pascal; categories are also slightly analogous to records in Pascal.)

Any symbol can be used as a feature name (in our implementation, any valid Lisp symbol was allowed), but there is one "built-in" feature name — `STEM` — which has special significance for the feature passing conventions (see Chapter 4). Hence a grammar should not contain a declaration of `STEM` as a feature (in the implementation, such declarations were accepted, providing that `STEM` was declared as a category-valued feature).

3.3.3 Word grammar rules

The word grammar is a feature grammar with rules of the form:

$$mother \rightarrow daughter_1, daughter_2 \cdots daughter_n$$

where *mother*, $daughter_1$, $daughter_2$, etc. are categories, and $n \geq 1$. Each rule is given a mnemonic name for convenience, and this is written before the left hand side of the rule, the whole rule being enclosed in parentheses. For example:

```
(Prefixing
   ((BAR 0)) -> ((FIX PRE) (BAR -1)) , ((BAR 0))
)
```

This rule can be read informally as "an item with the feature specification `((BAR 0))` can be made up from an item which has the features `((FIX PRE) (BAR -1))` followed by an item with the feature specification `((BAR 0))`". (See earlier discussions, and Appendix F, for more formal definitions.)

3.3.4 Variables

There are two types of variables allowed within the categories in the grammar — *rule category variables* and *feature value variables.*

Rule category variables Rule category variables range over specific categories, and are a short-hand which conflates a set of similar grammar rules. They are declared with a range of possible values that must be stated as a list of aliases. These variables do not increase the formal power of the grammatical formalism, but can be used to capture linguistic generalisations in rules. For example, in French both nouns and adjectives can take a plural morpheme `s` (which could be described with the category `((PLU +) (FIX SUF))`). This phenomenon could be described using the following alias statements and rules:

```
Alias   Adj  =  ((BAR 0) (N +) (V +))
Alias   Noun =  ((BAR 0) (N +) (V -))

(AdjPlural
      Adj[PLU +] -> Adj[PLU -], [PLU +, FIX SUF] )

(NounPlural
      Noun[PLU +] -> Noun[PLU -], [PLU +, FIX SUF] )
```

Alternatively, the two rules can be written as one by declaring a rule category variable:

```
Alias   Adj  =  ((BAR 0) (N +) (V +))
Alias   Noun =  ((BAR 0) (N +) (V -))

Variable  C  =  {Adj,Noun}
```

```
(Plural
      C[PLU +]  -> C[PLU -], [PLU +, FIX SUF] )
```

which is exactly equivalent in meaning to the fuller form, but might be deemed to describe the data more elegantly. (In the implementation, rules containing rule category variables are replaced by the full set of equivalent rules during grammar compilation, which emphasises the role of these variables as a mere notational convenience.)

Feature value variables Feature value variables, on the other hand, can be thought of as "holes" that are filled in during parsing, and are exactly the kind of variable which is customarily used in unification grammar. There are two types of feature value variables — *atomic-valued* and *category-valued* (category-valued variables are *not* the same as rule category variables). The distinction is directly parallel to that between the atomic-valued features and category-valued features described above. Atomic-valued variables are declared with an enumerated set of values, while category-valued variables are declared with the keyword `category` (or `CAT`):

```
Variable   ALPHA  =  {+,-}
Variable   ?AGR   =   category
```

(Associating ranges with feature value variables is again analogous to the use of types for variables in programming languages such as Pascal.) These sets of values indicate the range of allowable values for the variable in question — a variable cannot be assigned a value (in matching) which is outside this range (see Appendix F for precise details).

The main purpose of such variables, as discussed earlier, is to stipulate that the values of particular features must be identical. (From a computational viewpoint, the latter can be seen as *copying* values of features up (or down) the parse tree.) For example, a compound noun can be said to inherit its plural feature marking from the rightmost daughter. Using feature value variables we can write a rule that ensures that the compound noun will have the same `PLU` marking as its rightmost daughter:

```
Variable   ?X  =  {+,-}
Alias      N   =  ((BAR 0) (N +) (V -))
```

```
(NounCompound
    N[PLU ?X]   ->   N[PLU -],  N[PLU ?X]  )
```

Note that although atomic-valued variables can be thought of as a shorthand for a number of rules, one for each value in the range of the variable, category-valued variables cannot. This is because there is potentially an infinite set of categories that could be the value of a category-valued feature. It follows that atomic-valued feature variables could, in principle, be "compiled out" in a pre-processing stage, with each variable being replaced by its possible values; in practice, such a scheme would be hopelessly inefficient, since it would produce vast numbers of very similar rules. Category-valued variables could not be thus handled even in principle[5].

There are no typographical conventions built-in for specifying variables, although grammars may be easier to read if some convention is adopted, such as starting all variables with an underscore or question mark.

Although variables provide one way to equate the values of features, there are also various *feature passing conventions* (see Chapter 4 for more details).

One use of (atomic-valued) variables which is not at once obvious follows from the stipulation that a variable must have a particular range. That is, the range of values which a variable can be assigned is limited to a particular subset of the atomic feature values. This can very succinctly give the effect of *disjunction* in a rule. For example, suppose we wish a rule to apply only to those categories whose SUBCAT value is NP *or* PP (but not where the SUBCAT value is any of its other valid values). If we declare a variable

```
Variable  SIMPLE  =  {NP, PP}
```

then any category which contains a feature specification such as

```
(.... (SUBCAT SIMPLE) .... )
```

will apply to either of these two classes.

5 If we overlook this distinction between finite and infinite ranges, rule category variables and feature value variables are, at a suitably abstract level, minor variants of the same idea — an abbreviation for a larger set of rules.

3.3.5 Defining structures with grammar rules

Within contemporary linguistics, context free phrase structure rules are usually taken as stating *node-admissibility conditions* [Part90, p.450], which define the well-formedness of trees whose labels are atomic symbols. In order to define the well-formedness of a tree whose nodes are labelled with sets of feature specifications (categories), the definition of extension given in Section 3.2.2 is used, with the further constraint that a value can be the extension of a variable only if it lies within the range of that variable. In addition, the definition (also in that section) of how a rule licenses and labels a concatenation of items is adopted. (See Appendix F for full details.)

To complete the definition of well-formedness, we must also consider the notion of the *top category*, which corresponds to the *distinguished symbol* in a traditional context free grammar. One of the declarations in the grammar is the definition of a category as being *top*; for example:

```
Top = [BAR 0]
```

This states that a necessary condition for a sequence of morphemes to be acceptable as a complete word is that the grammar should assign to it a category which is an extension of the declared top category; in this example, that would demand that every word has at least the feature `BAR` with value `0`.

The grammar rules can then be thought of as assigning to each valid sequence of morphemes a tree whose terminal nodes (leaves) are associated with the morphemes in left-right order, and such that

1. The root of the tree is labelled with a category which is an extension of the top category;
2. Each terminal node is labelled with a category which is an extension of the category in the corresponding morpheme's lexical entry;
3. Each non-terminal node is licensed by some rule in the grammar, in the sense that if a non-terminal node N has a syntactic category C_0 and the licensing rule is $A \rightarrow d_1, d_2, \cdots, d_n$, then C_0 must be an extension of A, and N must have n daughter nodes $M_1, \cdots, M_n$ labelled with syntactic categories $C_1, \cdots, C_n$ such that C_i is an extension of d_i for each i from 1 to n.

In fact these definitions have to be augmented to take account of variables (Section 3.3.4), defaults (Section 3.3.6 below) and feature conventions (see Chapter 4); Appendix F gives a complete formal definition.

3.3.6 Feature defaults

For many years there has been a notion of default markings for linguistic features [Chom68], and this is still present in modern linguistic theories [Gazd85b]. These rely on the idea of a *default specification* for a particular feature — a value which is deemed to be present if no rule or lexical entry provides another value. For example, if we wished to indicate that all verbs are non-auxiliary (main) unless otherwise specified, we might state that the "default" value of the feature `AUX` is `-`. As another example, the regularity of the inflectional behaviour of verbs could be described by having it controlled by various features whose default values correspond to the normal, regular case. The essential point is summed up by the phrase "unless otherwise specified" — default values are to be used only when there is no information to the contrary from any other part of the linguistic description.

GPSG [Gazd85b] includes *Feature Specification Defaults*, a fairly general mechanism which would probably be computationally complex to implement. We have opted for a much simpler facility, which seems adequate for our purposes, and yet easy to implement. For any feature (either a category-valued feature or an atomic-valued one), a single value can be stated to be the default value for that feature. For example, the statement

```
Defaults  BAR 0, AGR Inf
```

declares default values for two features (`BAR` and `AGR`), where `Inf` could be an alias for some category. (Our implementation — see Chapter 7 — imposes the notational limitation that in such declarations, default values for category-valued features must be stated as single alias symbols.)

Wholly general defaults (such as Gazdar et al.'s) are difficult to characterise as a monotonic mechanism, since they depend upon some notion of priority of sources of information, although other rules or processes may use the default information once it has been inserted. That is, a default scheme makes sense only if the objects being manipulated can somehow be partitioned into a phase where other information is considered, and a phase where the default is used instead. In the use of inherited defaults (see, for example, [Gazd89]) the inheritance hierarchy defines the stage which separates default from non-default information, but we are not considering inheritance devices here.

Our defaults are very simple, which makes it slightly easier to define them precisely and declaratively. The essential idea is that we define a *default extension* of a category C to contain exactly the feature specifications of C together with one or more feature specifications which are supplied by the defaults, with the proviso that no feature may be supplied by default if the feature name already appears in C. The definitions of well-formedness given above then have to be altered to stipulate that the categories labelling the nodes of the tree are not just extensions of the categories in the rules, but default extensions which include feature specifications for all the features defined as having defaults. (See Appendix A for full formal definition.)

There is one slight complication which is worth mentioning (and which to some extent reflects the conflict of methodological criteria alluded to in Chapter 1). If the aim of our morphological rules was simply to characterise all the possible analyses of words, by assigning them structural analyses (trees labelled with categories), then it might be quite reasonable to allow all feature defaults to apply *after* every other source of linguistic information (e.g. feature grammar rules, feature passing conventions) has been used to create an entire analysis of a whole word. However, this would mean that the applicability of feature rules such as those discussed above could not be sensitive to information supplied by defaults. We decided that this was a less useful position than a slightly different approach where defaults were applied to each portion of a word as it was built, so that any rules which might be used to combine these portions into a large constituent could then be influenced by information supplied by defaults. We have therefore defined a scheme whereby defaults are checked and, where necessary, filled in once a feature rule has built a complete part of a word (and the feature passing conventions (Chapter 4) have applied). Feature values inserted by the defaults can thus affect the set of rules applicable to the constituent.[6] This may seem a rather procedural approach, but it can be given a declarative definition (see Appendix F).

---

6 In terms of the active chart implementation of the parsing mechanism — see Chapter 7 — the default checking is done whenever a complete (i.e. inactive) edge, other than a basic lexical entry, is entered into the chart.

Also, defaults do not apply to the syntactic categories of individual lexical entries. This was a deliberate omission, since the basic lexicon has a much more powerful mechanism for handling default information (see Chapter 5).

3.3.7 `MorphologyOnly` features

In much of the linguistic literature, morphology and the syntax of the sentence are discussed in a relatively separate manner, so that a detailed analysis of one of these areas can make whatever plausible assumptions are necessary about the other. If comprehensive linguistic analyses of both morphology and sentence syntax are required, the task is slightly more complicated. We discovered that there were various features which were useful for morphological description but which were irrelevant to the sentence grammar. The presence of these feature markings in categories which the sentence grammar was trying to manipulate was at best an inconvenience, and at worse distorted the sentence rules. We decided, therefore, to create a special class of features called "`MorphologyOnly`" which were purely internal to the morphology component, and which would be "invisible" to the sentence rules. This class of features is explicitly declared by the writer of the morphology rules, thus allowing the writer of the sentence grammar freedom to ignore the presence or absence of features which have been introduced by the writer of the lexicon solely to achieve the correct morphological forms. (In the implementation, all feature specifications declared to be `MorphologyOnly` are stripped from the overall category of a word before the result of lexical look-up is returned.) If no features are declared to be `MorphologyOnly`, then all features are deemed to be completely accessible by the sentence level rules. For example, to stipulate that no `INFL` feature specifications were to be seen by the sentence grammar, the declaration would be:

```
FeatureClass MorphologyOnly = {INFL}
```

Features mentioned in a feature class declaration must also be declared as features in the normal way.

There is a slight problem with this idea, which we did not resolve satisfactorily. As might be expected, the rules which define the internal structure of words (i.e. the word grammar and the feature passing conventions) refer explicitly to various features which are in the `MorphologyOnly` class. Hence, the tree structure generated for the word is well-formed providing these features are present with the correct values. If such features are removed, the resulting tree may contain a root category which is acceptable to the sentence grammar, but it is highly likely that it is ill-formed with respect to the rules which originally created it. Our implementation compromised by allowing two options for the result of lexical look-up — *either* the entire hierarchical decomposition of the word, with all the `MorphologyOnly` features still in place, *or* just the single root category of this decomposition (i.e. the syntactic label relevant to the sentence grammar), with all the `MorphologyOnly` features removed. (See Chapter 7 for fuller details.)

3.3.8 Other declarations

As mentioned earlier, a number of different types of declarations are required as part of the word grammar. As well as the declarations for feature names and values, variables of all kinds, aliases, defaults and `MorphologyOnly` features, there are a few other declarations which are better explained in conjunction with the mechanisms which they control or affect. These include `CatDef` and `LCategory` declarations (see Section 3.5 below on term unification), and the other feature class declarations (see Chapter 4 on feature passing conventions).

3.4 Varieties of unification

The outline of categories, unification and feature grammars given in Section 3.2 above relied on a particular cluster of ideas which have become commonplace within unification grammar (usually in connection with sentence syntax). There are, however, a few variants of these ideas, and our formalisms make some provision for a slightly different definition of *category* and *unification*. That is, there are two versions of our formalism (both of which were implemented), each relying on different basic feature structure mechanisms.

Most of our work went into the variation described earlier, which we refer to as the *unrestricted unification* version; the other variation (which was tested and used much less) is the *term unification* version. The two mechanisms are, at a suitably abstract level, formally equivalent, but in their normal usage they encourage different viewpoints of what a category represents.

3.4.1 Unrestricted unification

This method of representation and unification is based heavily on the GPSG model of syntactic features (cf. [Gazd85b, Ch. 2]), although it is also essentially the same as that of Functional Unification Grammar [Kay84, Kay85], PATR-II [Shei84], and many other formalisms.

In the unrestricted unification version there is no formal concept of *category types* — a category is simply represented as *any* set of feature specifications whatsoever. There are no constraints on which features can occur together in a category, so that the only notion of "well-formedness" for a category is that each feature name must appear at most once, and that each feature value must fall within the declared range of that feature. Of course, in any realistic grammatical descriptions, there will be patterns of cooccurrence amongst the features, and certain feature combinations will never occur in the same category, but this is not reflected in the formal mechanism in any way.

Consequently, the unification operation used to compute extensions of categories is very general — it can unify any two categories whatsoever, providing there is no clash between the feature specifications explicitly mentioned in the categories. All features which are not mentioned in a category are of equal status — none of them are deemed more suitable for inclusion than others. Hence, for example, the following two categories would unify, despite the intuition that one is describing a noun phrase and the other a verb:

```
((NUM  SING) (COUNT +) (DEFINITE +) (PRO +))

((TENSE PRES) (TYPE INTRANS) (MOOD ACTIVE))
```

This scheme, while conceptually simple and elegant, has two drawbacks. Linguistically, it is rather unsatisfactory — the linguist has ensure that each category is sufficiently well specified that it cannot "accidentally" unify with some unrelated category, and it fails to capture the generalisation that certain combinations of features occur whilst others do not. The extreme generality of this approach leads to computationally intensive processes. Not only is the basic operation of unification rather complex, any parser for a unification grammar has very little guidance in computing which rules are pertinent to a given sequence of constituents. (See Chapter 7 for a sketch of some of the techniques which can be used to alleviate this latter problem.)

3.4.2 Term unification

In work on first order logic, particularly on resolution (see [Robi65], [Bund83]), another definition of unification exists, and that notion has also been adopted in the programming language Prolog. In this approach, the structures being unified are *terms* within predicate logic; a term can be either a constant symbol, a variable symbol, or the combination of a *functor* and several arguments. For example, functor-argument terms might be written thus:

```
f(a, b, c)
loves(mikhail, raisa)
```

Arguments (but *not* functors) can be variables. An argument can itself be a functor-argument term, thus allowing nested (or even recursive) items:

```
f(a, g(h,a), f(d,e,f))
```

Two terms unify if either they are identical or there is a consistent way of substituting values (terms) for their variables which would make them identical. Hence two functor-argument terms unify iff:

1. They have identical functors
2. They have the same number of arguments
3. For each argument place, the corresponding values unify.

Although this definition of unification can still lead to a computationally intensive process, owing to the need to cater for the same variable appearing in both terms and to keep the variable substitutions consistent, it can be implemented more efficiently than the linguist's *unrestricted unification* described earlier. The crucial aspects are itemised in (1) and (2) above — there are certain quick and simple checks which can be made about two structures to see if they might unify, before detailed matching of their internal structures occurs. This leads naturally to the idea of using terms as grammatical labels, instead of the extremely general notion of a category as any set of feature specifications. For example:

```
noun(sing, count)
verb(past, active, transitive)
```

(This is, of course, exactly what is done in "logic grammars" such as Definite Clause Grammars [Pere80].) From the point of view of parsing with a grammar containing such structures, there are obvious ways of indexing potential candidates for unification — the functor (and number of arguments) can be used to index rules which might be relevant to (could unify with) a given item.

Within the logic community, it is normal to say that one term *subsumes* another when it is more general; that is, A subsumes B if there is a variable substitution in A which would make A and B identical. This is the direct counterpart of *extension* in unification grammar, though in the inverse direction. If B is an extension of A (contains more features), then A is more general than B. Hence, when logical terms are used as grammatical labels, the definitions of well-formedness for syntactic structures are comparable to those given for unification grammar, except that the categories in the rules must *subsume* the categories in the tree.

3.4.3 Comparing the two approaches

These two approaches to the representation of complex descriptive labels, and the variants of unification that are involved, are not totally dissimilar. It is even possible to simulate one system within the other, subject to suitable assumptions. If we have a linguistic description written on the basis of unrestricted unification, it could be re-written automatically (if somewhat cumbersomely) as a term unification description. Some very general symbolic label (e.g. `CATEGORY`) could be chosen as an all-purpose functor, and every feature name which appeared anywhere within the system would be allocated an argument place. All the terms in the term unification description would have exactly the same number of arguments, with one position for each possible feature. Each category in the original description would be restated as a term whose functor was `CATEGORY` and whose arguments were the feature values involved, with the argument positions indicating to which feature the values belonged. Features which were absent from a category in the original description would be given a variable value in the corresponding term, allowing them to unify with anything. This reconstructed description could then be manipulated using term unification, and would behave exactly as the original did under unrestricted unification.

Conversely, a description written in terms could be restated in unrestricted unification categories by replacing each term with a category in which there were the special features **FUNCTOR**, **ARITY** (to indicate the number of arguments), **ARG1**, **ARG2**, etc. For example

```
verb(past, X, intrans)
```

would become

```
((FUNCTOR VERB) (ARITY 3) (ARG1 PAST)
            (ARG2 X) (ARG3 INTRANS))
```

Again, this new version would, when handled using unrestricted unification, give the same effects as the original one did using term unification.

3.5 The term unification enhancements

After we had developed a fairly full description of English morphology using unrestricted unification, we decided to experiment with ways of introducing the essential ideas of term unification, but without revising our formalism radically to incorporate the traditional logic notation. That is, we opted to retain feature names, feature values and much of the notation normally used, but altered the way that these structures were handled, so that the underlying computations would be comparable to those of term unification.

If we had merely wanted to gain the processing advantages of representing categories as terms, we could have simply arranged matters so that an internal translation along the lines indicated above was carried out by our implementation, with term unification acting on an internal representation during the morphological processing. This was felt not to be enough, for two reasons. Linguistically, it does not introduce the notion of *category type* (i.e. naturally cooccurring family of features) which we felt was desirable to increase the perspicuity of our description. Computationally, a uniform (but hidden) translation into terms would (assuming that there is no special **CATEGORY** feature or other definitions which would structure the problem) necessitate every term having an argument for every feature in the system, resulting in very large terms.

The extra processing involved in matching such enormous terms might well cancel out any efficiency gains in the simpler algorithms.

We therefore introduced a formal declaration of *category type* to the descriptive mechanism[7]. In the term unification version, the grammar writer must include declarations of category types using the `CatDef` definition, which consists of an atomic name (a mnemonic for that category type) and a list of feature names that must appear on any such category. For example:

```
CatDef Noun has {CAT,PLU,COUNT,SUBCAT}
CatDef Verb has {VFORM,PN,TENSE,SUBCAT}
```

There is also the requirement that *each* category that appears in the lexical entries and word grammar rules *must* be of *one* and *only* one category type, though it need not specify all its features explicitly; moreover, it must be the case that any reference to a category must be such that the category type can be identified solely by the feature names it contains (without reference to their values). This does not mean that every category used in the linguistic description must explicitly mention *all* the features from some category type — all that is necessary is to use a subset of the features that uniquely defines which category type is intended (i.e. that is not also a subset of the features of any other category type). Category types are essentially playing the role that a functor (and its arity) would play in a term unification system.

These restrictions mean that it would not be possible to write a rule which generalised over exactly nouns and verbs, without either having a more general category type to which they both belonged, or using rule category variables (see Section 3.3.4 above). The cross-classification of nouns and verbs using the features `N` and `V` (as, for example, in GPSG [Gazd85b]) would not fit naturally into the restrictions of this scheme of category types unless either we never need to distinguish nouns from verbs, or else some other features are introduced to distinguish nouns and verbs; for example, we could write our description so that verbs contain the feature `VFORM` and all noun references contain `NFORM`, and include these features in the corresponding category type declarations.

The implementation (see Chapter 7 for more discussion) expanded the categories in the linguist's description so that each category contained

7 Category types are very similar to *sorts* in HPSG [Poll87], but are more motivated by computational efficiency.

variable values for those features that were not explicitly mentioned. This expansion of the basic category to the full category was done after all other abbreviatory mechanisms (such as aliases) had been applied. Notice that aliases are *not* the same as category types — aliases are a purely textual abbreviation which allow categories to be written more clearly, but they do not affect in any way the possible cooccurrences of features. Hence aliases can be used with either version of the formalism (unrestricted unification or term unification), and have the same import in either case.

Since we have retained the representation of a category as a set of feature specifications (features and their values), the definitions of extension and unification given earlier hold for both versions of the formalism — the *term* aspect shows up only in the range of structures which are created as categories to undergo unification, and in the processing optimisations that the implementation can make. In particular, in the term unification version one category can be an extension of another (or can unify with another) only if both are of the same category type.

Owing to lack of time, we did not develop an alternative description of English which made full use of the term unification mechanisms. The description given in this book (see Appendix D and Chapter 6) assumes unrestricted unification.

3.5.1 The top category

For the term unification variant, we also widened the definition of the "top" category (the distinguished label which all complete items must match). As stated earlier, when using unrestricted unification the category on the root of the tree spanning any whole word must be an extension of the top category declared in the word grammar. In term unification the top category is a *set* of (the names of) category types, and the category which is attached to a whole word (or potential word) must be of one of these types. This allows, for example, verbs and nouns to be defined to be distinct category types, but both to count as valid complete words.

3.5.2 `LCategory` declarations

As explained elsewhere, the morphological description of English was developed to integrate with a large grammar of English sentences developed by Briscoe et al. [Bris87]. Owing to various logistic problems, the specification for that project included an explicit term unification mechanism, at a stage at which we had already constructed a large English description using unrestricted unification. This meant that our dictionary made no attempt to ensure that categories assigned to words were "complete", in the sense of having specifications for some pre-defined set of features. The sentence level grammar (and parser) assumed that every syntactic category had some specification, even if only a variable, for every feature in some set; that is, it had something like the "category types" facility mentioned above. We therefore had to introduce an additional facility which would resolve this discrepancy by "padding out" categories with dummy values for features which would otherwise be absent. These dummy values should be of a form which would act as a variable for the sentence level grammar and parser, although they would have the status of constants within the morphological description. implementation, all such dummy values were symbols starting with @D.)

This was achieved using the `LCategory` declaration (which is used only in the unrestricted unification formalism). These declarations act on the overall category of a word when all morphological rules, defaults, and feature passing conventions have already applied. If any features listed in the `LCategory` declaration are not already present, then they are added with a special dummy value.

There are two forms of these, *simple* `LCategory` definitions and *feature* `LCategory` definitions. The first of these specifies that certain categories (as defined by a set of feature specifications) must also have specifications for certain further features. For example

```
LCategory ((N +) (V -)) => {PLU}
```

This ensures that any word whose category label includes `((N +) (V -))` also has some value for the feature `PLU`; if no such value is present at the time the comparison is made between the declaration and the category, a dummy value is inserted.

A feature `LCategory`, on the other hand, consists of a category-valued feature name followed by a category, then a list of features to be added. For example:

```
LCategory AGR () => {PLU,PERS}
```

This definition ensures that values of the category-valued feature AGR in categories assigned to whole words will contain values for the features PLU and PERS which are either supplied by the various descriptive mechanisms (which will already have applied) or are special **dummy** values. More precisely, any category that contains the named category-valued feature (AGR in the above example) with a value which is an extension of the specified category (the empty category () in the above example) is given dummy values for the listed features (PLU and PERS here) if no values are already present.

For example, suppose we have the simple LCategory definition:

```
LCategory ((N +)(V -)) =>
             {PLU, POSS, CASE, PRD, PN, PRO,
              COUNT, PART, NFORM, PER}
```

This definition ensures that the category of any noun returned by the lexicon will bear specifications for every feature on the right-hand side of the arrow (in addition to those on the left-hand side which trigger the completion). If the feature in question already exists, nothing happens, but if no specification is there, one is added, with as its value an atom to be interpreted by the sentence grammar as a variable. A noun such as dog is unspecified for case in its lexical entry, since non-pronominal nouns have no inherent case:

```
(dog dog ((V -) (N +) (FIX NOT) (POSS -) (PRO -)
          (PN -) (PER 3) (COMPOUND NOT) (BAR 0)
          (SUBCAT NULL) (INFL +) (PLU -)
          (NFORM NORM) (COUNT +) (AT +) (LAT +))
     dog
     NIL))
```

The LCategory statement above supplies variable-valued specifications for the CASE feature and others, giving dog the overall category:

```
((PART @D00021) (PRD @D00020) (CASE @D00019) (V -)
 (N +) (FIX NOT) (POSS -) (PRO -) (PN -) (PER 3)
 (COMPOUND NOT) (BAR 0) (SUBCAT NULL) (INFL +)
 (PLU -) (NFORM NORM) (COUNT +) (AT +) (LAT +))
```

As confessed earlier, LCategory declarations were added to the formalism as an afterthought to solve an immediate practical problem. Notice that they are different from the category definitions (`CatDef`) described earlier in Section 3.5, in that they do not interact in any way with other morphological mechanisms, and are a largely cosmetic device to allow an interface to a strict term unification grammar outside the morphological component. `CatDef`s, on the other hand, when employed, are an integral part of the morphological description.

In the longer term, a better solution would be to develop a proper term unification morphological description, and to coordinate its `CatDef` declarations with the category and feature requirements of the sentence grammar.

3.5.3 Simulating terms with a special feature

As mentioned earlier, some of the processing advantages of a term unification system can be attributed to the fact that every category has a single atomic label (its functor) which can be used both as a preliminary check to see if unification is feasible, and as a key under which relevant information (potentially matching grammar rules) can be indexed. Some of these advantages could in principle be gained even in an unrestricted unification system by ensuring that there is one feature which appears in every category, is atomic-valued, and never has a variable as its value. The values of this feature could then be used by the processing algorithms much as the functor of a logic term could be, to give a quickly accessible broad label for the category.

We did not devise our English description with a view to including such a feature, as there was no particular linguistic motivation for it. However, we did experiment with such a mechanism (in an earlier version of the description) by having an atomic-valued feature called `CAT` which appeared in all categories, and which was instantiated in all lexical entries. The lack of linguistic motivation for this feature was evident from the fact that we were able to add it uniformly to all lexical entries (morphemes) simply by having a lexical rule (see Chapter 5) which applied after all other lexical rules — that is, its presence or absence in a lexical entry was in all cases entirely predictable from the properly motivated syntactic features of the entry. This demonstrates that it would be feasible to incorporate this approach into a description of English morphology, which might in turn allow more efficient processing.

3.6 The role of the word grammar

We have presented a varied but integrated set of facilities for describing the hierarchical internal structure of words. At the heart of the mechanisms is the notion of a *feature grammar*, an idea which is now commonplace in other areas of linguistic description. If we assume that the two-level spelling rules described in Chapter 2 are capable of segmenting a morphologically complex word into its component morphemes, the rules (and supporting definitions) outlined in this chapter will specify how these morphemes can be grouped and how their morphosyntactic features can be combined.

In the next chapter we shall go on to consider how these rules can be simplified, by taking of advantages of regularities that occur in the configurations of features within the structures generated by the feature grammar.

3.7 An illustrative grammar

Our full English description is given in Appendix D (and discussed in Chapter 6), but the various facilities described in this chapter can be illustrated by the following "toy" grammar of English morphology (which assumes unrestricted unification). The FeatureClass WHead is explained in Chapter 4.

```
Declarations
 Feature V {+,-}          ; verbal items are + V
 Feature N {+,-}          ; nominal items are + N
 Feature BAR {-1,0,1,2}   ; level 0 is a word (see Ch. 6)
 Feature PN {PER1,PER2,   ; combined person-number for verbs
             PER3,PLUR}
 Feature PLU {+,-}        ; singular/plural for nouns
 Feature VFORM {EN,ED,    ; indicates part of verb
                ING,BSE}
 Feature AFORM {ER,EST}   ; adjectival variants
 Feature INFL {+,-}       ; whether available for inflection
 Feature FIX {PRE,SUF}    ; if a prefix or a suffix

 Alias        Noun    =    ((BAR 0) (N +) (V -))
```

```
 Alias        Verb    =    ((BAR 0) (N -) (V +))
 Alias        Adj     =    ((BAR 0) (N +) (V +))
 Alias        Prep    =    ((BAR 0) (N -) (V -))
 Alias        PNoun   =    ((BAR 2) (N -) (V -))
 Alias        Prefix =     ((FIX PRE)(BAR -1))
 Alias        Suffix =     ((FIX SUF)(BAR -1))

 Variable WORDS  = {0,1,2}

 FeatureClass WHead = {PLU,PN,V,N,VFORM,AFORM,INFL}
 FeatureClass MorphologyOnly = {INFL}

 Top = [BAR WORDS]         ; necessary marking for validity

Grammar

 (PREFIXING                ; a whole word is made of another
     [BAR 0] -> Prefix,    ; whole word preceded by a prefix
                [BAR 0] )

 (SUFFIXING                ; a whole word is made of another
     [BAR 0] -> [BAR 0],   ; whole word followed by a suffix
                 Suffix )
```

4 Feature Propagation in the Word Grammar

4.1 Beyond structural rules

The feature-based word structure rules defined in the previous chapter provide a very general way of defining the syntactic properties of combinations of morphemes. However, there are certain regularities about the relationships between feature values in English words which it seems inelegant to treat as the binding of arbitrary variables within categories. In this chapter, we develop ways of abstracting regularities away from the basic word structure rules, and expressing them as more general *feature passing conventions.*

This is of particular interest in the field of morphology in view of the widespread, though by no means universal, assumption that the structure of complex words may be properly described in terms of constituency and feature propagation. The trend in all branches of theoretical linguistics in recent years has been to abstract away from even relatively underspecified individual rule statements of the kind exploited by feature grammars, and instead to seek generality and expressive power in the interaction of conceptually modular portions of the grammar whose effects are not restricted to a single class of construction types. Thus, in the "Government and Binding" school of syntax, following Chomsky [Chom81], a number of components (such as Binding Theory, the Projection Principle, the Empty Category Principle, the Theta Criterion) are thought of as "conspiring" with the lexicon to produce a complex, multi-level, representation of sentence structure. And, more relevant to our current concern, in the framework of Gazdar et al. [Gazd85b] a more straightforward constituent structure is induced by the collaboration of various devices, including linearisation rules and, especially, universal and language particular principles which instantiate minimally specified categories with syntactic features.

Most recent work sharing the overall assumptions of our treatment of word structure has made extensive use of the notions of *feature* and *feature percolation* or *feature trickling* (depending on the conceptualised directionality of the copying process); some of this work will be reviewed in this chapter. In such approaches, featural correspondences between elements of a complex word are taken to be governed by general conventions referring to structural relations among those elements ("head", "branching node", "non-branching node", etc.), so avoiding the necessity of stipulating for each word how its properties are to be determined from those of its components.

4.2 Other theories of feature propagation

Our view of the role of feature distribution in the word grammar has been influenced by a number of other writers. However, we have not followed in a precise fashion any of their detailed proposals; rather, we see our rule formalisms, and the account of English morphology which makes use of them (Chapter 6), as being in the spirit of such work, freed from some of the more stringent theoretical demands felt by these linguists.

If one regards intuitions of internal structure in English complex words as motivating an analysis in terms of constituency, then it is unsurprising that such an analysis should seek to take advantage of some device for abbreviating and generalising over its descriptions. The structural configurations which can be assigned to complex words are far less varied than those which exist within sentences and phrases. Occasions when one would wish to permit a word (or part of a word) to have more than two immediate constituents are relatively rare, in English at least, and what variety does exist lies almost entirely in the range of categories which may appear in the three positions provided by a binary branching tree. If no mechanism is employed by which features (or morphological and syntactic information however described) may be shared or copied among those categories, then the number of word structure rules will be determined by the distribution of stems and affixes, in the worst case leading to a distinct word structure rule for each affix-stem combination that can be identified, a situation similar to that arising from Aronoff's Word-Formation Rules [Aron76]. However, if categories may be underspecified, and features propagated, then there is scope for a quite impressive reduction in the number of rules needed by the grammar. Among the linguists who have realised this, and attempted to formulate suitable mechanisms for generalising over structural configurations, are Lieber [Lieb80], Williams [Will81], and Selkirk [Selk82]. In view of the common appeal to feature propagation made in this tradition of morphological study, we now turn to a brief survey of some of the suggestions that have been made regarding categorial similarity, remarking on some areas of resemblance, and some respects in which they differ.

In sentence syntax, a *head* is a word or phrase which shares (and, on some views, determines) certain properties of the constituent which contains it; similarly, we could regard the "head" of a complex word as the element which has the greatest influence on that word's properties. This entails that, in prefix-stem combinations, the stem is the head, and in stem-suffix combinations, the suffix. Williams takes a forthright view of headedness and feature propagation, offering the "Right-hand Head Rule":

> In morphology, we define the head of a morphologically complex word to be the right-hand member of that word [Will81, p.248ff].

Features on the head of a word are identical to those of the word itself; thus inflectional suffixes are taken to be specified for the same features as the stems they attach to, and category-neutral prefixes need not have any features at all. There are a number of evident counterexamples to this generalisation, including the English "category-changing" prefixes such as `en` in `enslave`, and the Spanish category-neutral diminutive suffix described below. Williams has an appealingly simple account of the distribution of inflectional affixes:

> Morphemes which bear "syntactically relevant" features like `[tense]` and `[case]` must appear in the head position of words — otherwise their features will not "float" (via inheritance through heads) to a syntactic level. And head position of a complete word is the *final* position.

Selkirk suggests a revision to Williams' Right-hand Head Rule:

(4.1)

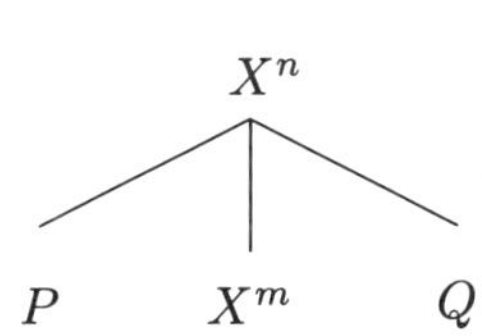

> In a word-internal configuration, where X stands for a syntactic feature complex and where Q contains no category

with the feature complex X, X^m is the head of X^n.
[Selk82, p.20]

Building on this definition of "head", she defines the following percolation mechanism [Selk82, p.76]:

1. If a head has a feature specification $[\alpha F_i], \alpha \neq u$ (i.e. "unmarked"), its mother node must be specified $[\alpha F_i]$.
2. If a nonhead has a feature specification $[\beta F_j]$, and the head has the specification $[uF_j]$, then the mother must have the specification $[\beta F_j]$.

That is to say, the notion of "head" is not defined in a purely configurational manner, as it is by Williams, but rather by taking into account the featural composition of the daughter categories. Thus, Selkirk's proposal is potentially more flexible than Williams' (and is similar to one of the conventions that we shall introduce in the next section). However, Selkirk and Williams both assume that the basic internal structure of complex words arises from a relatively rich grammar; Selkirk [Selk82, p.121] gives the rules as:

(4.2)

a. $X \longrightarrow Y^{af} X \quad X \longrightarrow Y X^{af}$

b. $X \longrightarrow X^r$

c. $X^r \longrightarrow Y^{af} X^r \quad X^r \longrightarrow Y^r X^{af}$

X, X^r, and X^{af} denote words, roots, and affixes of category X respectively.

Lieber [Lieb80] adopts a different stance concerning feature propagation in word structure. Unlike Selkirk and Williams, she proposes a single, general, constituency rule, which figures in the analysis of all complex words. She also differs in drawing no structural distinction between affixes, stems, roots, and words; affixes are identified simply by the presence in their feature matrix of a subcategorisation feature stating which category they may attach to, and on which side the attachment must be made. For Lieber, feature propagation is the only means by which morphosyntactic information may appear; the initial word structures provided by her "single context free rewrite rule" (op.cit.,p.47) are skeletal in the extreme, lacking even node labels. It is unclear how a context free rewrite rule could produce anything of this sort, and the rule responsible is not in fact given. A sensible reconstruction of the theory would be to label the nodes with empty feature sets:

(4.3) $() \longrightarrow ()\ ()$

Lieber's model is driven entirely from the lexicon, the empty node labels being filled by features which percolate upwards from lexical categories. Four conventions govern this process:

I All features of a stem morpheme including category features percolate to the first non-branching node dominating that morpheme. (ibid.,p.49)

II All features of an affix morpheme including category features percolate to the first branching node dominating that morpheme. (ibid.,p.49)

III If a branching node fails to obtain features by Convention II, features from the next lowest labeled node are automatically percolated up to the unlabeled branching node. (ibid.,p.50)

IV In compound words in English features from the right-hand stem are percolated up to the branching node dominating the stems. (ibid.,p.54)

Conventions I – III are intended to be universal, and convention IV language particular; Lieber gives examples of compounds in Vietnamese for which it is the left-hand stem whose features must percolate.

The first of Lieber's conventions is unvarying in its effect, and does no more than insert lexical features into the structure. The second is more interesting, stating that affixes have priority over stems in determining the properties of words in which they appear. Convention II thus subsumes derivational and inflectional suffixation of the familiar sort, and also the less common case of category-changing prefixes. Category-neutral affixes, like `counter`, which attaches to nouns (`counterweight`), verbs (`counteract`), and adjectives (`counterintuitive`) without affecting their category, and category-neutral suffixes like the Spanish diminutive `ito` (see (4.5) below) have, by hypothesis, no category features, and cannot therefore be the source of the features percolated by Convention II. It is for such cases that Convention III comes into play. It emerges from Lieber's elaboration of her Convention III that its intended interpretation is at variance with its literal wording. Consider her example (ibid.,p.52), the Latin **dixerāmus** (first person plural pluperfect of **say** — notice that the traditional "pluperfect" form is rendered by the combination of [-pres, +perf]):

(4.4)

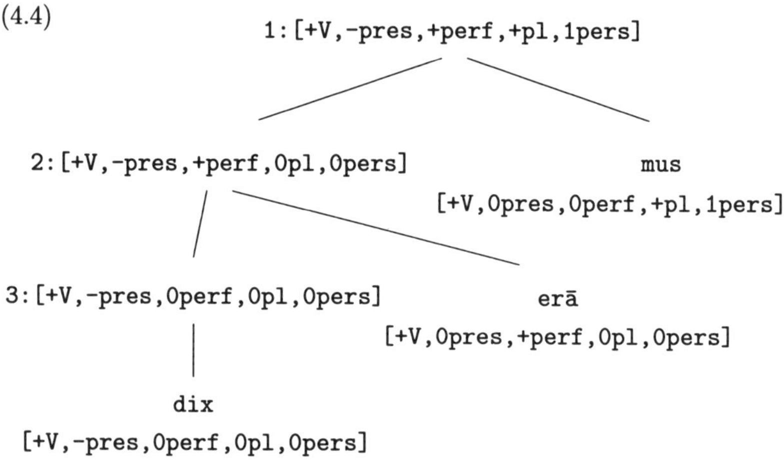

The tree in (4.4) (adapted from Lieber's (28a,b)) depicts the analysis[1] resulting from the application of Conventions I – III. There is an implicit distinction between a feature which is not present in some category, and a feature which is present but for which that category is "unmarked"; the notation "0<feature>" designates the latter case. The node we have indexed as 3, initially empty, receives the features +V and -pres from the stem dix by Convention I; this stem is unmarked for perf, pl, and pers, and so, therefore, is node 3. Convention II causes the features +V and +perf of the affix erā to be percolated to node 2, and the features +V, +pl, and 1pers of the affix mus to be percolated to node 1. These nodes are unmarked for just those features for which their respective affixes are unmarked. However, the first two conventions interact in such a way that no node "fails to receive features" or is "unlabelled", and Convention III, taken at face value, cannot apply. The intention is clearly that Convention III will supply features which are necessary

1 The non-branching node 3 is not permitted by Lieber's binary rule schema, but appears to be required by the reference to "the first non-branching node" in Convention I.

within a given category but which are not available via Conventions I and II, in (4.4) percolating `-pres` from node 3 to node 2 and `-pres`, `+perf` from node 2 to node 1. What must happen is for each node to "know" what features may appear in its label, and, if any of these cannot be percolated from the affix, for them to come instead from the "next lowest labeled node", or, equivalently in our terminology, the stem. This account naturally begs the question of how the completeness or otherwise of a node label is to be determined. It appears from Lieber's exposition (op.cit., p.53) that a pattern is defined for each category: "So although the noun `amīcus` "friend" is derived from the verbal root `am` which is specified for at least some of the verbal features, none of these features will percolate up to the branching node dominating `am` and `īc`, since this node will first receive the nominal feature matrix by Convention II [i.e. from the nominal suffix `īc`]." Morphological categories are thus not to be regarded simply as sets of features, but as comprising at least:

(i) a list for each (type of?) category indicating which features may be present,

(ii) some subset of those features, together with

(iii) the category feature that determines which "feature matrix" is to be satisfied.

It is this more complex information that the notions of "feature matrix" and "unmarked feature" represent.[2]

A further complication in Lieber's theory is that the conventions are intrinsically ordered; Convention III applies after Convention II, and only if the latter has not filled the mother node's feature matrix. By default, then, features propagate from affixes, only being drawn from stems when the required markings are not present in the affix.

In response to the counterexamples advanced by Lieber, Selkirk, and others to the Right-hand Head Rule, Di Sciullo and Williams [Di S87, p.26] introduce the notion of *relativised head*:

> The head$_F$ of a word is the rightmost element of the word marked for the feature F.

This proposal bears some similarities to those of Lieber and Selkirk; like both, it introduces a default element into the definition, and, like

2 Compare the discussion of "category types" in Section 3.5.

Selkirk's schematic definition (4.1), makes the operation of this default sensitive to linear order. It differs in admitting a quite drastic fragmentation of the notion "head" — a word may contain as many distinct heads as it has morphological segments, so that the rightmost element of a word will not necessarily be the head for the purpose of all feature propagation. The aim is to accommodate counterexamples, such as those in (4.5) below, to the unitary notion of headedness advanced in [Will81], to maintain some role for headedness in morphology, and to generalise over inflection and derivation. As we shall see, however, even so powerful an innovation is not in itself sufficient to account for some basic observations.

The category-neutral diminutive suffix of Spanish makes no contribution to the category of the word in which it appears (cited by [Di S87, p.26] from [Jaeg80]):

(4.5)	Adjective:	`poco`	`poquita`
		"little"	
	Noun:	`chica`	`chiquita`
		"girl"	
	Adverb:	`ahora`	`ahorita`
		"now"	

Di Sciullo and Williams suggest that:

> Because the left-hand elements of [(4.5)] are (by default) the rightmost elements of the forms marked for category specification, they are "$\text{head}_{\text{category}}$" (head with respect to category), and so the whole must agree with them in category. (op.cit.,p.26).

Furthermore, since there is not necessarily a single head in each word, the possibility now arises that each element of a word will be a head with respect to some feature or features. In this way, Di Sciullo and Williams are able to accommodate the cases of multiple inflectional suffixation which were not accounted for by the earlier formulation, such as the Latin `amabitur` (3rd person singular future passive "love"), in which "`bi` is the $\text{head}_{\text{future}}$ and `tur` is the $\text{head}_{\text{passive}}$." (op.cit.,p.27) (Presumably `tur` will also be $\text{head}_{\text{3rdperson}}$ and $\text{head}_{\text{singular}}$.) [3]

3 It is unfortunate that Di Sciullo and Williams' schematic illustration of rela-

The revision is not without its difficulties. Category-changing prefixes, as in **enslave**, still fall outside the revised definition; **slave**, being a noun, must be specified for category, thus being $\text{head}_{\text{category}}$; the prefix **en** will not be able to impose its verbal category upon the complex word. More serious are the consequences for the proposal of Williams [Will81] to account for the ordering within a word of inflectional and derivational suffixes. In the earlier work, any inflectional suffix had to appear as the head of a word, i.e. as the rightmost element, in order for its features to be "visible" to the syntax. Now that features expressing tense, agreement, etc. may pass from a suffix to the root of a word just as long as no instance of the same feature appears in a category to the right, this position cannot be sustained. Di Sciullo and Williams are aware of the problem:

> Suppose that alongside singular "boy" and plural "boys" there also existed unmarked "boy", neither singular nor plural. Then in the following compound the plural on the left element could mark the entire compound as plural:
>
> (4.6)
>
> 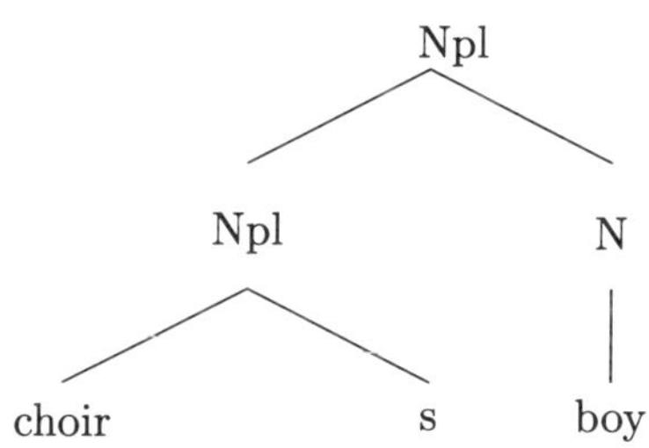
>
>
> ... To avoid this complication, we must assume that all nouns are marked for number.... And we must assume in general that if a feature is defined for a category, then all members of that category are marked for that feature. (op.cit.,p.27ff.)

However, even this general assumption regarding categorial completeness will be insufficient. Consider the ill-formed ***readingable**:

---

tivised heads (op.cit.,p.27,(11)) should fail to support their prose description of the facts; Y and Z, together with their associated feature matrices, appear to have been erroneously transposed.

(4.7)

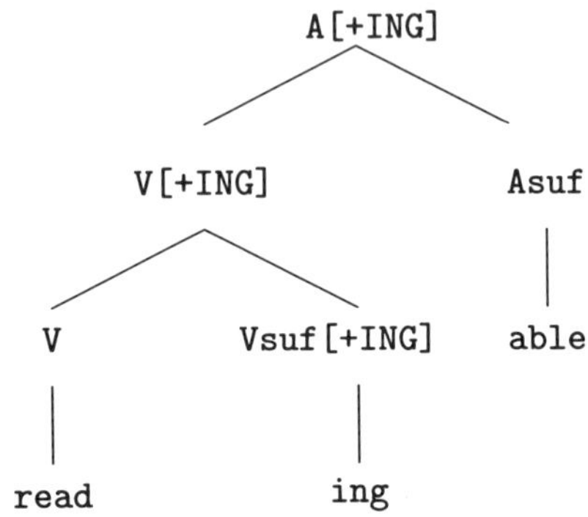

The suffix `ing` is the head$_{\text{ING}}$ of `reading`, and, because `able` is unspecified for `ING`, also the head$_{\text{ING}}$ of `*readingable`, this feature percolating to the `A` node.

Without making some further provision, Di Sciullo and Williams are faced with a dilemma; either `able` has no specification for `ING`, `ing` is the head$_{\text{ING}}$, and `*readingable` receives the specification `[+ING]`, or `able` is specified as `[-ING]`, is the head$_{\text{ING}}$, and `*readingable` receives the specification `[-ING]`. What must be done is to define, for each category permitted by the grammar, an exact set of features which must be present; every category must be marked for every feature in its domain, and for no other. The feature class for adjectives may then exclude `ING`, and so characterise `*readingable` as ill-formed. Note that this is a stronger condition than that acknowledged by Di Sciullo and Williams; they merely require that no category should lack a specification for some potential feature, whereas, in the general case exemplified by (4.7), it is necessary that no category should be specified for any spurious feature. Clearly, the terms "potential" and "spurious" can only be defined on the basis of some independently given feature class. The notion of "relativised head", like Lieber's third convention, demands of any theory in which it is embedded auxiliary assumptions concerning the possible and necessary featural composition of a morphological category.

A different aspect of the same problem my be seen in the following example:

(4.8)

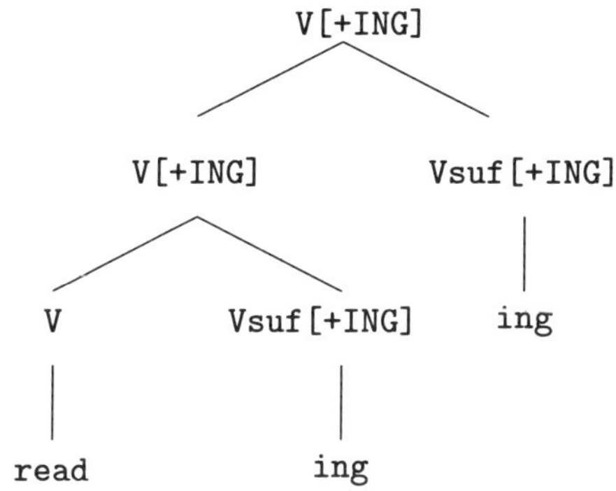

As in the previous account of suffix ordering in [Will81], there is no way of ensuring that identical inflectional suffixes will not be iterated. Even on the assumption that all categories are to be associated with a feature class, and that every category must be marked for every feature in its class, and only for those features, **readinging** will still be permitted.

Di Sciullo and Williams' account of multiple inflectional suffixes will require similar augmentation; according to their definition of relativised head, **amabitur** is correctly analysed as a future passive form, but so is ***amaturbi**. As far as the syntax is concerned, the two are interchangeable, each having the same features regardless of the order in which they are contributed by the suffixes.

4.3 Feature-passing conventions

The above discussion should have given a fairly clear picture of the sort of regularities in the feature markings of morphemes that can be captured by general principles of feature propagation. We thought it sensible to investigate how such feature passing conventions might be implemented and exploited within the style of word grammar we were proposing. The suggestions made in [Gazd85b] seemed to us to provide a suitable starting point, not so much for the detailed proposals made there for syntactic feature instantiation principles as for the underlying concepts of category structures and extension. However, our debt to that syntactic theory, and to a number of linguists working in theoretical morphology, should be clear in what follows.

We have devised three conventions, which interact with the word structure rules described in the previous chapter to produce correctly specified categories for words and parts of words. Two of the conventions refer to specific *classes* of features, so that their effects in a particular grammar depend on the use which the grammar writer makes of those feature classes; the third convention relies on a particular feature, so the grammar writer controls its effect by defining values for this feature in the lexicon. The conventions operate within binary branching rules only, rules with three or more daughters being by hypothesis unnecessary for a reasonably complete description of English word structure, and rules with a single daughter presumably always involving deviant feature dependencies that will require explicit stipulation. The conventions enforce correspondences between nodes in a *local tree* (i.e. a non-terminal node and its immediate daughters), and are stated by describing nodes using the familiar structurally based properties "mother", "right daughter", "left daughter", and "sister".

All of these conventions assume that unrestricted unification (see Section 3.4.1) is being used, as they depend crucially on the notion of a feature specification being "absent" from a category.

4.3.1 The Word-Head Convention

The first convention captures the notion that, in most circumstances, the right daughter is, in English, the "head" of the morphological construction. It relies on there being a class of features called `WHead` features, which the grammar writer is at liberty to define:

> The values of the `WHead` features in the mother must be the same as the values of the corresponding `WHead` features in the right daughter.

The Word-Head Convention is a straightforward analogue of the simplest case of the Head Feature Convention of [Gazd85b, p.94], and is similarly concerned with expressing an intuitive notion of centrality. "Head" is a familiar, though controversial, concept in morphology, and our analysis follows that of Williams [Will81] among others in taking it to be amenable to the simple structural definition implicit in the Word-Head Convention (cf. the discussion in Section 4.2 above). Such equality of feature values could, of course, be achieved using the feature variables in the word structure rules (Chapter 3). This observation suggests that, if a linguist wished to use our descriptive framework, but with relationships between features other than those we have defined, the correct approach would be to employ feature variables directly. However, as we shall see below, it may well prove difficult to achieve comparable generality.

In our description of English, the `WHead` set is:

```
{N, V, INFL, PAST, AFORM, VFORM, ADV, PLU, AT,
 NUM, REG, LAT, PRD, FIN, COUNT, QUA, PART, PRO,
 PN, PER, NFORM, POSS}
```

Some examples will clarify the kind of correspondence which the Word-Head Convention is designed to produce.

Suppose we have a word structure rule

```
[BAR 0]  ->  [BAR 0],  [FIX SUF]
```

and lexical entries which assign syntactic categories as follows:[4]

```
cup : [BAR 0, V -, N +, PLU - ]
+s  : [BAR -1, FIX SUF, V -, N +, PLU +]
```

(The feature `BAR` indicates whether an item is a bound or a free morpheme — see Section 6.4.) The rule would, on its own, license a tree of the form

(4.9)

```
                   [BAR 0]
              /              \
 [BAR 0, V -,            [BAR -1, FIX SUF,
  N +, PLU -]             V -, N +, PLU +]
      |                        |
     cup                       +s
```

Once the Word-Head Convention has been applied to the `WHead` features `V`, `N`, and `PLU`, the complete tree is as follows:

---

4 We are assuming an analysis in which there are two major category features `N` and `V`, with nouns, verbs, adjectives and prepositions being cross-classified using the four possible combinations of values for these features; see Section 6.9.1.

(4.10)

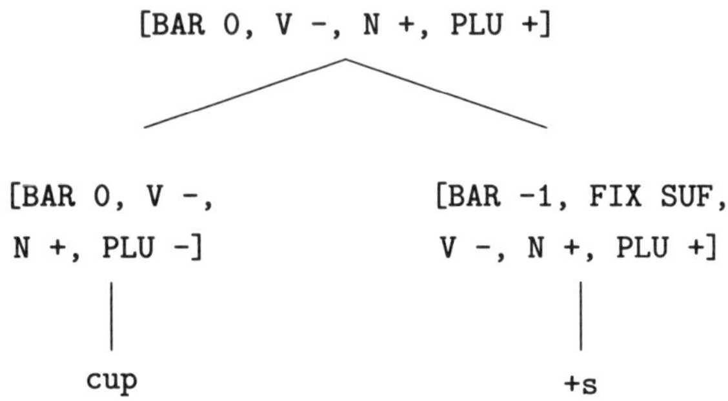

Note that, although both daughters contain (V -) and (N +), their presence in the mother is due to their presence in the right daughter. Derivational suffixation follows the same pattern, except that the major category features N and V often take different values on the right daughter (suffix) and on the stem; in such cases, the Word-Head Convention ensures that it is the suffix that supplies the major category features for whole word. For example, **happy** and **ness** combine to give **happiness**, with the marking [N +, V -] originating from the suffix.

Any feature specification given in word grammar rules must be compatible with the feature passing conventions; that is, the conventions are *not* merely a form of "default" mechanisms which fill in features left unspecified by the grammar rules (though they often have that effect). For example, if we try to analyse **cups** using the lexical entries and **WHead** feature set shown above in conjunction with either of the following (empirically incorrect) rules, the result is failure:

```
[BAR 0, PLU -]  ->  [BAR 0],  [FIX SUF]
[BAR 0, PLU -]  ->  [BAR 0],  [FIX SUF, PLU +]
```

The specification [PLU -] in the mother category of the rule conflicts with the requirements of the Word-Head Convention, since, according to the latter, if the specification [PLU +] is present in the suffix category, it must also be present in the mother.

The Word-Head Convention is also important in the treatment of prefixation. As stated earlier, in cases of prefixation the head is generally the stem rather than the affix; however, as this is the right daughter the Word-Head Convention gives suitable effects (see Chapter 6 for more detailed and realistic examples).

4.3.2 The Word-Daughter Convention

Although the Word-Head Convention accounts for a great many feature correspondences, there are some we should like to enforce which lie outside its power. Certain properties of some complex words are determined by the stem, regardless of whether this also happens to be the head. Consider the matter of subcategorisation; a verb which in its uninflected base form is transitive does not undergo a change of subcategorisation when an inflectional suffix is attached; `+s`, `+ing`, and `+ed` all preserve this property.[5] In order to reconcile this observation with a strict equation of *head* and *suffix*, one which maintained that the suffix is the sole source of a word's syntactic properties, we should have to multiply the entries for each inflectional suffix so as to supply a distinct suffix for each subcategorisation class. Furthermore, we should face the problem of ensuring that, for example, the interrogative complement `+ing` only attaches to interrogative complement verb stems. It is to cope with such non-head feature dependencies that the Word-Daughter Convention is provided. There is a class of `WDaughter` features to which this convention applies, and for each `WDaughter` feature:

(a) If the feature exists in the right daughter, then its value must be the same in the right daughter and the mother.

(b) If the feature does not exist in the right daughter, but does exists in the left daughter, then its value must be the same in the mother and the left daughter.

Hence this convention will have no effect if the linguist does not define any features to be in the `WDaughter` class.

Unlike the Word-Head Convention, this convention introduces an element of preference into feature distribution. Its first clause is equivalent to the earlier convention, and instantiates the mother in the same way, except that each `WDaughter` feature is treated individually. If no specification for a given `WDaughter` feature is found in the right daughter, one will be taken from the left daughter. The special head-like status of the

5 We are assuming that, for the purposes of the sentence grammar, a passive participle like `devoured` in `devoured by the guests` remains transitive in terms of its `SUBCAT` feature specification, and that a metarule produces objectless VPs in which such transitive passives may appear. This analysis was used in the sentence grammar for which our lexicon was intended — see Chapter 6.

right daughter is thus reflected in this convention too, though the name refers to "daughter" rather than "head".

The first clause enables this single convention to account for instances where a feature specification that would in some words be taken from the stem must instead be taken from the suffix. Typical examples occur in derivational affixation; the adjectival suffix `+able` attaches to transitive verb stems, "detransitivising" them, and the verbal suffix `+ize` attaches to adjectives, producing transitive verbs. If we assume that we still have the very skeletal suffixing rule given earlier, together with the set of `WHead` features given, and that `SUBCAT` is a `WDaughter` feature, then possible trees, after application of the Word-Head Convention but prior to application of the Word-Daughter Convention, would be as in (4.11) and (4.12):

(4.11)

```
                 [BAR 0, V +, N +]
                  /             \
   [BAR 0, V +, N -,     [BAR -1, FIX SUF, V +, N +,
     SUBCAT NP]                SUBCAT NULL]
         |                          |
        read                      +able
```

(4.12)

```
                 [BAR 0, V +, N -]
                  /             \
   [BAR 0, V +, N +,     [BAR -1, FIX SUF, V +, N -,
    SUBCAT NULL]                SUBCAT NP]
         |                          |
      regular                      +ize
```

Once the Word-Daughter Convention has applied, the `SUBCAT` value will be passed up correctly, as in (4.13) and (4.14):

(4.13)

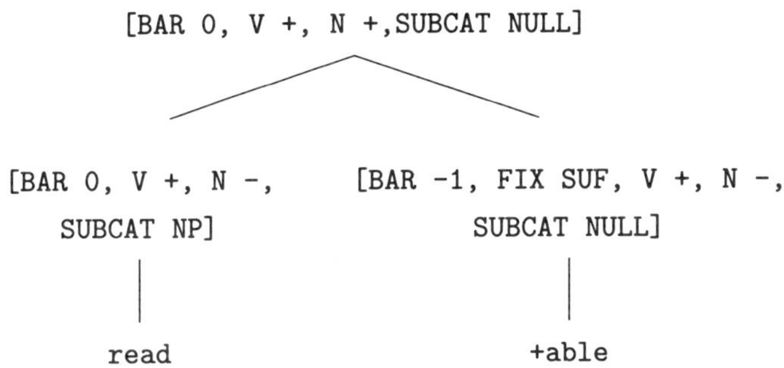

(4.14)

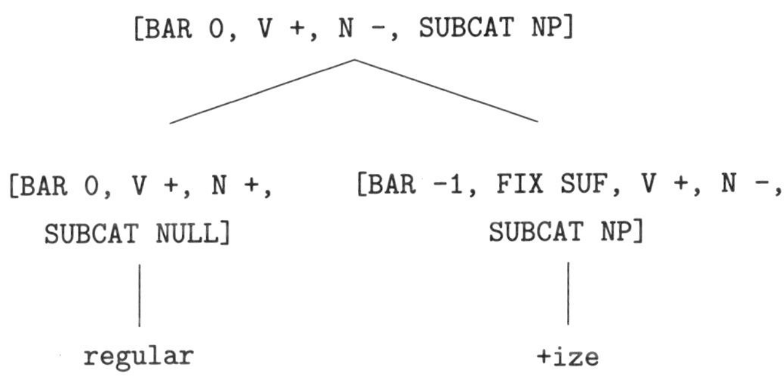

In these examples, the SUBCAT specification of the right daughter is present in the mother, along with the specifications for all of the right daughter's WHead features, and hence the subcategorisation class of the derived word correctly differs from that of the stem which it contains. (It must be emphasised that these are merely simple illustrative examples, and do not purport to capture the full complexity of English morphology.)

An inflectional suffix such as +ing is not lexically specified for SUBCAT. This fact, together with the declaration of SUBCAT as a WDaughter feature, allows the relevant specification in the stem category (left daughter) to be transferred to the mother, correctly forming transitive present participles such as reading. See Chapter 6 for further examples and discussion.

As before, a conflict between feature specifications explicit in rule categories and the requirements of the Word-Daughter Convention results in failure; thus, a rule such as

```
[BAR 0, SUBCAT VP]  ->  [BAR 0],  [FIX SUF]
```

permits the analysis of neither `reading` nor `regularize`, as the former involves a stem, and the latter a suffix bearing values for `SUBCAT` which are inconsistent with that in the rule.

The Word-Daughter Convention bears an obvious resemblance to the effects of relativised heads in Di Sciullo and Williams' theory of morphology, described in Section 4.2 above. Di Sciullo and Williams do not state explicitly that all features are to be distributed in that way, but if that were the case, their version could be implemented within our feature propagation regime by declaring the `WHead` feature class to be empty, and placing all features in the `WDaughter` class.

4.3.3 The Word-Sister Convention

The third of our feature passing conventions is concerned not with dependencies between mother and daughter, but with a dependency between sister nodes. It is a commonplace observation that affixes are in effect subcategorised for the type of stem that they may attach to. In most cases, the criterion is morphosyntactic; `+ing` attaches only to non-inflected verbs, `+ness` to adjectives, and so on. English does furnish instances of partly phonological stem selection, however; the verbal derivational suffix `en` attaches only to monosyllabic adjectives whose final segment is a stop, and the separation of morphosyntax from phonology and spelling in our framework means that effects of this type may be achieved only indirectly, by making the appropriate distinction between the lexical categories of, for example, `light` (allowing `lighten`) and `heavy` (disallowing `heavien`).

The Word-Sister Convention is stated as follows:

> When one daughter (either left or right) contains a specification for the feature `STEM`, the category of the other must be an extension (in the sense defined in Chapter 3) of the value of `STEM` in its sister.

This convention is defined in terms not of a feature class, but of a single feature, `STEM`, which is category-valued. If a grammar writer does not wish to take advantage of the Word-Sister Convention, then no `STEM` feature specifications should be inserted in the lexicon.

This convention allows attachment possibilities to be controlled as follows: the lexical category of an item (most sensibly an affix) contains a STEM specification in which the value serves to pick out just the set of categories to which that item is to attach. To return to an example cited above, the distribution of the nominal suffix +ness can be restricted as shown in the example (4.15):

(4.15)

```
                [BAR 0, N +, V -]
                 /             \
[BAR 0, V +, N +,        [BAR -1, FIX SUF, N +, V -,
  AFORM NONE]                STEM [AFORM NONE]]
      |                           |
    happy                       +ness
```

The value of STEM, [AFORM NONE], is a subset of the category which is sister to the one in which it appears, and so the attachment is permitted. If (as is the case in our English description) only uninflected adjectives are specified as (AFORM NONE), nominalisations like *happierness and *arriveness are prevented, the former because happier is specified as (AFORM ER), and the latter because arrive, as a verb, has no AFORM specification at all (see (4.16), (4.17)):

(4.16)

```
                   UNDEFINED
                 /           \
[BAR 0, V +, N +,        [BAR -1, FIX SUF, N +, V -,
   AFORM ER]                 STEM [AFORM NONE]]
      |                           |
   happier                      +ness
```

(4.17)

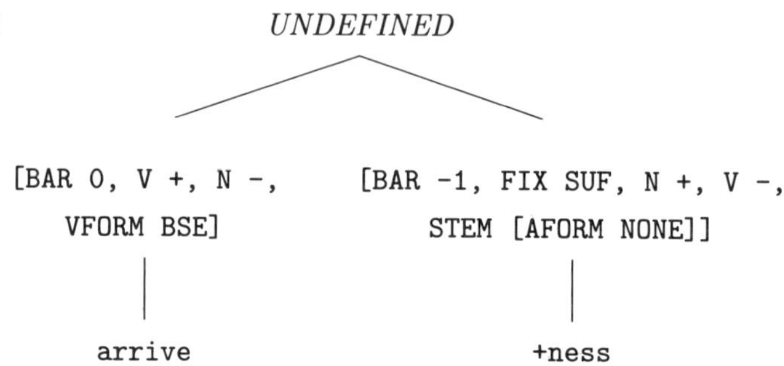

Note that STEM must not be a WHead or WDaughter feature; we do not want it to percolate to the mother, as its effect is local to immediate sisters in a local tree.

As well as giving a very natural and flexible way of indicating compatibility between adjacent constituents of a word (not just adjacent individual morphemes), the Word-Sister Convention gives a way of describing one of the most familiar and salient phenomena in English affixation; the ordering of derivational before inflectional suffixes. This will be described in more detail in Chapter 6.

4.4 Usefulness of conventions

The mechanisms outlined in the previous section, in particular the Word-Sister Convention, effectively subcategorise affixes for the stems to which they may attach. This circumvents many problems mentioned in our review of related feature propagation work. English suffixes may be given a STEM value which prevents attachment to inflected stems, thus disallowing constructions in which an inflectional suffix appears non-finally. Inflectional suffixes may be provided with feature specifications subject to both the Word-Head Convention and the Word-Sister Convention, thus marking any word in which they are the right daughter as inflected, and preventing the attachment of further suffixes. (See Chapter 6 for fuller details of this analysis.)

When taken together with the word structure rules (Chapter 3), the feature passing conventions describe the internal hierarchical structure of words, as well as indicating how the features of the whole word depend on those of its component morphemes. In the next chapter we turn to the rather different topic of lexical redundancy.

5 Lexical Rules

5.1 Lexicon expansion

In addition to the morphographemic rules described in Chapter 2, and the feature rules described in Chapters 3 and 4, the system makes available a further family of devices which are referred to collectively as *lexical rules.* Their function can most easily be understood in terms of a distinction between the form in which the lexicon is originally written, and the form in which this basic description is manipulated by the various morphological rules and conventions. As mentioned in Chapter 1, a distinction can be made between the content of lexical entries that the linguist writes, and those which are the result of a lexical look-up operation. Moreover, in principle there may also be an intermediate representation for the lexicon which mediates between these two essential stages. We have chosen, both in our abstract model and our implementation, to introduce such an intermediate representation, for computational efficiency and for conceptual clarity.

The basic lexical entries as written by the linguist are *pre-processed* (or to use the more common term, *compiled*) into an *expanded* lexicon, which is likely to contain more detailed explicit information. This lexicon is then the representation upon which spelling rules, word structure rules and feature passing conventions operate. (In the implemented version, pre-processing also provides an opportunity to convert the machine representation of the entries into an efficient internal form for the spelling rules to handle — see Chapter 7 — but this is of little linguistic interest.)

Lexical rules operate during this pre-processing phase — they define the relationship between the (usually underspecified) lexical entries written by the linguist, and the forms on which full morphological processing operates.

5.2 The role of lexical rules

A person setting out to write a usefully large lexicon is faced with a number of problems. One is that, typically, the majority of entries will be for entirely regular words, with contents that are (to a degree that will vary with the analysis adopted) predictable; it is wasteful of both time and effort to construct such entries individually and completely. Another is that details of the analysis are liable to change. In practice, the content of an entry may well not be stable throughout the process of dictionary creation. This becomes more likely when, as was the case with the work described here, dictionary development proceeds in parallel with work on a sentence grammar intended to operate with information taken from its entries.

It is practical problems like these that lexical rules address. Their purpose is to modify the dictionary by manipulating individual lexical entries according to patterns specified by the linguist. Lexical rules are of three kinds:

- Completion Rules, which may be thought of as adding predictable information to individual entries.
- Multiplication Rules, which build new entries according to some existing template.
- Consistency Checks, which permit the writer of a lexicon to state conditional well-formedness constraints on entries.

As explained earlier, they are applied during the compilation phase of lexicon construction, when entries as specified by the lexicon writer are processed into an intermediate form for use by the morphological rules.

In addition to the practical motivation for lexical rules, viz. that they facilitate the construction and maintenance of large dictionaries, they may also be thought of as having a theoretical motivation, that of providing a means of stating certain simple linguistic generalisations not expressed by the word grammar or spelling rules. We shall return to these topics below, after describing the form of the rules and the manner in which they apply to the lexicon.

5.3 Format of lexical rules

The three types of lexical rule share the same basic form — a rule consists of a *pattern* which describes a class of lexical entries, together with an *action* specifying what is to be done if the pattern matches a given entry. The pattern follows broadly the form of lexical entries, with sub-parts for each of the five fields.[1] Where lexical rule patterns differ from lexical entries is in their ability to include *conjunction* and *negation*, and in the behaviour of *variables* which occur within them. (Note that, whereas lexical entries may be written in either of the two forms described in Chapter 3, lexical rule patterns must be stated in the Lisp-style syntax, without aliases).

In a lexical rule, a *variable* is any symbol whose first character is the underscore "_". Variables are bound to whatever items they match when the pattern is compared with an entry, and they may be used to denote that item later in the match or in a rule action. A variable consisting of the underscore alone, however, receives no binding and may thus be used to match anything, like the "anonymous variable" of Prolog. Other variables must have a consistent binding throughout an application of a rule.

Variables are of three kinds:

1. A variable which occurs inside a syntactic category, in the position of a feature value, and which matches a feature value in an actual lexical category.
2. A variable which occurs inside a syntactic category, alongside a set of feature specifications, and which matches a *set* of feature specifications in a lexical category.
3. A variable which appears as an entire field of a lexical entry, and matches the corresponding field of an actual entry.

5.3.1 Variables matching feature values

The behaviour of the first kind of variable is fairly straightforward, being directly comparable to the feature grammar variables described in Chapter 3. For example, the pattern

```
((N _val1) (PLU _val2) (V -))
```

contains two variables `_val1` and `_val2`, and it would match a lexical category such as

```
((N +) (PLU -) (V -))
```

1 See Chapters 6 and 7 for an explanation of the various fields, and Appendix A for full details of the rule notation.

with _val1 bound to "+" and _val2 bound to "–".

Within a pattern, a feature specification can be negated by attaching a tilde to it, so that

```
(~(N +))
```

will match any category which does *not* have the feature specification (N +). Bindings established within a negative pattern such as ~(N +) above are not passed on through the match, but bindings originating outside a negation may be passed into it. Thus

```
((N _val) ~(PLU _val))
```

matches any one of

```
((N -))
((N +))
((N +)(PLU -))
((N -)(PLU +))
```

but none of

```
((N +)(PLU +))
((N -)(PLU -))
((PLU +))
((PLU -))
```

(Recall from Chapter 3 that a feature cannot appear more than once in a category.)

5.3.2 Variables matching parts of categories

The second kind of variable, which matches a *set* of feature specifications) can occur only at the *end* of a pattern which describes a lexical category; hence

```
((N -)  (V +) _things)
```

is a well-formed pattern (in which _things is to match any feature specifications other than (N -) and (V +)), but

```
((N -) _things (V +))
```

is not a well-formed pattern. (This does not conflict with the definition in Chapter 3 of a category as an *unordered* set of feature specifications — these patterns are templates which may match categories, but they are not genuine categories in their own right.) Matching occurs from the left of the pattern, and such a variable is defined as matching all the feature specifications which remain when it is encountered, regardless of where they occurred in the lexical category. It follows that only one such variable may appear in a pattern, and exactly one binding for that variable will result from a successful match.

Some examples of syntactic category matching illustrate these points. Since the order of feature specifications within a category is not significant,

```
((N -)(V +) _rest)
```

matches

```
((V +)(PLU -)(N -)(INFL +))
```

with `_rest` bound to `((PLU -)(INFL +))`; a variable may bind to an empty feature list, and so

```
((N -)(V +) _rest)
```

matches

```
((V +)(N -))
```

with `_rest` bound to `( )`.

```
((FIX _fix) ~(BAR _) _rest)
```

matches

```
((FIX SUF)(N +)(V -))
```

with `_fix` bound to `SUF`, and `_rest` to `((N +)(V -))`. The presence of the tilde "~" (negation) means that

```
((FIX _fix) ~(BAR _) _rest)
```

does not match

```
((FIX SUF)(BAR -1)(N +)(V -))
```

since the pattern is constrained by the negation of its `BAR` feature to match only categories unspecified for `BAR`.

5.3.3 Variables matching parts of entries

The third kind of variable, which matches an entire field of a lexical entry, can appear as part of a larger sort of pattern, which matches an entire lexical entry. For example:

```
(be _ ((V +)(N -) (VFORM BSE)) _SEM _)
```

would match any entry whose citation form was `be`, with any phonological form at all (the underscore variable), with the syntactic features listed, and anything at all in the fifth field; the variable `_SEM` would become bound to whatever was in the semantic (fourth) field of the entry.

This style of variable has not been used very much in our description of English, as we have not investigated manipulations of fields other than the syntactic category. As can be seen in Appendix D.4, the only variable of this variety that we use is the "anonymous" variable, underscore.

5.3.4 Complete patterns

As just indicated, the patterns which match syntactic categories within lexical entries can appear as components of larger patterns which match entire lexical entries. For example:

```
(_ _ ((N +)(V -) ~(PLU _) _rest) _ _)
```

would match all entries with the features `(N +)` and `(V -)`, but which lack any specification for `PLU`; the underscores match any value at all in the other four fields.

Such full-size patterns may be negated (using the tilde symbol) and conjoined (using the keyword `and`); for example

```
~(be _ _ _ _) and (_ _ ((N -)(V +) _rest) _ _)
```

would match all entries whose citation form is not "`be`" and whose syntactic category is an extension of `((N -)(V +))`. That is, negation may appear either in an individual feature specification (as described earlier) *or* on the pattern for an entire entry; conjunction may appear only between patterns for entire entries (see Appendix A).

5.4 Completion Rules

Completion Rules are used to add information to partially specified entries. Any entry matched by the pattern is *replaced* by one constructed on the basis of an *entry skeleton* in the action. An entry skeleton has the same general form as a lexical entry, but may contain in any field the ampersand character "&", indicating that the content of that field is to be the same as that in the original entry. Entry skeletons may also contain variables which have appeared in the corresponding pattern, and so have been bound to parts of the entry in the matching process.

A lexicon in which nouns are to be given (in the regular case) a singular marking can exploit a Completion Rule of the following form to add the desired information:

```
(_ _ ((CAT N) _rest) _ _)  =>
            (& & ((CAT N)(NUM SING) _rest) & &)
```

An entry like the following:

```
(dog dog ((CAT N)) dog nil)
```

will then be overwritten as:

```
(dog dog ((CAT N)(NUM SING)) dog nil)
```

The precondition binds the variable `_rest` to the empty list, the first, second, fourth and fifth fields are copied unchanged, and the entry skeleton inserts the specifications `(CAT N)` and `(NUM SING)`.

Such a simple Completion Rule would not be compatible with an analysis in which irregularly inflected word forms were explicitly inserted in the lexicon by the linguist. Consider English irregular plurals such as `men`, `geese`, `children`, etc. The lexicon writer might allocate these words entries such as:

```
(men men ((CAT N)(NUM PLU)) MAN nil)
(geese geese ((CAT N)(NUM PLU)) GOOSE nil)
(children children ((CAT N)(NUM PLU)) CHILD nil)
```

The rule given above would attempt to rewrite these as:

```
(men men ((CAT N)(NUM PLU)(NUM SING)) MAN nil)
(geese geese ((CAT N)(NUM PLU)(NUM SING)) GOOSE nil)
```

```
(children children ((CAT N)(NUM PLU)(NUM SING))
                                        CHILD nil)
```

giving rise to unintended conflicting feature values. In fact, it is part of the definition of what constitutes a well-formed syntactic category that it must contain no two feature specifications with the same feature, so these putative "expanded" entries would be malformed, and rejected from the lexicon.

As the negation facility in preconditions allows a lexical rule to be further restricted, entries for irregular plural nouns will not be affected if the rule is revised to the following:

```
(_ _ ((CAT N) ~(NUM PLU) _rest) _ _) =>
        (& & ((CAT N)(NUM SING) _rest) & &)
```

However, any entries already specified with (NUM SING) will receive a duplicate copy of that feature specification giving rise to the same difficulty seen above.[2] In cases like this, it is neater, and more useful, to leave the negated feature value unspecified:

```
(_ _ ((CAT N) ~(NUM _) _rest) _ _) =>
        (& & ((CAT N)(NUM SING) _rest) & &)
```

The precondition now matches only noun entries that bear no NUM specification.

The situation outlined above arises in our description of English; **man**, **child**, **knife** and other nouns with irregular plural forms are entered once in the singular and once in the plural, distinguished by their value for the feature PLU:

```
(knife knife ((V -)(N +)(PLU -)) KNIFE NIL)
(knives knives ((V -)(N +)(PLU +)) KNIFE NIL)
```

Nouns with no plural form are entered as singular only:

```
(behalf behalf ((V -)(N +)(PLU -)) BEHALF NIL)
```

2 At a suitably abstract level, where categories are genuinely *sets* of feature specifications, this is not really a problem; in a practical implementation, where they may be implemented as lists (in which duplicates may occur), it is something of a nuisance. Indeed, the implementation described in Chapter 7 signals an error if duplicate feature names occur in an entry, regardless of whether they have the same value.

Similarly, nouns with no singular are entered as plural only:

```
(scissors scissors ((V -)(N +)(PLU +)) SCISSORS NIL)
```

Other, regular, nouns are entered with no number specification:

```
(sausage sausage ((V -)(N +)) SAUSAGE NIL)
```

on the assumption that they can acquire a plural marking by the addition of an ordinary inflectional suffix such as `+s`. If this inflection is to happen correctly, we have to ensure that although regular nouns like `sausage` do take the plural suffix `+s`, those like `knife`, which have listed plurals, do not. Our word structure rules and feature passing conventions rely on the value of the feature `INFL` in the category of a word to control inflectional suffixation; items which have `(INFL +)` may take an inflectional suffix, while those that have `(INFL -)` may not. In more detail, this is achieved by supplying the plural suffix with a value for `STEM` that includes `(INFL +)` (which informally means "combines only with items marked `(INFL +)`" — see Section 6.8 for further details):

```
(+s +s ((FIX SUF)(V -)(N +)(PLU +)
              (STEM ((COUNT +)(INFL +)))) S NIL)
```

The Completion Rule which adds the appropriate `INFL` specification to entries is triggered by the presence of `PLU`:

```
Add_INFL_MINUS_PLU:
      (_ _ ((PLU _plu) ~(INFL _) _rest) _ _) =>
               (& & ((INFL -) (PLU _plu) _rest) & &)
```

The variable `_plu` binds to either "+" or "–", so preserving the value in the new entry. Hence, irregular noun entries are expanded thus:

```
(knife knife ((V -)(N +)(PLU -)(INFL -)) KNIFE NIL)
(knives knives ((V -)(N +)(PLU +)(INFL -)) KNIFE NIL)
(behalf behalf ((V -)(N +)(PLU -)(INFL -)) BEHALF NIL)
(scissors scissors ((V -)(N +)(PLU +)(INFL -))
                                           SCISSORS NIL)
(sausage sausage ((V -)(N +)) SAUSAGE NIL)
```

The majority of noun entries are unaffected, being, as yet, unspecified for `PLU`. In order for `sausage`, etc. to be handled correctly by the sentence grammar, its number will need to be stated; a further Completion Rule adds `(PLU -)` to all noun entries that lack a value for this feature:

```
Add_PLU_MINUS:
   (_ _ ((V -) (N +) ~(PLU _) _rest) _ _) =>
           (& & ((N +) (V -) (PLU -) _rest) & &)
```

All noun entries now have the required number information:

```
(knife knife ((V -)(N +)(PLU -)(INFL -)) KNIFE NIL)
(knives knives ((V -)(N +)(PLU +)(INFL -)) KNIFE NIL)
(behalf behalf ((V -)(N +)(PLU -)(INFL -)) BEHALF NIL)
(scissors scissors ((V -)(N +)(PLU +)(INFL -))
                                           SCISSORS NIL)
(sausage sausage ((V -)(N +)(PLU -)) SAUSAGE NIL)
```

Finally, another Completion Rule augments regular noun entries with (INFL +) so as to permit suffixation:

```
Add_INFL_PLUS:
   (_ _ (~(INFL _) _rest) _ _) =>
           (& & ((INFL +) _rest) & &)
```

(In our full description, this rule is slightly more complex, as its pattern takes account of other features which are not relevant to the current issue — see Appendix D.) Typical entries then have these contents:

```
(knife knife ((V -)(N +)(PLU -)(INFL -)) KNIFE NIL)
(knives knives ((V -)(N +)(PLU +)(INFL -)) KNIFE NIL)
(behalf behalf ((V -)(N +)(PLU -)(INFL -)) BEHALF NIL)
(scissors scissors ((V -)(N +)(PLU +)(INFL -))
                                           SCISSORS NIL)
(sausage sausage ((V -)(N +)(PLU -)(INFL +))
                                           SAUSAGE NIL)
```

Two related points are illustrated by this sequence of applications — the ordering of Completion Rules is significant, and their interaction permits a simple but powerful form of default feature instantiation.

The first of these points can be seen from a comparison of the results just shown with those obtained from applying the same rules in a different order. Starting from the same set of user-written entries, if Add_PLU_MINUS were applied first, it would produce the following derived entries:

```
(knife knife ((V -)(N +)(PLU -)) KNIFE NIL)
(knives knives ((V -)(N +)(PLU +)) KNIFE NIL)
(behalf behalf ((V -)(N +)(PLU -)) BEHALF NIL)
(scissors scissors ((V -)(N +)(PLU +)) SCISSORS NIL)
(sausage sausage ((V -)(N +)(PLU -)) SAUSAGE NIL)
```

Note that the negative PLU pattern in this rule restricts it to the last of these entries. All noun entries would now be specified for PLU, and so would be subject to the rule Add_INFL_MINUS_PLU, giving:

```
(knife knife ((V -)(N +)(PLU -)(INFL -)) KNIFE NIL)
(knives knives ((V -)(N +)(PLU +)(INFL -)) KNIFE NIL)
(behalf behalf ((V -)(N +)(PLU -)(INFL -)) BEHALF NIL)
(scissors scissors ((V -)(N +)(PLU +)(INFL -))
                                         SCISSORS NIL)
(sausage sausage ((V -)(N +)(PLU -)(INFL -))
                                          SAUSAGE NIL)
```

Here, what was intended to be a regular noun entry for sausage has been rewritten as one that does not permit suffixation. The presence of (INFL -) prevents Add_INFL_PLUS from applying to rectify the error, and sausage, along with every other regular noun, is incorrectly prevented from taking the plural suffix +s.

The ability of Completion Rules to act as default statements relies on their procedural interpretation, together with the presence of negative feature specifications in their pattern. Thus, Add_INFL_MINUS_PLU effectively states that the default value of INFL in categories specified for PLU is -. The fact that this rule applies before Add_INFL_PLUS allows it to "override" the later rule.

It is important to realise that the basic interpretation of Completion Rules has no notion of "default" built into it — they can be used to add default information because the use of negation and the "wild-card" variable allows the linguist to write patterns which mean "if this feature does not have a value already then add one". In fact, the basic definition of the effect of a Completion Rule does not even stipulate that features must be added, since a rule *replaces* the matched entry with the revised version (perhaps these rules should have been called "Replacement Rules"). Hence a Completion Rule could be used to *alter* the values of features within the lexicon (e.g. changing all nouns to adjectives!), or to *remove* features from entries. Although these alternative usages are perhaps of little linguistic interest, they are extremely useful in certain practical situations, where the rules can be used as a special-purpose language for editing large lexicons in a systematic way (see further comments on this in Section 5.8 below).

5.5 Multiplication Rules

Multiplication Rules extend the lexicon by constructing additional entries, typically differing in some predictable way from an existing one. They are similar in form to Completion Rules, except that the "action" component consists of a *list* of entry skeletons as described above. Any entry matched by the pattern of a Multiplication Rule remains unchanged, but one or more additional entries are constructed according to the entry skeleton list, and inserted into the lexicon following the original. In general, such rules are employed to create similar entries with varying feature markings; negation and disjunction are not available within the syntax field of lexical entries, and Multiplication Rules make it possible to express the type of generalisation that could be achieved with these devices, albeit in an indirect manner.

English verbs have a common form for their uninflected "base" or bare infinitive, first and second person singular and plural and third person plural of the present tense; the following Multiplication Rule takes an initial base form entry and produces from it three additional entries covering the other cases:

```
(_ _ ((CAT V)(VFORM BSE)(INFL +) _rest) _ _)
 =>>
 (
  (& & ((CAT V)(PN PER1)(TNS PRES)(INFL -) _rest) & &)
  (& & ((CAT V)(PN PER2)(TNS PRES)(INFL -) _rest) & &)
  (& & ((CAT V)(PN PLU)(TNS PRES)(INFL -) _rest) & &)
 )
```

As the rule simply copies the other fields of the entry, it may be interpreted as stating that plural and first and second person variants of present tense verbs have the same form, phonology, semantics and other information as the base. An alternative, and perhaps more natural, interpretation, is that a given verb form is associated with four morphosyntactic categories; the resulting entries thus contain information that might well be compressed into a single entry, given a richer language for describing categories in terms of disjunctions and negations of sets of features.

Multiplication Rules differ from Completion Rules in three respects: whereas Completion Rules replace the original entry with a new one, Multiplication Rules retain the original in addition to those newly created; Multiplication Rules, but not Completion Rules, are able to relate a basic entry to more than one additional entry; and all the Multiplication Rules apply, notionally simultaneously, to the same set of lexical entries — no Multiplication Rule ever applies to the output of any other Multiplication Rule. This last point means that the order in which Multiplication Rules are written is irrelevant, since they cannot feed or bleed each other. The motivation for this restriction is the need to prevent infinite reapplication; if Multiplication Rules were able to apply to an entry which had itself been created by some such rule, it would be difficult to guarantee that no recursion would arise from their interaction. Note that the problem could not be circumvented by automatically checking the patterns and entry skeletons of Multiplication Rules, as the output of a Multiplication Rule also depends on the contents of the original entry; checking for guaranteed termination of a set of recursively-applicable Multiplication Rules would almost certainly equivalent to the halting problem for Turing machines.

A further difference between Completion Rules and Multiplication Rules is therefore that the latter cannot be used to provide default-style behaviour.

5.6 Consistency Checks

Unlike Completion and Multiplication Rules, Consistency Checks do not extend the lexicon; rather, they provide a means of verifying that entries have been constructed correctly, either by the writer or by the other lexical rules. The pattern and action components of a Consistency Check have the same form, and they are connected by the keyword `demands`. The interpretation of a Consistency Check is that any entry which matches the pattern must also match the action. If it does not, then the entry is (linguistically) ill-formed, and must be omitted from the expanded lexicon. If both patterns match, the entry is retained unchanged. It is important to notice that there are two different notions of well-formedness regarding lexical entries. The basic notion is imposed by our definition of what constitutes a lexical entry, in that it must have the four linguistic fields outlined earlier — citation form, syntactic category, phonological form and semantic form — with a fifth extra field in the implemented system. The content of the third field must meet the formal definition of a syntactic category, and the other fields must contain suitable symbolic expressions. There is also the notion of *linguistic* well-formedness, which may depend on the linguistic analyses being used, and may involve quite idiosyncratic constraints or dependencies between the values of features in an entry. Consistency Checks are used to ensure that the expanded lexicon contains only entries which meet these *linguistic* well-formedness constraints.

In an analysis that makes use of the two boolean valued features `N` and `V` to encode the major category of lexical items (see Section 6.9.1), one would probably wish to ensure that any entry specified for `V` should also be specified for `N`, and vice versa; this requirement can be stated in the two rules:

```
V_MustHave_N :
    (_ _ ((V _) _rest) _ _)  demands
                        (_ _ ((N _) _rest) _ _)

N_MustHave_V :
    (_ _ ((N _) _rest) _ _)  demands
                        (_ _ ((V _) _rest) _ _)
```

As with the other types of lexical rule, Consistency Checks may be regarded as embodying linguistic statements, such as "past participles of verbs are necessarily unmarked for tense". However, the analogy with devices such as the Feature Cooccurrence Restrictions (FCRs) of GPSG [Gazd85b] should not be pushed too far; a properly written basic set of entries, together with correct Completion and Multiplication Rules, should construct linguistically well-formed entries without any intervention from the Consistency Checks, and Consistency Checks have no power to construct entries. That is, our mechanisms have no counterpart of the "free instantiation of features" that makes FCRs necessary in GPSG.

5.7 Application of lexical rules

The lexical rules are applied to each entry in turn, and each type of rule applies *en bloc*, all Completion Rules preceding all Multiplication Rules, which in turn precede the Consistency Checks, or, as an alternative, with the Multiplication Rules preceding the Completion Rules, but the two main types of rule (Completion and Multiplication) cannot be intermingled and Consistency Checks are always last. It is most effective to apply Consistency Checks after other lexical rules have had the opportunity to introduce errors.

As within rule sets, the order of application follows the order in which the rules are stated. It should be clear, moreover, that rules sets written with one order in view will not, in general, have the same effect when another order is employed.

When Multiplication Rules are used in combination with Completion Rules, care must be taken to ensure that they are compatible. When Completion Rules precede Multiplication Rules, the latter must reproduce the effects of the former. This can be illustrated in the following example, in which we assume an analysis in which `FIN` distinguishes between finite and non-finite, `INFL` controls the attachment of inflectional suffixes (as described in Section 5.4 above), `AGR` is a category-valued feature stating the type of subject that a verb takes, and subcategorisation is ignored. Suppose we have basic regular verb entries of the form:

```
(write write ((CAT V)) WRITE NIL)
```

and we have the following Completion Rules:

```
Add_BSE:
   (_ _ ((CAT V) ~(INFL _) ~(FIN _)
                 ~(VFORM _) _rest) _ _) =>
      (& & ((CAT V)(INFL +)(FIN -)(VFORM BSE)
            _rest) & &)

Add_FIN:
   (_ _ ((VFORM _vf) ~(FIN _) _rest) _ _) =>
      (& & ((VFORM _vf)(FIN -) _rest) & &)
```

```
Add_INFL_MINUS_FIN:
   (_ _ ((FIN _fin) ~(INFL _) _rest) _ _) =>
      (& & ((INFL -)(FIN _fin) _rest) & &)

Add_FIN_PLUS:
   (_ _ ((CAT V) ~(FIN _) _rest) _ _) =>
      (& & (CAT V)(FIN +) _rest) & &)
```

A Multiplication Rule intended to create entries for present tense verbs agreeing with plural, first person, or second person subjects would have to be written as follows:

```
Multi_Person_Agreement:
   (_ _ ((VFORM BSE)(FIN -)(INFL +) _rest) _ _)
   =>>
    (
     (& & ((FIN +)(INFL -)(PAST -)
           (AGR ((CAT NP)(CASE NOM)(PLU +)))
           _rest) & &)
     (& & ((FIN +)(INFL -)(PAST -)
           (AGR ((CAT NP)(CASE NOM)(PER 1)(PLU -)))
           _rest) & &)
     (& & ((FIN +)(INFL -)(PAST -)
           (AGR ((CAT NP)(CASE NOM)(PER 2)(PLU -)))
           _rest) & &)
    )
```

That is, both the pattern and entry skeletons contain whatever feature specifications (here for `VFORM`, `FIN` and `INFL`) are added to entries by Completion Rules.

If `Multi_Person_Agreement` is made to apply *prior* to the Completion Rules, then its pattern will not match entries such as that for `write`; for this rule ordering, a different version of the rule would be needed.

In our description of English, Completion Rules precede Multiplication Rules, for the reason that entries often need to be quite fully "fleshed out" before they contain sufficient information to properly constrain the application of Multiplication Rules, and the default style of Completion Rule is used extensively to achieve this.

5.8 Lexicon management

As hinted in earlier sections, lexical rules allow one to simplify the tasks of lexicon creation and maintenance by removing information from the entries themselves and centralising it in a form that is easier to modify. A lexicon which has been written with certain assumptions about the featural content of entries can be "edited" into an alternative form by writing special purpose rules (usually Completion Rules) which add, remove, or replace features according to certain patterns.

For example, the lexicon which we created used a fairly sophisticated theory of syntactic features, based on GPSG, but we were able, at the request of another project, to transform it into a similarly sized lexicon with much simpler syntactic categories simply by creating a single Completion Rule which applied after all other lexical rules and removed all features except those encoding major category and subcategorisation.

Less trivially, it is sometimes the case that a lexicon is being developed in parallel with a sentence grammar, and changes to the linguistic analysis adopted in the latter may well have repercussions on the former. For example, one version of a sentence grammar may encode the subcategorisation class of a verb as an atomic value of the feature `SUBCAT`:

```
(see see ((CAT V)(SUBCAT TRANS)) SEE NIL)
```

A subsequent revision might depart from this approach, replacing it with a valency-style analysis like that of Shieber [Shie86, p.27], in which the subcategorisation of a verb is encoded in a list. `SUBCAT` is redeclared as category-valued, and two more such features, `FIRST` and `REST`, introduced. The central idea is that `FIRST` and `REST` together implement a list in the manner of "`car`" and "`cdr`" in Lisp; `FIRST` takes a syntactic category as its value, and `REST` takes a list, either another `FIRST-REST` pair, or an empty list, denoting the end of the list. In the sentence level grammar, the value of `SUBCAT` would be treated as a stack, in which the top element corresponds to a syntactic category with which the verb must combine, whereupon the stack is "popped", and the next item "exposed". The intention is to permit the sentence grammar to use very general rules, by moving information concerning verb subcategorisation from the syntax to the lexicon (cf. the proposals made in [Poll87]). This leads to lexical entries such as:

```
(see see ((CAT V)
          (SUBCAT ((FIRST ((CAT NP)(CASE ACC)))
                   (REST ((FIRST ((CAT NP)(CASE NOM)))
                          (REST ()))))))) SEE NIL)
```

Further experimentation in the sentence grammar may lead to other modifications to this scheme, perhaps decomposing (CAT V), (CAT NP), etc. into appropriate specifications for N, V, and BAR, in the type of feature system described in Chapter 6.

In such a situation, lexical rules permit the user to retain a constant set of basic entries, modifying the final lexical representations indirectly by changing the rules which create them during lexical pre-processing. In the case under consideration, a basic entry might be:

```
(see see () SEE vtrans)
```

where the atom "vtrans" in the extra fifth field encodes both the category and the subcategorisation properties of the word. The following Completion Rule produces a version of the entry suitable for a grammar requiring atomic values for SUBCAT:

```
expand_vtrans_1:
  (_ _ () _ vtrans)  =>
  (& & ((CAT V)(SUBCAT TRANS)) & &)
```

In order to accommodate a change in the sentence grammar towards the list-based representation, the rule would instead be:

```
expand_vtrans_2:
  (_ _ () _ vtrans) =>
  (& & ((CAT V)
        (SUBCAT ((FIRST ((CAT NP)(CASE ACC)))
                 (REST ((FIRST ((CAT NP)(CASE NOM)))
                        (REST ()))))))) & &)
```

In this way, the essential classification of a word may be isolated from what are often the more volatile aspects of lexical entries, permitting different levels of detail to be distinguished in a type of data abstraction.

5.9 The advantages of lexical rules

It should be clear from the above discussions that lexical rules fulfil both a theoretical role, allowing the explicit statement of linguistic generalisations about lexical entries, and a practical role, permitting the expansion of a conveniently terse lexicon into a more detailed version, and also providing quite powerful tools for maintaining or editing a large lexicon.

In our overall model (both theoretically and in the implementation), lexical rules operate on the lexicon specified by the linguist to create a more detailed lexicon for subsequent use by the various morphological mechanisms described in Chapters 2, 3 and 4.

We will now discuss our particular description of English, which employs all these linguistic formalisms in an integrated way.

6 A Description of English

6.1 Preamble

The preceding chapters have defined the various kinds of rules and conventions which we devised for the description of morphological and lexical phenomena, particularly those of English. We can now demonstrate the application of these mechanisms, by outlining and giving the motivation for a linguistic description of a non-trivial subset of English. These rules and lexical entries were developed along with a large sentence grammar within the general framework of GPSG (see [Bris87], [Bogu87], [Grov89]), and are thus not a description of morphological issues in isolation. Indeed, some of our decisions were directly influenced by the requirements of the sentence grammar, as may become clear later. The description evolved through many intermediate versions (see [Ritc87c] for details of an early one), and many of the later additions (particularly in the lexical rules) were made by the authors of the sentence grammar without particular regard for morphological issues. Most of the original description was based on a lexicon of about 7,000 commonly occurring morphemes, but the dictionary has since grown to over 62,000 entries.

The sentence grammar is large and complex. In particular, it requires many lexical distinctions to be drawn, each of which is expressed in the featural content of the categories affected. This presents an expository problem; in order to represent accurately the operation of the lexical and morphological rules, it would be necessary to present examples whose categorial complexity would obscure the very patterns which it is our intention to display. Accordingly, we shall often take the liberty of suppressing without comment feature specifications whose inclusion would be an irrelevant distraction.

6.2 Overview of the model

The descriptive framework we are assuming has been described in great detail in the preceding chapters, but we will give a brief summary before presenting our discussion of English morphology.

There are the following aspects to a full description:

1. Lexical entries. Each item in the basic lexicon constructed by the grammar writer must contain at least a representation of the orthographic form of the phrase, word, or morpheme in a suitable lexical alphabet (see Chapter 2), and a category (set of syntactic feature specifications) as defined in Chapter 3.
2. Lexical rules. There are Completion Rules which add predictable information to individual entries, Multiplication Rules which create new predictable entries, and Consistency Checks which vet the internal linguistic content of entries. Chapter 5 gives fuller details.
3. Word structure rules. There are unification grammar rules which define how morphemes may combine, in terms of their feature values, as described in Chapter 3.
4. Feature classes. The various features which appear in syntactic categories may be allocated to various special classes, and the feature passing conventions (Chapter 4) will operate on these features accordingly.
5. Spelling rules. Two-level morphographemic rules (Chapter 2) must be written to ensure that concatenations of lexical forms have the correct surface spelling.
6. Defaults. Any feature may be given a simple default value, which will be used if no other value is available (Section 3.3.6).
7. Top category. The linguist must decide what combination of syntactic features counts as the criterion for a fragment being a whole word (Section 3.5.1).

When testing a linguistic description using the implemented system (Chapter 7) there are various other notational trimmings (aliases, variable declarations, etc.), but the above summary covers all the decisions which have direct linguistic content.

6.3 What is a morpheme?

As should have become clear from earlier chapters, particularly Chapter 3, we prefer to decompose words into their parts where there is a good linguistic motivation for doing so. Despite many years of linguistic research, there is still no widely accepted definition of what constitutes a "morpheme". One possible approach posits highly abstract entities underlying words, so that, for example, the word `men` is deemed to be composed of two "morphemes", namely the morpheme `man` and the morpheme `plural`. Such an outlook detaches the issue of morpheme composition from the issue of structural form (whether written or spoken), and is somewhat incompatible with our attempt to adopt rules of structural combination (such as those in Chapter 3). We chose instead to treat a word like `men` as an atomic "morpheme" in its own right, which would nevertheless have a syntactic feature indicating plurality, and should have a semantic entry similar or identical to that for `man`. That is, we have separated the concrete form of a word (which might be quite idiosyncratic) from the allocation of morphosyntactic labellings such as "plural", and have described them at separate levels. This is not a compromise, but a fairly principled distinction which gives a cleaner description.

Adopting this approach still leaves the lexicon writer the task of deciding exactly which items are to be decomposed and which are to be treated as atomic. For example, consider the word `children`. Unlike `men`, this word could be segmented into an obvious stem `child` and a concrete suffix `ren`. To incorporate such a segmentation into our framework, we would need either to create a plural morpheme `ren` which attached *only* to the stem `child` (which could be done via the `STEM` feature — Section 4.3.3), or else devise a spelling rule (or rules) which would ensure that the surface character sequence `ren` would correspond to the lexical `s` (or some other standard plural ending) in just the right context. Although either of these solutions is possible within our formalisms, we decided that they were less elegant than simply entering `children` in the lexicon as an atomic item, with a plural marking among its syntactic features.

Notice that this is not merely a question of practical convenience or computational complexity (although the latter might be an interesting candidate for a working formalisation of the notion of linguistic "elegance"). Deciding to decompose an orthographically idiosyncratic word (e.g. `destruction`) is not a option to be taken lightly, as it could complicate the various rules in a manner which would be unattractive even to those linguists unconstrained by the limitations of an implementation.

A slightly more complicated example is provided by sets of words such as `retract`, `detract`, `tractable` or `receive`, `deceive`, `conceive`, etc., where there might (under some traditional schemes) be thought to be a central stem ("tract" or "ceive"). We decided *not* to decompose these words, because although their internal composition is very regular orthographically (i.e. the spelling rules would be straightforward, perhaps even non-existent), we could see little motivation at the other levels of the model. This is because our criteria for considering a word to be morphologically complex are stricter than many. Among them, and by no means the least important, is the assumption that, for our purposes, a complex word is one which may be subdivided not only in form but also in meaning. Although we did not investigate the question of a compositional semantics for words (i.e. defining the meaning of a word on the basis of the meanings of its component morphemes), we intended that the word structure (morphotactic) rules would in principle reflect semantic regularities, and could perhaps be developed to have associated semantic effects, much as is commonly done for sentence level syntax. To this end, the formal definition of well-formedness for a word (see Appendix F) specifies a *tree* as the internal structure of a word, and in the implementation (see Chapter 7) it is possible to define the result of lexical look-up to be this tree. This hierarchical internal structure of the word could in principle be used as the basis of compositional semantic rules for English words.[1]

It is extremely doubtful whether classes of word such as `conceive` could be given a sensible compositional semantics which would allow the meaning of prefix and stem to combine as desired, while preserving the ability of the prefix to combine in the same manner with other stems. In other words, the problem to be solved is to show how the `con-` of `conceive` can be the same as, or at least related to, the `con-` of `concede`, `consider`, or `confuse`. Naturally, this is not to deny the interest of such questions, but merely to observe that, given a view of the lexicon in which the entry for a morpheme is a repository of morphosyntactic, phonological, and semantic information, and in which the different types of information extend over the same domain, they present some notable difficulties. In any event, to turn for the moment to purely practical matters, decomposing words like `deceive` would be of little benefit either to the size of our dictionary (since the additional prefix and stem entries would detract from the saving that could be

1 An experimental system using this semantic interface has been devised by Briscoe, Grover and Carroll.

achieved by omitting entries for the regular nominalisations **`conception`**, etc.) or to the speed and efficiency of lexical analysis.

A further interesting class of examples is that where a word is treated *both* as an atomic item *and* as a complex word to be decomposed. For example, the word **`establishment`** appears in our lexicon as a whole word, for use in sentences such as:

> **`This establishment must be closed immediately.`**

However, the stem **`establish`** and the suffix **`ment`** also appear separately, and our rules allow these to combine to form a word with the same surface form (orthography). The combined form is supposed to be appropriate for sentences like:

> **`The establishment of a charitable fund was agreed.`**

That is, the first case is regarded as semantically idiosyncratic, whereas the latter is deemed to be a systematic formation of a noun from a verb.

It is perhaps misleading to use the phrase "morpheme" in connection with our lexical entries, since some of our entries are very far from any traditional notion of morpheme. It would be better to use the more neutral term *atomic lexical entry* to describe our basic units. The description (lexical entries, lexical rules, spelling rules, word structure rules) was developed as an integrated whole, and choices about what should count as a separate lexical item were dependent on decisions about the various rules needed. Although the criteria sketched above were relevant, the overall (informal) notion of "elegance" was applied to the description *as a whole*, not just the list of lexical entries in isolation. As remarked earlier, we also had to make decisions which were compatible with a comprehensive and linguistically principled sentence grammar.

An atomic lexical entry is regarded as containing four linguistically significant fields (see Chapter 7 for details of what was actually stored in the data files):

1. Citation field. This is a sequence of characters in a (pre-defined) *lexical alphabet*. It could contain non-English alphabetic symbols (for example, we use the plus sign "**`+`**" to mark most affixes), including spaces (so that phrases such as "**`New York`**" or "**`by and large`**" could be included as single items). These forms constitute the "key" for looking up entries, and the spelling rules operate on them, in the manner outlined in Chapter 2.

2. Syntactic features. This is a single *syntactic category* in the sense of Chapter 3, and is used by the word structure rules to determine combinations of morphemes.
3. Phonological Field. This is a representation of the pronunciation of the word or part of word represented in the entry. As we are not exploring phonetic or phonological issues, we do not actually take any account of this field (dummy symbols are put there in the implemented version).
4. Semantic field. This is an arbitrary expression in whatever semantic representation language is chosen by the lexicon writer. As with the phonological field, we take no interest in the content of this field.

Hence we are able to put virtually any word, fragment of word, or phrase into the lexicon, subject only to the constraints that:

1. There must be spelling rules which would relate surface forms to the lexical form(s) in the correct way; this was a constraint on the content of the citation form.
2. There must be word structure rules which combine lexical items in the correct way; this was a constraint on the content of the syntactic category.
3. Any lexical rules which are defined should operate correctly; this was a constraint on the whole lexical entry.
4. The number of different analyses produced should accord with the needs of a suitable sentence level grammar.

It could be argued that the analyses produced for any word should also conform to a native speaker's linguistic intuition about the word, but we can regard compatibility with a sentence grammar as being a more formalised version of this stipulation.

As commented earlier, decisions about the content of any one of the components of the description always had to be compatible with the content of the others, so the constraints were really mutual constraints, rather than being imposed on the lexicon by the rule sets.

This arrangement does not allow for disjunction (lists of alternatives) as part of the basic entry format, so where a single citation form (e.g. `bank`) could have more than one syntactic category, it was necessary to have separate entries. Similarly, if a single syntactic form might have more than one semantic form, this would, had we been concerned with semantics, have necessitated separate entries for each meaning, unless the lexicon writer opted to place a *list* of semantic forms, representing a disjunction, in the semantic field. (This would be quite possible, as the system places no restriction on what may occur in the semantic field in a lexical entry.) These restrictions are not as awkward as they might seem. It would be feasible to introduce notational schemata for writing lexical entries with alternatives within their components, regarding these as a abbreviation for a larger set of our atomic entries.

6.4 Stems and affixes

It is traditional practice to subclassify morphemes into at least two sets of items — *stems* and *affixes* (split into *prefixes* and *suffixes*). Some analyses draw a further distinction, employing a class of *roots* as well, but we found no need for this. We also made no distinction between the notions of *stem* and *word*. That is, we take the stem of both `rediscover` and `discovering` as being the verb `discover`. Hence *stem* is a recursive category — `rediscovering` consists of a stem-suffix pair `rediscover` and `ing`, and `rediscover` itself comprises a prefix-stem pair `re` and `discover`. As part of this approach, we have elected to treat as unanalysable those forms which contain no subcomponent capable of functioning as an isolated word (cf. remarks earlier on "`tract`").

Stems can be thought of as *free* morphemes, and affixes as *bound* morphemes. Affixes depend upon the presence of other word segments for their completeness, and are unable to appear alone in a sentence, whereas stems can appear as independent words. Hence, nothing appears in our dictionary which is not either an affix or a self-contained word.

Within our system of syntactic features, we have used the feature `BAR` to distinguish affixes from stems. In GPSG [Gazd85b], the values of `BAR` indicate (very loosely speaking) the "size" of a constituent — `(BAR 0)` indicates a word, `(BAR 1)` a phrasal constituent of a particular type, and `(BAR 2)` a phrasal or clausal constituent. The intention is that linguistic generalisations derived from $\bar{\text{X}}$ Theory [Jack77] can then be accommodated in rules. We have extended the range of values of

`BAR` below the word level, so that `(BAR 0)` indicates a stem, and `(BAR -1)` indicates an affix. We found no need for `(BAR -2)`. Also, there is a feature `FIX` — prefixes have the marking `(FIX PRE)`, while suffixes, unsurprisingly, are marked `(FIX SUF)`.

6.5 Morphographemics

A full list of the spelling rules can be found in Appendix D.1, together with brief remarks outlining their purpose. A few general points are worth making about the practical assumptions underlying these rules.

The rules are assumed to operate on a sequence of characters in the pre-defined *surface alphabet*, with any extraneous characters that might have resulted from the input of the data on a computer (e.g. line feeds, extra spaces) removed. We did contemplate making the rules more general, to cater for such bizarre characters, but this was dismissed on the grounds that these are not properly linguistic issues, and that the task of writing what is known in computer science as an "itemiser" or "tokeniser" is better tackled in a good systems programming language, not a linguistic formalism. Punctuation marks such as commas were also assumed to have been removed. Hyphens were given no special treatment, with the result that hyphens appearing in surface words would match lexical entries only if the spelling rules and default pairs explicitly permitted the correspondence. In our rules (Appendix D.1) hyphens in the lexical entries were allowed to match nothing at all (lexical `data-base` matching surface `database`), and surface hyphens could match lexical spaces (lexical `data base` matching surface `data-base`).

We also did not give a proper treatment of the upper-case/lower-case distinction, which is perhaps a more linguistic issue. The word `labour` is not the name of a British political party, whereas `Labour` is. There are relatively few instances like this, where the case of the characters in a word indicates that it refers to one lexical entry rather than another, so our lack of a thorough analysis of the problem is not a major defect. Our implementation (Chapter 7) treats upper- and lower-case characters as distinct in the spelling rules, so if the input text contains ordinary words which are capitalised (e.g. at the start of a sentence), these will not match the lower-case lexical forms, since a special spelling rule has not been included to make that match.

6.6 Lexical rules and defaults

The full list of lexical rules is given in Appendix D.4. These are mainly Completion Rules, with a few Multiplication Rules which are largely similar to the illustrative examples given in Chapter 5.

There are also a small number of feature defaults, as follows (the feature name is followed by its default value):

```
BAR 0
COMPOUND NOT
FIX NOT
```

Each morphologically complex word resulting from the application of a word grammar rule therefore bears these values, unless the rule in question demands otherwise. The default values of `BAR` and `FIX` are never overridden by specifications in the left-hand side category of a rule, but rules responsible for compound words have left-hand side categories whose value for `COMPOUND` is distinct from `NOT` (see Appendix D.3). The rules `PREFIXES` and `SUFFIXES` (Section 6.10) do not override the `COMPOUND` default, and so all non-compound words bear the specification `[COMPOUND NOT]`.

6.7 Syntactic features

The complete word grammar (see Appendix D.3) uses about fifty features, and Appendix B explains their intended usage. However, only a relatively small number of these features were morphologically motivated — the majority appeared in lexical entries solely to satisfy the needs of the sentence grammar. Such features (e.g. `CASE`, `SUBCAT`) would be passed up from the lexicon, via the word grammar, but would not directly affect the morphological rules. This is a slight over-simplification, since the workings of the Word-Sister Convention (see Chapter 4) mean that virtually any feature marking participates (albeit rather vacuously) in determination of correct morpheme combinations. Features which were included solely for morphological purposes without any relevance to sentence grammar (such as `INFL`, whose purpose is simply to constrain possible affixations) were declared to be in the `MorphologyOnly` feature class, and thus were invisible to the sentence grammar rules (in the computational implementation, they were "stripped off" before the result of the look-up was returned). The following features were purely morphological in that sense:

`{AT, LAT, FIX, INFL, REG, COMPOUND}`

Another feature of relevance only to the morphology is `STEM`, which in this description does not happen to appear in the categories of complete words, and so may be omitted from the `MorphologyOnly` declaration without affecting look-up.

6.8 Inflection and derivation

No formal distinction is made in our analysis between inflection and derivation — both consist of the attachment of affixes to stems, governed by the application of various rules and conventions, using a single rule of suffixation (see Section 6.10). In both traditional grammar and some generative grammar the two are often taken to be distinct processes, yet there seems to be no good reason for ascribing radically different properties to them as far as English is concerned. Anderson [Ande88] summarises many of the arguments for and against this position in the general, cross-linguistic, case.

However, there are two facts about English word structure that must be taken into account:

1. No suffix may follow an inflectional suffix.
2. Derivational suffixes alter the category of the word they attach to, while inflectional suffixes preserve the overall category, modifying its morphosyntactic properties.

We have captured both these regularities using the feature passing conventions (Chapter 4) interacting with the syntactic features of the individual lexical entries, without recourse to the division of affixation between two levels of the morphology, or between the morphology and the syntax.

The restricted distribution of inflectional suffixes results from the use of the feature `INFL` ("inflectable") to control suffixation — `(INFL -)` behaves in a way which means "cannot take further suffixes" and `(INFL +)` gives the effect "can accept further suffixes". Inflectional suffixes, and non-analysed inflected forms like `am`, `went`, and `worse`, are lexically specified as (INFL -), indicating that they are not further inflectable. Other words and suffixes are specified as (INFL +). The effect is to partition the dictionary into two subsets, one containing items which must not be followed by a suffix, while the other is unrestricted in this respect. Also, suffixes are given a STEM value which indicates what sort of INFL marking they require on the stems to which they attach (this uses the Word-Sister Convention of Chapter 4). These markings prevent, for example, regular inflectional suffixes (which will have a STEM value containing (INFL +)) attaching to irregular stems. For example, the lexical entry for the plural suffix +s contains a STEM value [N +, V -, COUNT +, INFL +], which ensures that this affix will attach only to items with these feature specifications in its syntactic category. Only nouns that are neither plural nor irregular singular forms will have the specification (INFL +), so combinations like **houses** will be permitted, but not those like ***geeses**, ***gooses**. Further, only countable nouns (**egg**, **letter**, etc.) have the specification (COUNT +), so the combination of a non-count noun such as **impatience** with the plural suffix is prevented.

In order to ensure that derivational suffixes precede any inflectional suffix, the former are given a marking (INFL +), and the latter (INFL -); also, INFL is declared, in the terms of Section 4.3.1, to be a WHead feature, which means (informally) that when a suffix is attached to a stem, the overall word takes on the same INFL value as the suffix. This means that the attachment of an inflectional suffix, marked (INFL -), causes the resultant word not to match the STEM values of inflectional suffixes, thus preventing more than one inflectional suffix appearing in a word — ***houseses**, ***worsest**, ***wenting**, ***biggester**, ***readingable**, etc. are correctly excluded. On the other hand, the attachment of a derivational, (INFL +), suffix produces a positive INFL marking which allows further suffixation.

The tree in (6.1) depicts a failed analysis within this scheme:

(6.1)

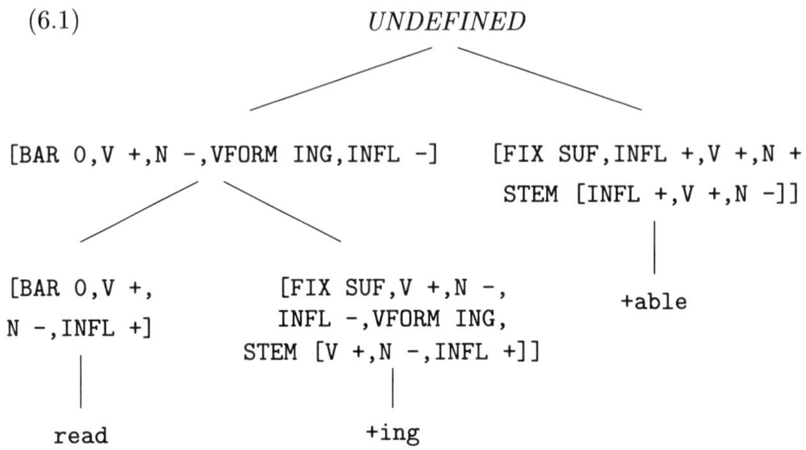

The appearance of specifications for **INFL** in lexical entries is, in most cases, due to the application of a Completion Rule adding predictable information (see Appendix D.4). Any entry, for example, that contains the specification (PLU +) also acquires the specification (INFL -), as do entries for inflected adjectives and adjectival inflectional suffixes with the feature **AFORM** (see later section on adjectives), and those for irregular verbs and verbal inflectional suffixes that are specified for the feature **VFORM**, among others.

This insertion of information by Completion Rules is an illustration of the importance of ordering to the correct operation of lexical rules. The rules which add the specification (INFL -) to plural nouns and to irregular single nouns are ordered *before* another rule which adds (PLU -) to entries for nouns that do not so far have a specification for PLU. Hence the original entry for a word such as **house** (as defined by the lexicon writer) has no marking for plurality at all, and the Completion Rules automatically flesh it out with the markings for a singular noun which may bear a plural suffix. A plural noun, on the other hand, is defined initially to be (PLU +), and acquires the additional specification (INFL -), as will a noun which has only a single form, or whose plural is irregular.

The **STEM** feature and the Word-Sister Convention allow quite fine control of affixation, as exemplified by our treatment of the distinction between stems and affixes according to whether they are "latinate" or "native". Certain suffixes, including **+ation**, **+ative**, **+ion**, **+ive**, attach only to stems specified as (LAT +), where LAT is a feature intended to reproduce some aspects of the traditional distinction between latinate and non-latinate stems. Words whose lexical entries contain (LAT -) cannot take such affixes; for example, the verb contain nominalises as containment rather than *containation. Other suffixes, notably inflectional ones, are not thus restricted, attaching freely to (LAT -) and (LAT +) stems.

The very productive family of suffixes +ation, +ative, etc. is parallel to the less productive set +ion, +ive, etc. The formal similarity between the two classes has led some linguists to treat them as morphologically related. We have chosen to list them separately in the lexicon, since taking presentation to be the concatenation of present, +ate, +ion would be awkward without also allowing the existence of *presentate as an independent word. The different distributions of the two classes of suffix are expressed by means of a feature AT, present only in entries that are also specified as (LAT +). (The specification (AT +) is added by a Completion Rule to all lexical entries containing (LAT +) but without a specification for AT.) The STEM value of +ion and +ive is [V +, N -, INFL +, AT -], which restricts these suffixes to attaching to inflectable verbs with the marking (AT -). The STEM value of +ation, +ative, +ator, and +atory is [V +, N -, INFL +, AT +], and so these suffixes may attach only to inflectable verbs marked as (AT +) (and hence (LAT +)). Verbs such as invent are marked as [LAT +, AT -], thus taking, for example, +ion to form invention; present is marked as [LAT +, AT +], thereby taking e.g. +ation to form presentation. Note that the requirement given by the Word-Sister Convention (that the category label of the stem must be an extension of the STEM value of the affix) allows some economy in the statement of these restrictions; there is no need to specify that +ion and +ation attach only to stems marked as (LAT +), as no other stems are marked for AT.

The features AT, LAT and INFL are all classed as MorphologyOnly features — present purely for morphological or lexicon-internal purposes, and invisible to the sentence grammar.

Further affix-stem restrictions may be imposed by manipulating the content of lexical categories and the value of STEM. A recent suggestion from the theoretical literature, intended to supersede the problematic Level Ordering Hypothesis of [Seig74] and [Alle78], can be found in [Fabb88]; this could be implemented quite straightforwardly by extending the inventory of features and assigning appropriate lexical STEM specifications to suffixes.

6.9 Classifying words

6.9.1 Major classes

Following practice within the GPSG framework, we used the features V and N to cross-classify nouns, verbs, adjectives and prepositions. Nouns have the features [N +, V -], verbs have the features [V +, N -], adjectives [N +, V +] and prepositions [N -, V -]. Affixes and phrasal projections of these categories will also have these markings (remember that our lexicon is not restricted to holding only words or parts of words). As mentioned earlier, the distinction between affix, word and phrase is marked using the BAR feature.

6.9.2 Nouns

Count nouns are distinguished from mass nouns chiefly for the convenience of the sentence grammar. Only one inflectional affix is included for nouns — +s (the plural suffix) is restricted, via its STEM marking, to attaching to count nouns.

Pronouns and proper names have in common the property of functioning as complete noun phrases, despite being single words. One method of expressing this fact would be to provide such words with lexical entries that effectively assign them the category NP (i.e. a category containing the features [N +, V -, BAR 2]). Alternatively, the sentence grammar could contain rules which allow a noun phrase to consist solely of one pronoun or proper name. The latter option has been chosen here.

Pronouns are distinguished from other nouns by the feature specification (PRO +), and proper names have the marking (PN +) (other nouns having the value - for these features).

6.9.3 Verbs

Our treatment of verb forms is based on [Warn85]. Finite verbs are distinguished from others by their value for the feature FIN; thus **is**, **went**, **throws** are all (FIN +), and **be**, **going**, **thrown** are all (FIN -). Non-finite verbs are specified for the feature VFORM; the suffixes +ing, +ed are (VFORM ING) and (VFORM EN) respectively, appearing in (regular) present participles, gerunds, past participles and passive participles. The infinitive to is regarded as a verb, and has the specification (VFORM TO). The "bare infinitive" or *base form* of the verb is marked as (VFORM BSE). This variant also functions as the stem for inflections and derivations. Completion Rules (see Appendix D.4) add the specification (INFL -) to any entry containing a FIN specification, or any value for VFORM other than BSE, so that none of these may be further suffixed (see discussion of INFL in Section 6.8 above). Finite verbs are specified for PAST; irregular past tense forms and the regular suffix +ed bear the specification (PAST +), while the present tense forms, including the third person singular suffix +s, have the marking (PAST -). Passives are distinguished from past participles, and gerunds from present participles by their value for the feature PRD.

Information concerning the type of subject which a given verb must take is encoded in the value of the feature AGR; this is a category-valued feature (see Chapter 3), and the subject must match the value supplied (such matching is of course an issue for the sentence grammar — our lexicon merely supplies the information for use at that level). For example, SING3 is declared to be an alias for the category for third person singular NPs — [N +, V -, BAR 2, PER 3, NFORM NORM, PLU -] — and the entry for the third person singular present tense suffix +s contains the specification (AGR SING3). The irregular verbs is, does, etc. also bear this specification. Other values for AGR may appear in verb entries; for example, surprise has an entry specified as (AGR S), and another entry specified (AGR IT), where S and IT are aliases for the sentential and dummy pronoun subject respectively.

6.9.4 Adjectives

The two main inflectional possibilities that exist for adjectives are those forming comparatives and superlatives. The lexicon contains entries for +er and +est, with the feature specifications (AFORM ER) and (AFORM EST) respectively. Many adjectives appear only as phrasal comparatives or superlatives (that is, in phrases like more intelligent, but not *intelligenter). The feature INFL (see Section 6.8) restricts the distribution of these two suffixes — adjectives such as intelligent receive the specification (INFL -) (meaning "cannot be inflected") via a Completion Rule triggered by the presence in their entries of the value NONE for the AFORM feature. This then prevents the suffixes, which have a STEM value containing (INFL +), from attaching to these stems. Inflectable adjectives, such as clever, have the specification (INFL +) ("can be inflected"), and so accept the suffixes. As the suffixes themselves have the marking (INFL -), which is passed on to the combined form (via the Word Head feature passing convention), no further inflection is possible (preventing, for example, *cleverester).

A further suffixation process is that which forms adverbs like quickly from adjectives. The suffix +ly is taken to be an adjectival suffix (like +er and +est), except that it has (ADV +) instead of an AFORM marking (indicating its "adverbial" nature). This is, by our criteria, an inflectional suffix, in the sense that it renders the stems it attaches to uninflectable. However, unlike +er and +est, it is able to attach to adjectives such as intelligent (although it may not attach to inflected adjectives as in *clevererly).

Some adjectives, such as alike, are restricted to predicative positions (compare e.g. "they are alike" with "*they are an alike couple"), while others are restricted to prenominal position (e.g. chief in "the chief problem" but "*the problem is chief"). The former are marked as (PRD +), and the latter as (PRD -). The majority of adjectives are able to appear in either context, and are not supplied with any PRD specification in the lexicon.

6.9.5 Prepositions

Prepositions are of little interest morphologically, as they cannot serve as stems for affixation, and there are no prepositional affixes[2]. The lexicon contains several types of entry for prepositions, however. Those for which certain lexical items are subcategorised (the so-called "case-marking" prepositions) are specified for the feature PFORM; thus, the to that appears in the complement PP of verbs like give is (PFORM TO). Prepositions that can serve as verb particles have the specification (PRT α), where α is the lexical form of the particle in question — (PRT OUT), for example.

Words like outside are treated as pronominal prepositions, having the category [BAR 0, V -, N -, PRO +]. Like pronominal nouns, they have the same distribution within sentence structure as their correspond-

2 We assume that e.g. within, into and outside are not profitably analysable into consistently interpretable subparts — see Section 6.3.

ing phrasal category.

The inability of prepositions to appear as stems in complex words results from the values of STEM in affix entries, none of which can be extended into a category which appears in the lexicon and which contains the features [V -,N -]. Also, as commented earlier, there are no prepositional affixes. The fact that prepositions neither undergo affixation nor are derivable by affixation from other categories obviously demands explanation; what is the reason for this asymmetry in the categorial inventory? Unfortunately, we have no answer, beyond the conjecture that there is a connection with the status of prepositions as "closed-class" items.

6.9.6 Determiners and minor items

The class of determiners is a heterogeneous one. The articles **a**, **an** and **the** are minor category items, whereas others are treated as members of the category of adjective.

There are also lexical items which do not fall within the major categories provided by the features N and V. Such items have no phrasal projections, and so also lack a specification for the feature BAR. Generally, their category consists simply of a SUBCAT specification in which the value is a symbol corresponding to the word in question. For example, **and** has the category (SUBCAT AND). The articles **a**, **an** and **the** have more informative markings; for example, **a** has [SUBCAT DETN, QUA +, DEF -, AGR SING], where SING is an alias for singular nominal phrases, the value of DEF indicates that a NP which has **a** as a daughter will be indefinite, and the SUBCAT and QUA specifications generalise across other determiners.

6.10 The word grammar

The distinguished symbol for the word grammar is the (underspecified) category

```
(FIX NOT)
```

That is, any item whose value for FIX is NOT counts as a word. This specification is added by a Completion Rule to all entries not otherwise marked for FIX, and is inserted either explicitly or by default into the result of each word grammar rule application, so that all words, simple or complex, are acceptable to this declaration. Hence the only items not to receive the marking (FIX NOT) will be the affixes, which reflects their status as "bound morphemes".

The word grammar is economical, both in the number of rules it employs and in the amount of information stipulated in each rule, with further feature values being determined by word grammar defaults and the feature passing conventions described in Chapter 4 (together with the allocation of various features to the classes WHead and WDaughter and the STEM markings of the lexical entries).

6.10.1 Basic affixation

There are just two rules for affixation, and these are shown below. Each is labelled with a mnemonic name, and introduces two daughters.

```
( PREFIXES
   [] ->
         [FIX PRE, BAR -1],
         [BAR 0] )

( SUFFIXES
   [] ->
         [BAR 0],
         [FIX SUF, BAR -1] )
```

The rule "PREFIXES" states that an item may consist of a prefix followed by a word. The specification (BAR 0) is inserted by default, and so the sequence of prefix and word is itself classified as a word (i.e. an item specified as (BAR 0)). Similarly, the rule "SUFFIXES" states that a word may consist of another word, followed by a suffix.

Both rules, in conjunction with the feature class definitions given in Section 6.11 and the feature passing conventions described in Chapter 4, admit configurations of morphemes in which categorial identity is established between the mother and right-hand daughter. The intention here is to capture the often stated and much discussed generalisation concerning the "headedness" of complex words in English, namely that in stem-suffix pairs it is the suffix which determines the overall syntactic and morphological properties of the word, while in prefix-stem pairs it is in the great majority of cases the stem. Exceptions like becalm (verb formed from adjective), `outbid` (transitive verb formed from intransitive), and `enslave` (verb formed from noun) are beyond the scope of this grammar, though not of course beyond the scope of the general descriptive mechanisms provided within our system. Here, as elsewhere, it is important to remember that the analysis of English morphology being described is just one among many that could be formulated. To maintain the simplicity of our word grammar, we have listed such items explicitly in the lexicon.

None of the rules introduces more than two daughters. This predicts that, for any word which may be segmented into the morpheme sequence $X-Y-Z$, either $X-Y$ or $Y-Z$ is itself a word (ignoring the effects of the spelling rules). This prediction is of course for the most part borne out by English; exceptions such as `embolden` (which contains neither `*embold` nor `*bolden`) are not within the scope of this grammar, and are therefore listed explicitly as items in the lexicon. It is important to emphasise, however, that this is again just an accident of this particular description, and is not a formal limitation on our rule notation; as defined in Chapter 3, a rule may have any number of categories on its right-hand side. (The full grammar, together with all the relevant declarations, can be found in Appendix D.3).

Although we have made considerable use of the feature passing conventions, a lexicon writer who wished to avoid them could simply refrain from using the feature `STEM`, and declare the feature classes `WHead` and `WDaughter` to be empty. It would then still be possible to have some control over feature passing within rules by explicitly equating feature values using the variables within the categories, as discussed in Chapter 3.

6.10.2 Non-branching rules

There are two rules which handle "zero-derivations" — that is, where a word is related to another *without* the addition of a concrete (phonologically or orthographically realised) morpheme. The two words have identical forms, but different syntactic markings. The feature passing conventions do not apply to single-daughter rules, since, typically, such rules are intended to have the effect of changing lexical feature specifications, and so any non-default features that are desired to appear on the mother must be placed there explicitly. That is, we have to rely on the fact that a feature value variable (see Chapter 3) must take consistent bindings throughout a rule, thereby imposing equality between values on the mother node and values on the daughter node. In the next two rules, symbols starting with a question-mark "?" have been declared to be feature value variables.

The first such rule creates adjectives from passive verbs:

```
( PAS-TO-ADJ
    [N +, V +, AFORM NONE, INFL -,
     QUA -, ADV -, AGR ?agr, SUBCAT ?sub] ->
            [BAR 0, N -, V +, VFORM EN, PRD +, AUX -,
             AGR ?agr, SUBCAT ?sub] )
```

The other rule of this kind creates adjectives from present participles:

```
( ING-TO-ADJ
    [N +, V +, AFORM NONE, INFL -,
     QUA -, ADV -, AGR ?agr, SUBCAT ?sub] ->
            [BAR 0, N -, V +, VFORM ING, PRD -,
             AUX -, AGR ?agr, SUBCAT ?sub] )
```

6.11 Feature conventions

In this description, the `WHead` features are as follows:

```
{N, V, INFL, PAST, AFORM, VFORM, ADV, PLU, AT,
 NUM, REG, LAT, PRD, FIN, COUNT, QUA, PART, PRO,
 PN, PER, NFORM, POSS}
```

Most of the features which play a part in our description are members of the above set. The `WDaughter` features are:

```
{SUBCAT, AUX, AGR, INV, NEG}
```

6.12 Illustrative examples

The best way to demonstrate the interactions of all the various devices, particularly the word grammar rules and the feature conventions, is to present some example analyses.

(6.2)

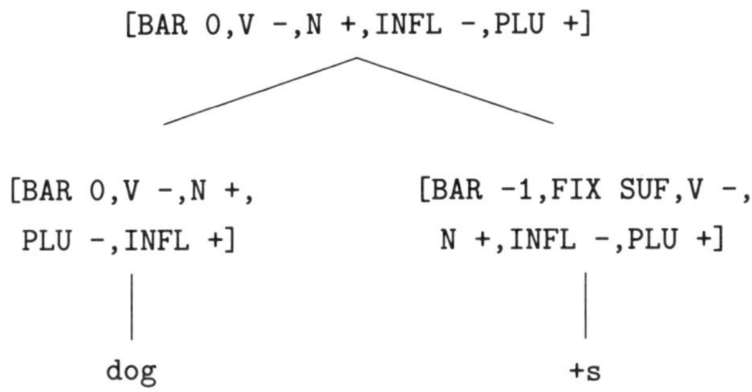

The complex word dogs is composed of the stem dog and the plural noun suffix +s (the lexical boundary marker symbol "+" being suppressed by the spelling rules). The syntactic category assigned to dog in the tree in (6.2) is an extension of the left-hand daughter category in the rule SUFFIXES, and the category dominating +s is an extension of the right-hand daughter.[3] BAR is inserted into the resulting category by a word grammar default as it is neither mentioned explicitly in the rule nor subject to a feature passing conventions, and the remaining feature specifications arise via the Word-Head Convention acting on the category of the lexical entry for the suffix. BAR is not a member of the WHead set, since we do not wish its value to be identical in mother and suffix. The presence of (V -) and (N +) in the mother category is due to their presence in the right daughter, via the Word-Head Convention. One factor which distinguishes inflectional from derivational suffixation is that, with inflection, the *major category features* (i.e. N and V) of the stem and the suffix have identical values, while this is not the case with derivation. Informally, the effect of attaching +s to dog is to change it from an inflectable singular noun to a non-inflectable plural noun. INFL is declared as a MorphologyOnly feature, and the corresponding specification in the mother's category is not available to the sentence grammar, but (PLU +), (N +), (BAR 0), and (V -) are available to ensure the correct distribution of the word, proper subject-verb agreement, etc.

Another example of inflectional suffixation is shown in (6.3):

3 In view of the extensive discussion of the Word-Sister Convention in Section 6.8 above, we shall assume its effects without further remark, and shall omit the STEM marking from categories to simplify the diagrams.

(6.3) `[BAR 0,V +,N +,AFORM EST,INFL -]`

```
        [BAR 0,V +,N +,AFORM EST,INFL -]
             /                    \
[BAR 0,V +,N +,              [BAR -1,FIX SUF,V +,
AFORM NONE,INFL +]           N +,AFORM EST,INFL -]
        |                             |
      happy                          +est
```

Here, a superlative adjective is formed by the attachment of the superlative suffix **+est** to an adjective in its basic uninflected form. The spelling rule `Y-to-I` comes into operation, giving rise to the surface form **happiest**. The category of the superlative contains specifications originating both in the word grammar defaults — `(BAR 0)` — and in the **WHead** features of the right daughter. In particular, its status as a superlative is encoded in its **AFORM** specification, associated ultimately with the suffix in its lexical entry; the sentence grammar thus has the information necessary to place **happiest** in the correct syntactic environment (e.g. **the happiest professor**, but not ***as happiest as the professor** or ***happiest than the professor**). As before, the **WHead** feature specifications of the stem are "lost", making no direct contribution to the category of the overall word.

Derivational suffixation follows the same pattern — see (6.4):

(6.4)

```
          [BAR 0,V -,N +,PLU -,INFL +]
             /                    \
[BAR 0,V +,N -,AT +,         [BAR -1,FIX SUF,V -,N +,
VFORM BSE,INFL +]            PLU -,INFL +]
        |                             |
     restore                        +ation
```

The derived noun **restoration** consists, under our analysis, of the verb **restore**, in its uninflected base form, and the nominal suffix **+ation**, with the `Elision` spelling rule deleting the final `e` of the stem and the boundary marker of the suffix. The Word-Head Convention ensures that the relevant features are the same on the suffix and the mother. Here, the effect is rather more dramatic, in that the equating of features results in a mother whose category differs more drastically from that of the stem. The "verbiness" of `restore` is not represented in the category of `restoration`, which is indistinguishable from that of a simple noun like `dog` in the example above. As such, it, too, may bear further suffixes, producing `restorations`, etc. One of the predictions of this type of analysis is that there are no affixes which, for example, attach only to nouns that are derived from verbs; such information is not present within the mother category, and it is only that category which can determine the possibility of affixation.

As stated in Chapter 4, in cases of prefixation, the head is generally the stem rather than the affix. The analysis below illustrates how features are distributed by the Word-Head Convention in such words:

(6.5)

```
                 [BAR 0,V +,VFORM BSE,INFL +]
                      /                \
  [BAR -1,FIX PRE]                [BAR 0,V +,N -,
         |                       VFORM BSE,INFL +]
         |                               |
        dis-                          assemble
```

The affix has made no morphological or syntactic contribution to the category of the word in which it appears, though, clearly, any extension of the present system to include the semantics of complex words would take into account its meaning in specifying that of the whole. Both `assemble` and `disassemble` are therefore assigned the same syntactic category, and will share the same distribution.

Inflectional suffixes appear in configurations of the sort shown in (6.6).

(6.6) 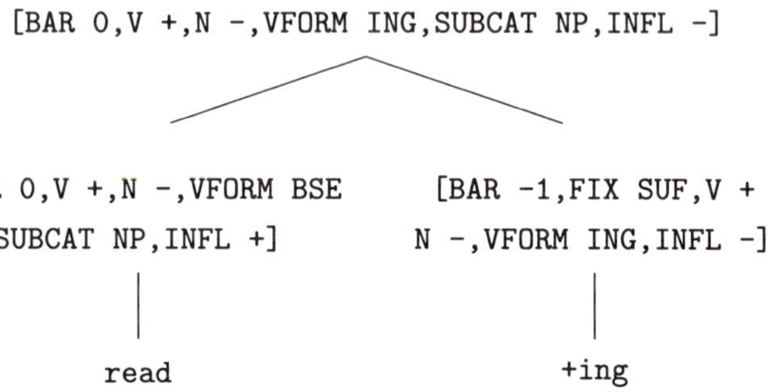

An inflectional suffix such as **+ing** is not lexically specified for SUBCAT. This fact, together with the declaration of SUBCAT as a **WDaughter** feature, allows the relevant specification in the stem category to be transferred to the mother, correctly forming a transitive present participle.

Our **WDaughter** feature class also includes AUX, INV, NEG, and AGR. Like SUBCAT, they must on some occasions share the same value in mother and non-head daughter. The suffix **+ing**, for example, attaches to both auxiliary and non-auxiliary verbs; its lack of an inherent AUX specification allows that of the stem to be present in the mother, so that **reading** is (AUX -) and **having** (AUX +). Verbal derivational suffixes, on the other hand, are all lexically specified as (AUX -), with the result that no derived verbs are auxiliaries. INV and NEG are **WDaughter** features for the same reason. Depending on the suffix, inflected verbs have the AGR specification of either the suffix or the stem. **Walking**, for example, has an AGR specification [BAR 2, V -, N +, NFORM NORM] while **walks** receives the fuller AGR specification [PLU -, PER 3, CASE NOM, NFORM NORM, N +, V -, BAR 2], the lexical AGR specification of the suffix. There are, in fact, three variants of the verbal suffix **+s**, one of which occurs in configurations where the subject of the verb is a normal NP (as in **walks** above), and the others where the agreement is with a "non-standard" subject, either sentential (as in **that we shall fail appears unlikely**) or expletive **it** (as with **snows**, and **appears** when the sentential subject is extraposed). The reason for this duplication is that, in each case, the inflected form of the verb must bear a value for its AGR feature that is more instantiated than that of the stem to which it attaches — a finite verb such as **walks** or **appears** must agree with a subject (i.e. a NP with the specification (CASE NOM)), while a non-finite variant is not so restricted — and the necessary additional specifications vary between the different subject types.

6.13 Over-generation

The Word-Sister Convention can be used to capture finer distinctions than those discussed in Section 6.8. English verbs vary in their regularity, from the largely suppletive paradigm of `be` to the wholly regular `walk`. Mid-way between these two extremes lie a number of verbs which behave regularly with respect to present participlespresent participle and third person singular present tense inflections, but which have an exceptional past participle and past tense form; `go`, `stand`, `come`, etc. are typical cases. It would be going too far to mark these lexically as `(INFL -)`, as that would block words such as `going` and `stands`, unless special entries for the relevant suffixes were created, a solution which has nothing to recommend it. One alternative would be to do nothing at all about such semi-regular verbs; the consequence would be that both the lexically listed past forms `went`, `gone`, `came`, `come`, `stood` and the suffixed past forms `goed`, `standed`, `comed` would be then be well-formed. To some extent, this might be excused as harmless over-acceptance; as these latter forms are never likely to be encountered in practice, their theoretical existence is no problem. In some circumstances, such behaviour might even be welcomed as mimicking the errors of human language-learners. But things are not so simple; any over-acceptance of this sort risks producing unexpected false ambiguities, as when a valid string like `seed` is segmented as `see+ed` (i.e. as a past form of the irregular `see`, whose correct version is `saw`), one `e` having been deleted by the spelling rules, on the model of `agreed`. In order to avoid this, verbs like `come`, `go`, `stand` and `see` are specified as `(REG -)`, while fully regular verbs are `(REG +)`. The `STEM` specification of `+ed` is `[STEM [V +, N -, INFL +, REG +]]`, and so the stems in question will not be suffixed.

6.14 A caveat

We have constructed, for a fragment of the English lexicon, a linguistic description which meets as far as possible the usual criteria of generality and elegance, although it has occasionally been tempered with practicality. The rules, declarations, and entries in Appendix D formed the data for an experimental implementation (see Chapter 7), so they can be regarded as fairly well tested by linguistic standards. However, the description was constantly being revised, and more recent work by others [Grov89] has continued to introduce amendments (particularly to the set of lexical rules). This means that, despite our best efforts, there may be some inconsistencies between the theoretical discussions here and the actual working version as specified in Appendix D. However, we believe that the general ideas are adhered to consistently.

7 The Implemented System

In this chapter, we give an outline of practical software (a collection of Lisp programs) that embodies the mechanisms described in Chapters 2, 3, 4 and 5 in a usable fashion. This is not a complete user manual or an implementor's guide (see [Ritc87b], [Ritc87a] for definitive details) but describes how the theoretical techniques can be combined in a working system.

The aims of carrying out this implementation were twofold. From a practical point of view, we wanted to construct a properly engineered dictionary handler that could be used by others to build natural language parsing systems or front-ends without any loss of linguistic generality or elegance. There was also the theoretical aim of defining in complete detail an integrated set of mechanisms for describing lexical phenomena, confirming that these formalisms were both computationally feasible and empirically useful. Both these aims made it crucial to distinguish clearly between the substance (or limitations) of the formalisms, and the way that we had chosen to use these mechanisms in our own description of the English lexicon. When some particular device was considered, it was important to decide whether this was something linguistically general (which should be reflected in the definitions of the software) or merely a useful way of getting our English rules to operate correctly (which therefore should show up solely in the English-specific rules). This distinction (which may seem trivially clear when baldly stated) can be maintained only with great care, and is sometimes blurred in linguistic analyses or illustrative natural language programs. Our attention was concentrated on this issue by the fact that we were committed to producing a general-purpose tool that could be used by a wide variety of computational linguists.

The original intentions of the project were that it would rely where appropriate on the results of existing research (for example, the work on two-level morphology — see Chapter 2). Although this was possible to a large extent, it was found that many results had to be adapted to match our requirements, sometimes quite radically, and there was a significant amount of research effort involved in deciding how best to integrate various proposals from the linguistic literature. Throughout the project there was continuous interaction between theoretical requirements (coverage, perspicuity etc.) and practicalities (speed of recognition and compilation, compatibility with earlier versions, robustness and speed of implementation, etc.). It is important in implementing such a system that the program should directly reflect the theoretical mechanisms, and that realistic linguistic descriptions should be processable in a reasonable time. Hence, some time was spent looking at various alternative implementations and sometimes the details of the formalisms were modified for computational reasons.

7.1 Facilities provided

The software allows the user to specify, by writing appropriate data files, all the components of the linguistic model, namely:

- a set of atomic lexical entries;
- a set of lexical rules which express redundancy relations within the lexicon (see Chapter 5);
- a set of two-level morphographemic rules (see Chapter 2);
- a set of feature grammar rules for word structure (see Chapter 3);
- definitions of feature classes to which the feature passing conventions apply (see Chapter 4).

A lexicon containing around 7000 commonly occurring morphemes was developed[1], along with an integrated set of feature declarations, lexical rules, morphographemic rules and word grammar rules. Further details of these can be found in the appendices.

The files containing these linguistic descriptions have to be compiled using various pre-processing programs, and then loaded into a Lisp runtime system. This provides various Lisp functions which allow the manipulation of these rules and entries, including the following facilities:

- looking up a single morpheme in a lexicon without using any morphological analysis;
- carrying out morphographemic segmentation on a word (using a lexicon) without any morphotactic (word grammar) processing;
- looking up a word in a lexicon using full morphological analysis;

1 This figure represents the state of the lexicon in summer 1987; it was subsequently increased to over 60,000 in work by Briscoe, Boguraev, Grover and Carroll [Bogu87].

Figure 7.1
The implemented system: the user's files are processed into intermediate forms, which, once loaded, provide the facilities listed at the foot of the diagram

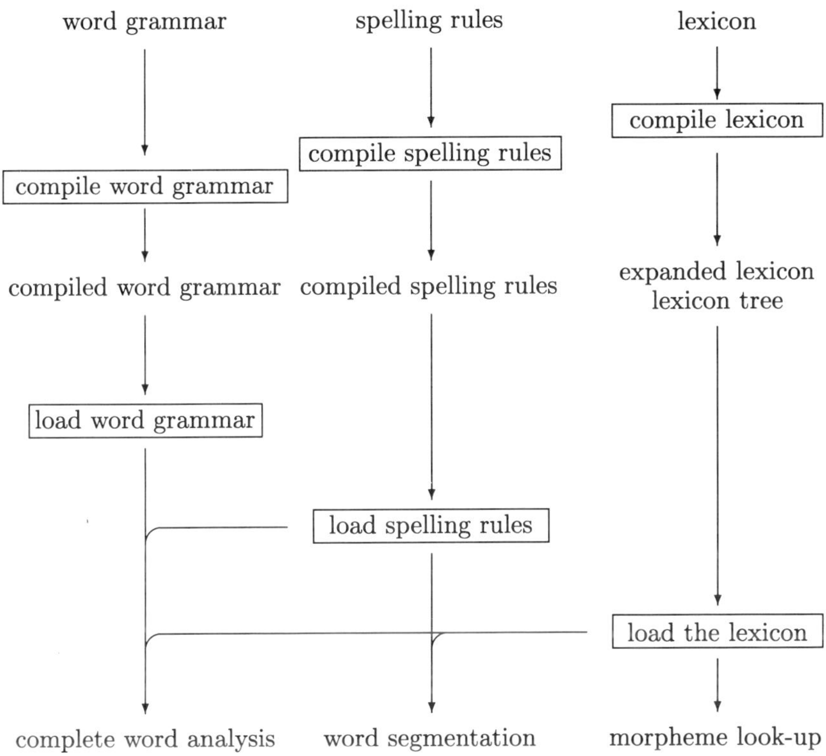

- concatenating the lexical forms of a sequence of morphemes using the morphographemic rules to generate corresponding surface forms;
- comparing a sequence of lexical symbols and a sequence of surface symbols in order to determine if they are acceptable to the morphographemic rules.

Figure 7.1 shows the relationship between user description files and (some of) the facilities which process these files and use their results.

7.2 The lexicon

7.2.1 Lexical entries

Within generative linguistics, grammarians have typically assumed that the lexicon would contain whatever the sentence grammar required. As mentioned in Chapters 1 and 6, this usually meant that a lexical entry consisted of three main fields — a phonological field, a syntactic field and a semantic field — together, sometimes, with other components such as morphological information and a list of exceptional or idiosyncratic information. In trying to devise a fairly general format which would allow most users of the system to build systems to suit their theoretical inclinations, we settled for a total of five fields:

Citation form : Because we were interested in an access method which relied on conventional keyboard input in normal orthography (i.e. written input rather than spoken or phonetically represented input), this field (which does not normally figure in linguistic treatments) was in fact a "key" field, in the sense that the look-up process matched sequences of citation forms against input strings using the spelling rules (see Chapter 2).

Phonological form : This field was felt to be necessary for compatibility with linguistic practice, and could contain an arbitrary expression. Our software carried out no processing on it.

Syntactic features : The information in this field is actively processed by the various rules, both lexical redundancy rules (see Chapter 5) and morphotactic analysis (see Chapters 3 and 4). The field should contain exactly one "category" in the sense defined in Chapter 3 — i.e. a set of feature specifications.

Semantic structure : This field, like the phonological field, is included merely for generality and to allow possible extensions to the system; its contents are not processed by the morphological rules, and although it would in principle be possible to manipulate them in a limited way using lexical rules, this does not occur in our description of English (in which there are dummy mnemonic symbols in all the semantic fields).

Miscellaneous field : Whereas the other four fields can be characterised in terms of a specific linguistic purpose, this field is purely practical, with no real theoretical import. As mentioned earlier, our aim was that the software would allow a wide variety of applications, and it seemed realistic to assume that some users would wish to include in lexical entries information other than that covered by the four linguistically defined fields. This all-purpose repository was therefore incorporated, even though we made no use of it; in the English description, it contains the empty marker `NIL` throughout (but see Section 5.8 for an illustration of how it could be used).

Although the rules in our description essentially manipulate only the citation form and the syntactic features, the look-up process returns entire lexical entries, so that the other three fields, although not actively influencing the computation, do appear in the result, and could be used by some later stage of processing.

The system allows the linguist to write individual lexical entries in a rather Lisp-like notation (although some "syntactic sugar" is available to render syntactic categories more readable), such as:

```
(some
    sum
    ((DET +) (DEFINITE -))
    (LAMBDA P (LAMBDA Q (EXISTS X (AND (P X) (Q X)))))
    "quantified indefinite determiner"
)
( man man  N[PLU -] MAN nil)
( men men  ( (N +)(V -)(BAR 0) (PLU +)) MAN nil)
( afterwards AftuwEdz PP AFTERWARDS nil)
( saw  sO  V[VFORM fin,PAST +]   SEE nil)
```

where `N` (in the entry for `man`) is an abbreviation (or *alias*) for `((N +)(V -)(BAR 0))`, `V` (in `saw`) abbreviates `((V +)(N -)(BAR 0))`, and `PP` abbreviates `((V -) (N -) (BAR 2))`.

As discussed in Section 6.3, the question of what counts as a morpheme is not trivial, particularly in view of our aim to allow great flexibility to a potential user of our system. We have taken a fairly pragmatic approach, which is best explained in terms of *atomic lexical entries* rather than using the more contentious notion of "morpheme". The scheme is as follows:

- Each entry must contain exactly one citation form, one phonological form, one syntactic category, one semantic structure, and one other item.
- There is no requirement of dissimilarity between parts of lexical entries; in particular, the same citation form may appear in more than one entry.
- The spelling rules segment input strings into a corresponding sequence of lexical entries, but these are then treated as atomic items by the word grammar.

Hence the way in which a given citation form may be associated with different meanings or with different syntactic specifications is for there to be several entries, each with the same citation form — `bank`, for example, might appear several times in the lexicon, once for each meaning of the word. Also, the point about segmentation is to emphasise that although an entire phrase (e.g. "`make fun of`") could be given its own lexical entry (by allowing spaces in the lexical alphabet), it would not be possible (since entries are atomic as far as the word grammar is concerned) for the various inflected forms of this phrase (e.g. "`making fun of`", "`makes fun of`") to be handled systematically by the morphotactic rules of the analyser (although it might be possible to arrange morphographemic rules which would match the appropriate surface string to the phrasal form in the lexicon). The choice of which items should merit entries has been left to the linguist who constructs the linguistic description (with the restriction that every lexical entry must have a non-null citation form).

It is important to distinguish between the notion of "morpheme" (or *atomic lexical entry*) which is built in to the system, and the descriptive question of whether a particular word should count as a single morpheme or a combination of morphemes. For example, in our analysis of English morphology, the word `division` is listed separately in the lexicon, rather than being derived from the obviously related `divide`. There is in principle no reason not to decompose such items; the choice of how far to segment words is the user's. There is of course a trade-off between the number and complexity of spelling and grammar rules and the separate listing of such irregular forms. (See Section 6.3 for fuller discussion.)

A citation form must be a string over the (explicitly declared) lexical alphabet, which may contain any normal keyboard characters, although various non-alphanumeric characters require special treatment. All characters specified in the citation form must be dealt with by the spelling rules, if only as default pairs, otherwise no analyses involving that form will be found. It is the responsibility of the user to ensure that any particular context to which the spelling rules allude is identifiable by the analyser. One technique which can sometimes be useful is to add a special character to the lexical form in a position to which certain spelling rules must refer exactly; for example in the case where spelling changes occur adjacent to the morpheme `ing`, the user can specify a citation form of `+ing` and hence refer to the `+` in the spelling rules that relate to that context. It is important to notice that "boundary" symbols such as this "+" have no special status either in our theory or in the implementation. It is up to the linguist (i.e. the user) to define all such symbols in the appropriate alphabets, and to include spelling rules to handle them, so that lexical symbols are always associated with surface symbols (possibly null).

In earlier versions of the system, there was no provision for allowing the user to equate two positions within the syntactic category in a lexical entry by specifying the same variable name in both positions. This is perhaps a slightly unfortunate restriction, but did not cause problems for our description of English morphology. Strictly, the software did allow the inclusion of variables (in the sense of Section 3.2.2) within a syntactic category in a lexical entry, but the implementation did not attempt to equate the values of identically named variables within a lexical entry. However, it was still useful to include variables within entries to get the effect of *disjunctions* of feature values, as described in Section 3.3.4.

7.2.2 Lexical rules

All three sorts of lexical rule described in Chapter 5 were implemented; that is, Completion Rules (for adding predictable features to the syntactic fields of user-specified entries), Multiplication Rules (for constructing new lexical entries whose presence and content are predictable from others) and Consistency Checks (which ensure the lexical entries are internally consistent before they are added to the lexicon).

As the basic meaning of these rules is fairly procedural, the description in Chapter 5 is an accurate outline of the implemented version.

Multiplication Rules may be defined (and hence applied) before or after the Completion Rules, but the two types may not be intermingled. Consistency Checks are defined and applied last of all. Within each set of rules, the order of application is the same as the order in which the rules are specified, so Completion Rules may "feed" or "bleed" each other in the manner outlined in Chapter 5.

The name associated with each rule was useful for practical purposes such as debugging.

7.2.3 Compiling the lexicon

The lexical rules are used to pre-process the lexical entries, but are not used in the actual process of morphological analysis (i.e. in dictionary look-up). The pre-compilation phase thus expands the basic lexicon written by the user, using Completion Rules to expand entries, Multiplication Rules to insert further entries, and Consistency Checks to eliminate any linguistically malformed entries. In addition, during this pre-compilation, the expanded lexicon is re-formatted into a suitably indexed form (the *lexicon tree*) which will facilitate the scanning of citation forms during morphographemic analysis (hence pre-processing is necessary even if no lexical rules are being used).

The lexicon tree uses a standard technique for indexing sequences of symbols ([Knut73, pp. 481-490] defines such a structure as a *trie*, [Char85] describes it as a *discrimination net*, and [Thor68] outlines its use for lexical strings). The constructed index is a tree in which each node is labelled with a character, certain nodes are marked as possible "end nodes" (which need not be terminal nodes in the tree) and the characters attached to the nodes of any path from the root of the tree to a marked end node represent a lexical citation form. For example an index tree for the citation forms `car`, `carp`, `coat`, `cone` and `care` would be as shown in figure 7.2. A "`.`" marks an end node (at which point the lexical entries containing that citation form would be attached).

The scanning process to match a simple string against the index can then be carried out from left to right, character by character, starting at the root of the tree. At each stage, the current character in the string indicates which node to select from the daughters of the current node. If the scan is at an *end node* when the end of the string is reached, that sequence of characters has been recognised.

There is some scope for optimisation of this scanning process, de-

Figure 7.2
a lexicon tree

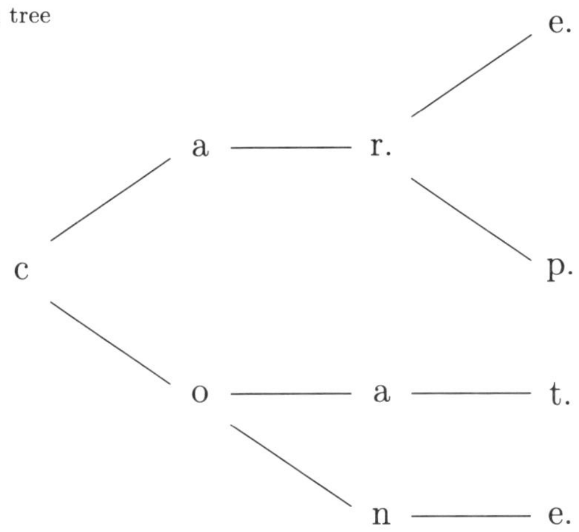

pending on what constructs are available in the programming language. For example, the representation must allow some way of selecting the next node on the basis of the currently-scanned symbol. There are various ways of implementing this as a look-up table (e.g. a hash-table, an association list). The better of these allow the choice to be done in time logarithmically related to the size of the alphabet, but at the time of implementation (1984) such devices were not standard in all Lisps. Since our implementation was intended to be easily portable to various versions of Lisp, this was one case where we opted for a possibly less efficient method.

When morphographemic rules have to be interposed between the lexical tree and the surface string, the process is more complicated — see Section 7.5.2 below.

The user may compile separate lexicons and then load the compiled forms together for later use. This can be useful as an organisational approach, to ease debugging, or to avoid space restrictions which the lexicon compiler may run into when compiling large lexicons. There is a slight loss in look-up efficiency with this approach, although if the partitioning of the lexicon is done according to the initial letter of the citation form, this adverse effect will be negligible.

There is also a facility for splitting the lexical entries into different files, though they will still be compiled into the same lexicon. Lexical files (or in fact any of the files) may contain an `#include` compiler directive followed by a file name. The compiler will simply treat it as if the data in the included file appears at that point. This facility can also be used to share declarations between the word grammar and a lexicon.

7.3 Spelling rules

7.3.1 History

A fairly full implementation of the two-level morphographemic formalism, was carried out with the following limitations: no Kleene star constructs were allowed — only "one or more" iterations were included; it was not permitted to specify optional elements within a context; and certain keyboard characters (e.g. square brackets) were not allowed in the alphabets unless specially quoted. As described in Chapter 2, in the earlier implementations of such rules (e.g. [Kosk83a], [Kart83a]), users had to write spelling rules as transition tables for transducers. Apart from being extremely difficult to do, this can be relatively unprincipled, and can lead to confusion if the rules are simultaneously stated in the high-level rule notation, with no guarantee of consistency between the alternative statements. After Koskenniemi's later work [Kosk85], we implemented a rule compiler that allowed the user to specify rules of the form described in Chapter 2. The problem with the original implementation of this basic compiler was its speed — it was very slow. It took around twenty minutes to compile our description (about 16 rules) into automata.

The compiler was in essence very simple. After expanding all abbreviatory devices (sets and variables), it converted the regular expressions in the contexts of rules into standard finite state automata where each transition was labelled with a pair consisting of a lexical and surface character and then built an automaton for each rule in a way dependent on the rule type. The automata built were (or should be) equivalent in overall effect to the ones the user specified directly in previous versions of the system. The main problem was that the automata had to run continually, to give the effect of reapplying the rule at each step of the scan. This meant that instead of a simple translation from a regular expression to an automaton which recognised the particular pattern described by the rule, arcs had to be added which allowed the rule to restart at each stage in the match. What was required was not an automaton that recognised just the language generated by the regular expression, but an automaton which matched that pattern embedded anywhere within a string; i.e. a matcher for the *closure* of the pattern had to be created. For this reason, the typical automaton that came out of the compilation process was very large — each state typically had arcs for all pairs in the alphabet. This was in contrast to the transducers that a linguist might specify directly (e.g. [Kart83b]), which contained set mnemonics that were not expanded until run time. As these automata were non-deterministic, the compiler went on to determinise them, which is a computationally expensive task. In our compilation of around 16 spelling rules, conversion to basic automata took about 2 minutes and determinising took 18 minutes. After determinising it is advisable to minimise the automata, which again is a standard and simple transformation. In our system this was not implemented, not because it was not needed but because we were already looking for alternative ways of compilation. Minimisation would never reduce the number of state transitions needed to recognise (or reject) a string but would reduce the number of states in an automaton. In the description of the implementation of the KIMMO system [Kart83a], a way of merging automata was described. This was experimented with, but still resulted in a large automaton that took an unacceptably long time to determinise.

In the compiler described in [Kart87], a technique similar to our earlier implementation is used, but with the addition of an *elsewhere principle* which allows many arcs to be grouped together and hence reduces the size of the automata significantly. This means that determinising and minimising take less time, but slightly increases the processing carried out by the interpreter.

After some experimentation we decided to follow the work of Bear [Bear85] so that instead of closures of patterns being created, simple patterns were created and each rule is *re-started* at each stage in a match. Also following Bear's work the generated automata from the compilation are not simple classical automata but are a special form of automaton where the states are marked and hence require a special interpretation (see Section 7.3.4 for a detailed description).

One very important criterion we had when looking for better compilation processes is that the semantics (and syntax) of the high level rules must not change. So although this later version used a different compilation (and interpretation) method to the one first described by Koskenniemi [Kosk85], no change was required in our rule notation and our actual description.

We also spent some time looking at alternative spelling rule notations. These all fell into the paradigm of two-level morphology but used different notations and interpretations. The only one carried through to full implementation was that described in [Blac87] (see Section 8.1.4). However it was decided not to incorporate this fully into a public version of the system and it existed only in an early experimental version.

7.3.2 Compilation of spelling rules

The compilation procedure which we eventually adopted produces a form of automaton which is not the classical type, but a slightly more complex form. In this formalism each state is marked with typing information which is used by a special interpreter. Also, although the two-level framework is often referred to as using *transducers* (with a connotation of a translation process), in our look-up process we do not employ the automata as transducers but as acceptors. This means we do not use the automata to *generate* the lexical tape from the surface tape (or vice versa) but use the automata to "accept" tapes based on the surface string and the concatenation of lexical forms.

Before the actual compilation starts some amount of pre-processing takes place. The spelling rules are first checked for syntactic errors, and then the rules are "multiplied out" by replacing each variable with its possible values (since variables have finite explicitly declared ranges, this is not problematic). This means that each user-written rule is now represented by a *set* of rules.

Next, the set of *feasible pairs* is found. Feasible pairs are all pairs of lexical and surface characters that are used in the description. This set is found by finding all *concrete pairs* (i.e. pairs not containing sets) in the rules and then adding the *defaults* set. The *defaults* set is made from the identity pairs of the intersection of the lexical and surface alphabets and any pairs specifically declared as default pairs. The feasible pairs set is important to the expansion of set mnemonics in other pairs, and is effectively the alphabet of the automata.

The new structure built from the rules is reminiscent of a conventional finite state machine. It does however have a slightly more complex interpretation with special classes of state. Any state can be marked with either of two properties, TERMINAL or LICENCE (or may be left unmarked). The machine is non-deterministic as determinising would probably make the compilation stage take too long. Even then non-determinism would still exist in the continuous re-application of the rules.

The exact compilation procedure depends on the rule type, in the following way:

Context Restriction Rules :

```
pair => LC --- RC
```

The compilation produces patterns which recognise the set of symbol pair sequences characterised as

```
LC pair RC
```

`LC` is converted into an automaton in which no state is marked TERMINAL or LICENCE. `RC` is also converted to an automaton, in which the starting state is marked LICENCE, the final state is marked TERMINAL and all other states have no markings. Lastly an arc, labelled with `pair`, is added to join the two context automata.

Surface Coercion Rules :

```
pair <= LC --- RC
```

The automaton for such a rule does not describe acceptable sequences, but effectively looks for erroneous patterns. A pattern is made from this which recognises strings that have the given contexts and lexical character but do not have the specified surface character. Automata are built for `LC` and `RC`, and the last state of `RC` is the special state ERROR. The two contexts are joined by arcs for all feasible pairs that have the same lexical character as the rule pair but a different surface character. All states in the automaton are unmarked.

Composite Rules :

```
pair <=> LC --- RC
```

> This is effectively made up of the combination of the two above rules. An automaton is made from `LC` in which all states are unmarked. Two different automata are created for `RC`. First an arc labelled with `pair` is added from the end of `LC` to one automaton representing `RC` starting with a LICENCE state and ending in a TERMINAL state. Secondly, arcs for all feasible pairs that have the same lexical character as `pair` but different surface characters, are added from the end of `LC` to the start of another automaton representing `RC`. This second `RC` automaton ends in ERROR and has no marked states.

Although the automaton for each rule is created independently they are all added into the same structure, with duplicate arcs being removed as the arcs are added. This means that there is one structure representing all the spelling rules (although all states are labelled with the name of the original rule from which they arose, to assist in debugging). This structure, however, is not "minimised" in any formal sense but will allow some (initial) arcs from different rules to be merged.

In addition to the rules, transitions are also added to this automaton for all *unrestricted pairs*, from the initial state to a state marked as both LICENCE and TERMINAL. *Unrestricted pairs* are all pairs in the feasible set that do not have an associated Context Restriction (or Composite) rule. This means that restricted pairs are allowed only when in their appropriate context.

7.3.3 An example of compilation

To illustrate the process here is a example of the compilation of a simple spelling rule into an automaton. The feasible set is

```
{a:a, b:b, c:c, d:d, e:e, ... y:y, z:z, +:0, +:e}
```

And the rule to be compiled is

```
Example
   +:e <=> {<{ c:c s:s } h:h> s:s x:x z:z } --- s:s
```

This rule is a Composite Rule so we use the third method of compilation described above. The automaton built for this rule effectively deals with recognising two forms of patterns — one that allows the pair `+:e` to appear only in specified context and one that checks to see that if the context exists, then only `+:e` is within it.

The first task is to convert the left context into an automaton. This automaton will be shared between the two pattern matchers. The algorithm for producing an automaton from a regular expression can be found in many text books on formal language theory and automata (for example [Hopc79, p.32]). Thus an automaton which represents the above left context is:

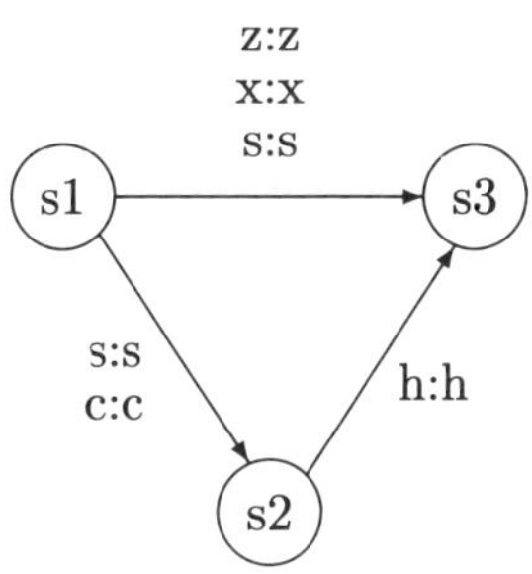

Note the non-determinism in the two possible transitions from *s1* for the symbol `s:s`. The next stage is to build *two* automata for the right context, both the same but with different start and end states. The start of the first automaton (*s4*) is marked LICENCE and the end state of that automaton (*s5*) is marked TERMINAL. The second automaton for the right context is unmarked (*s6*) and ends in an ERROR-state. This gives the following:

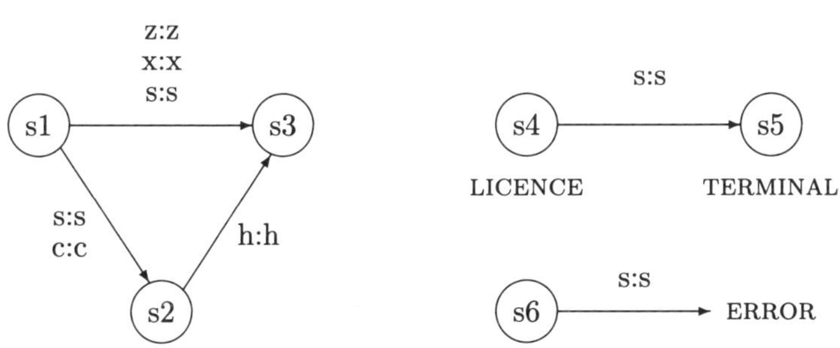

ERROR is a special state, the usage of which is described below in the interpretation section. Now we must join the left context automaton to the first right context one by adding a transition from the end of the left context one (*s3*) to the start of the right (*s4*) labelled with the rule pair (`+:e`). Also, in order to detect places where the left and right context exist but the rule pair does not, the end of the left context (*s3*) must be connected to the start of the second right context automaton (*s6*) by a transition for each feasible pair that has the same lexical character but a different surface character to that in the rule pair. In this example the only feasible pair which meets this criterion is `+:0`. Thus the complete automaton, with these final two arcs added, that represents the sample rule is

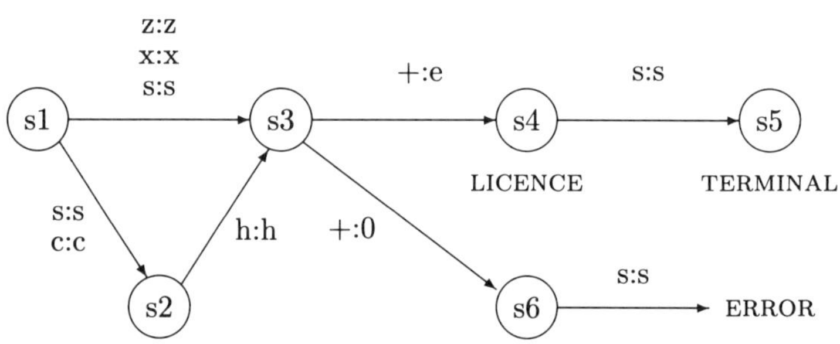

All other rules are compiled in a similar way and are combined into the same (non-deterministic) "automaton" (i.e. their initial states are merged). Transitions for unrestricted pairs are then added, as described at the end of Section 7.3.2.

7.3.4 Interpretation of automata

The interpreter maintains a set of *configurations*, where a configuration corresponds to a possible analysis of the input being scanned. That is, the non-determinism introduced by there being different possible analyses is handled by a breadth-first search. Each configuration consists of a set of what could be called *rule-states*. There are two types of rule-state — a *simple state* consists of a single automaton state, and a *commit group* consists of a set of automaton states. The initial configuration of the machine starts with one rule-state, consisting of one simple state — the initial state of the automaton. At each stage of the match all states in each rule-state of the configuration are tested against the given pair to find a new set of automaton states for that rule-state. A configuration typically consists of only 3 or 4 rule-states when our spelling rules are used, so it could be said that 3 or 4 rules are potentially active at any time in a single analysis. After a move, the new configuration must meet some simple conditions to be valid, then some post-processing is done before the configuration is returned ready for the next match. In describing the computation, we will say that a symbol-pair is *licensed* if there is a Context Restriction Rule for that pair whose left context is satisfied by the pairs immediately to the left (or if it is an unrestricted pair). A new configuration must pass the following conditions:

- It must contain at least one simple state that is marked with LICENCE. (Indicating some rule potentially allows the current pair.)
- It must not contain the state ERROR in any of its rule-states. (No rule has blocked.)
- All commit groups in a configuration must be non-empty. (The right context for a previously licensed pair has continued to be valid.)

After it has passed these tests the following modifications are made before it is passed on to the next stage in the match:

- Simple states which are marked TERMINAL are removed. (These represent the completion of a Context Restriction Rule.)
- Commit groups containing a state marked TERMINAL are removed. (This represents the successful completion of one of a set of Context Restriction Rules, any of which would allow the same pair.)
- All remaining simple states marked LICENCE are collected into a new commit group. (These represent Context Restriction Rules at least one of whose right contexts must match.)

A complete surface to lexical match is valid if the eventual configuration contains no commit groups. This will have the effect that each pair must first be licensed in a match before it is accepted and any post-conditions (from the right context) on the licence must also be met (via the commit groups) before the complete strings are accepted.

7.3.5 Other implementations

As indicated in Chapter 2, Koskenniemi's original work has continued to be developed along with Kaplan, Karttunen and others. [Kart87] describes a very sophisticated implementation of two-level morphological rules, with the following features which go beyond what we have implemented:

1. Mnemonics may be defined for regular expressions of symbol-pairs.
2. Rules may be checked for various forms of conflict (e.g. context expressions which define intersecting sets) as part of the compilation process, and some of these conflicts may be resolved by the compiler.
3. The compilation process makes thorough use of classical transducers, which not only permits the checking process, but allows a much simpler and more efficient interpreter for the compiled form.
4. "Diacritic" symbols may appear in lexical entries but affect only those rules which explicitly mention them.
5. The rule writer may specify how variables in rules are to be instantiated, to enforce identity or non-identity of values.
6. There is a third rule type which allows statements of the form "lexical symbol `l` is never realised as surface symbol `s` in the context `LC ___ RC`".

Antworth [Antw90] describes a carefully engineered system available on various personal computers. It greatest drawback is that it essentially implements the state of two-level morphology in 1983, in that it demands that the user explicitly write transducers as transition tables, instead of there being a compiler which will convert high-level rules to that lower-level form.

7.4 The word grammar

The unification-based feature grammar formalism described in Chapter 3 was implemented, including the feature passing conventions of Chapter 4. Like the morphographemic spelling rules, the word grammar rules must be pre-compiled before being loaded into the Lisp program which is to perform the morphological analysis. Various manipulations are carried out during compilation — the replacement of aliases with their full form, and the expansion of rule category variables by the insertion of one copy of the rule for each possible value of the variable. Feature value variables are not expanded at compile time but are bound during morphological analysis (look-up) by unification. Most of the word grammar compilation process involves setting up structures that will allow the analyser to operate more efficiently (see Section 7.7 below). Both varieties of unification (see Section 3.4) were implemented, although only one version can be used at any time (the unification mechanism is selected when creating the Lisp programs, prior to any compilation of linguistic rules).

7.4.1 Notation for categories and rules

The system allows two possible notations for syntactic categories (this is true in either the unrestricted or term unification version of the system). One is a simple Lisp-like notation where categories are simply lists of feature value pairs, where a feature value pair is a two-element list containing an atomic feature name and its value (atomic, category or variable). For example:

```
((N +) (V -) (BAR 0) (PLU +) (COUNT -))
```

Alternatively, categories can be written in a style closer to that typically used in GPSG [Gazd85b], where categories consist of a name (which is optional, and is an alias for some features) followed by a *feature bundle* in square brackets. For example assuming `Noun` is an alias for `((N +) (V -) (BAR 0))`, the above category could be written in either of the following ways:

```
Noun[PLU +,COUNT -]
[N +,V -,BAR 0,PLU +,COUNT -]
```

In both notations, the order in which features are given is arbitrary — a category is an unordered set of feature value pairs.

All categories returned or printed by the system are given in the Lisp-like form, as finding an appropriate alias to use would be a non-trivial task in general. Internally, the GPSG form is transformed into the Lisp-like form during analysis, and this Lisp-like form is further translated into a more efficient internal representation, which can be systematically converted back to the Lisp-like form before being returned by the analyser. When a category is being converted into its internal representation, variables are converted to a standard internal form. Feature names, values and user variable names are atomic symbols; even if the user includes numerals in rules or lexical entries, these are treated by the system not as integers but as Lisp symbols which have a print name which consists of numerals.

Word grammar rules consist of a mother category (left hand side) and one or more daughter categories (right hand side). Rules with a null right hand side are not allowed.

The distinguished category of the word grammar should be declared (using the keyword `Top`); if no explicit declaration is given, a default of the empty category is used, thus treating all structures that span the whole input as valid analyses.

7.5 The analysis process

The analysis of a word takes place at two levels. The lower level is the segmentation of the word into morphemes using the spelling rules. These morphemes are then fed into a parser that checks them against the word grammar, using feature passing conventions where appropriate. Lexical rules have already applied during the pre-compilation of the lexicon, and are not applicable during analysis, but various other mechanisms (feature defaults and `LCategory` definitions) are applied at various stages.

7.5.1 The word grammar parser

The analyser uses the word grammar rules to find all possible structures for a given word (or surface form). A valid analysis, in keeping with the definitions in Chapter 3, is a tree structure as follows:

- Each leaf node is labelled with two linguistic items — one is the full lexical entry for an individual morpheme, and the other is a syntactic category which is an extension of the syntactic category in the lexical entry. In the implementation, leaf nodes are also labelled with the key-word `ENTRY` to distinguish them from non-leaf nodes.
- Each non-terminal node (in addition to pointers to its daughter nodes) has attached to it a symbol naming a grammar rule of the form $A \rightarrow d_1, \ldots, d_m$, and a syntactic category which is an extension of the mother category A and to which the feature defaults have applied. Also, the categories labelled on its

daughter nodes must be extensions of the daughters $d_1, \ldots, d_m$. If the rule has only two daughters (and unrestricted unification is used) the node must conform to the feature passing conventions.

- The category label on the root node must be an extension of the distinguished category of the word grammar.
- The tree must span the entire input, in the sense that the terminal nodes of the tree, taken left to right, give rise, via their associated lexical entries, to a sequence of lexical citation forms which correspond, via the spelling rules, to the surface string. (Unless the string segmentation options are selected — see Section 7.5.4 below.)

A further condition is that the tree contains the minimum features that are required to meet these conditions. That is, it might well be the case that a particular string could give rise to a large, even infinite, class of trees, if redundant features were added systematically to nodes in the tree; however, we define the tree to be such that the above characterisation would be false if any features were removed. The consequence of this (rather necessary) aspect of the definition is that the categories labelled on to the nodes of the tree must be computed by the analyser using unification. The unification of two categories is, by definition (Section 3.2), the minimal category which is an extension of both, and so achieves the necessary result.

The sequence of morphemes resulting from the segmentation stage is parsed using the word grammar and an *active chart parser* (for general description of chart parsing see [Wino83, pp. 116-129] and [Thom84]). The chart is implemented to run bottom-up, as it was found in earlier versions of the system that running bottom-up was faster than running top-down. This seemed to be because there was no very effective indexing method for word grammar rules. This decision was an informal, empirical one, and it is unclear whether there is any principled reason for choosing either strategy.

The basic analysis algorithm is as follows (this is a simplified version of the algorithm — the actual implementation includes various efficiency measures):

Parse Function

```
1  Initialise structures
2  Find first morpheme(s) of string and add to agenda
3  while agenda not nil
4      take first edge from agenda and make it current
5      if current edge is complete (inactive)
6          check feature conventions and apply defaults
7      if feature conventions are satisfied or
8          current edge is incomplete (active)
9          combine current edge with edges in chart, adding
10             any resulting new edges to the agenda
11         Add current edge to chart
12 Find full parses
```

Line 9 requires further expansion. The combination with other chart edges is as follows:

Combine Function

```
1  if current edge is complete
2      check each incomplete edge ending at the place
3          where the current edge starts. If current label
4          can unify with the next-required category on the
5          incomplete edge construct a new edge and add it to
6          the agenda
7      Propose the label of this new edge to the grammar (see below)
8  else if current edge is incomplete
9      if there is no further morpheme yet at its right end
10         call the morpheme segmenter (with arguments as
11             described below) to fetch set of next morphemes
12         for each next morpheme found
13             build a new vertex (attaching the results passed by the
14                 morpheme segmenter) and a new edge and
15                 add that edge to the agenda
16     check each complete edge starting at the place
17         where the current edge ends. If current's next required
18         category can unify with the complete edge's label
19         then construct a new edge and add it to the agenda
```

Thus the chart extends itself (line 10) only on demand (line 8) and hence will not blindly search possible dead ends in segmenting a string but will search only where it may give rise to a complete word (i.e. where the parser is still making progress from left to right).

Proposing a category to the grammar (line 7) is the process of retrieving all rules which are relevant to building constituents starting with that category (i.e. the normal bottom-up method of accessing a grammar). This occurs at this juncture only in the unrestricted unification version of the system. The term unification version scans the grammar for relevant rules only when new morphemes are found. That is, line 7 is omitted from the term unification parsing algorithm, and proposing categories to the grammar occurs instead after line 15 when a new lexical edge is added to the agenda. (See Section 7.7.2 below for more details of how this mechanism operates.)

7.5.2 Morpheme segmentation

The segmentation function finds the next morphemes (there may be several possibilities starting at a particular point in the string) given a surface string (i.e. the remaining surface symbols) and a spelling rule configuration (i.e. the internal state of the two-level rule handler). The current remainder of the surface string is compared against the lexicon tree (represented as a set of subtrees following from the current position in the lexicon tree), for the next possible morphemes. The basic searching of the lexicon subtrees is done by a recursive function which returns as its result a set of structures, each structure consisting of a list of lexical entries (all with the same citation form), a surface string (the new remainder of the original surface string) and a configuration of the spelling rule interpreter. These results are used in the interface to the chart — see Section 7.5.3 below — and the latter two parts are used in subsequent calls to the segmenter.

The algorithm is best described in two stages. The procedure **next-morphemes** is the external interface — given a sequence of symbols in the surface alphabet (i.e. part or all of a surface form) and a configuration of the spelling rule interpreter (in the sense described earlier), it returns a set of structures, each of which represents a set of next morphemes from the front of the string. Each of these structures contains 3 parts:

1. The lexical information (i.e. one or more lexical entries) all associated with the same citation form.
2. The remainder of the original string when the surface counterpart of this citation form has been removed from the front.
3. A spelling rule configuration suitable for a subsequent call of **next-morphemes** (when it is necessary to find citation forms following on from this one in the string).

Notice that the various sets of morphemes may correspond to the scanning of different amounts of the surface string. The top level function is

```
next-morphemes(string, config)
    results := empty set
    scan(string, root of lexicon tree, config)
    scan(0.string, root of lexicon tree, config)
```

Here "0.*string*" means the concatenation of the null symbol 0 with the string. The variable *results* is global to the calls of **scan** and acts as an accumulator for the various result structures.

The real work is done by the recursive procedure **scan**.

```
scan(string, node, config)
    if node is marked as an end-node
    then
        results := results + [all entries at node, string, config]
    for each L in the lexical alphabet which could form a feasible pair
            with the first symbol S in string,
        node' := nextnode(node, L)
        if node' ≠ NIL
        then
            Try to generate a new configuration config' from
            config and L : S
            if this succeeds
            then
                string' := string less its first symbol
                scan(string', node', config')
                scan(0.string', node', config')
```

In this, **nextnode** steps one link further along the lexicon tree, allowing for the special case of the null symbol (which might have arisen as a possible feasible pairing):

```
nextnode(node, char)
    if char = 0 (i.e. null symbol)
    then
        return(node)
    else
        if node has a daughter linked to it by char
        then
            return(that daughter)
        else
            return(NIL)
```

Notice that the two recursive calls to **scan** in **next-morpheme** are *both* made, and the results from both calls added to the set of results. The restriction "which could form a feasible pair" means that only subtrees with valid lexical characters are searched, thus pruning many of the branches of the lexicon tree, and also caters for the possibility of arbitrary null symbols on the lexical side in a fairly controlled way. Various linguistically uninteresting optimisations are possible in implementing the search for the appropriate subtrees.

As mentioned above, the morpheme segmentation is done only on demand (from the word grammar parser) and all possible segmentations of a word are not found, as this would be computationally expensive. See Section 7.7 below for an outline of some of the optimising techniques.

7.5.3 Interfacing the segmenter and the chart

The results of the segmentation process cannot easily be represented simply in the classical *well-formed sub-string table* normally used in a chart parser. The problem with word segmentation is that the basic analysis path is not linear but may have many branches. The segmentation function, as sketched above, takes the remainder of the surface string and a spelling rule configuration and returns a list of possible next morphemes, each with its own remainder and new spelling rule configuration (or suitable end-markers where appropriate). This reflects the fact that the presence of a particular morpheme may be hypothesised only subject to subsequent morphemes being compatible with whatever processing the spelling rules had to perform in order to postulate this morpheme; the spelling rule configuration "remembers" these outstanding commitments upon which the next step in the segmentation depends. As can be seen from the algorithm given above, when lexical entries have been found with the same citation form *and* by the same matching process, the entries are grouped together (e.g. `ache` in figure 7.3). On the other hand, it may not be possible to group identical surface string remainders together, since it is possible that identical remainders might correspond to significantly different spelling rule configurations (e.g. nodes 3 and 4 in figure 7.3). Hence, when the chart is extended to the right by building a new vertex, that vertex must have attached to it the string remainder and spelling rule configuration that were current at the right hand end of the morpheme whose right vertex this is. This attached information can then be passed to the morpheme segmentation

Figure 7.3
Directed graph of possible morphemes

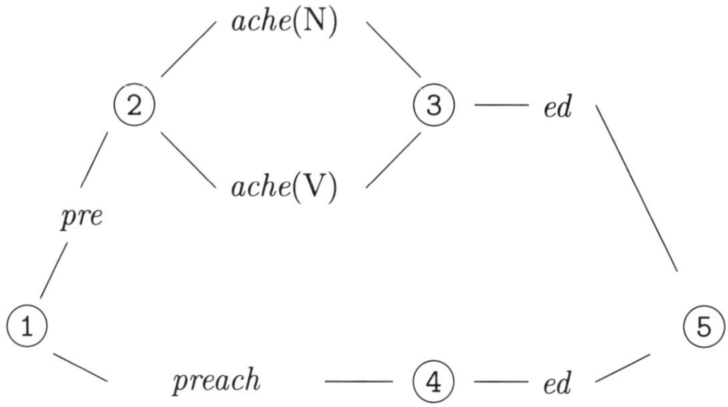

function when it is next called to extend the chart still further to the right.

What actually occurs when looking up morphemes is that the base chart is built as a directed graph structure rather than as a simple ordered sequence of vertices, with all paths through the chart connected to one *end* node, vertex 5 in the example. Thus given the surface form `preached` we may get the basic chart built as in figure 7.3

Note that the two edges labelled `ache` both join vertex 3, rather than splitting the search space again, because they both have the same citation form, and will be found by the same morphographemic processing (from left to right). Vertex 3 will have attached to it the string remainder and configuration which were passed back by the segmenter when it returned the two `ache` morphemes. However, Vertices 3 and 4 are represented as different even though they have the same following morpheme, since they have resulted from different sequences of computations of the spelling rules. It was decided that to find out where vertices in the chart could join up was too difficult. In theory, vertices can be merged only if they have the same remaining surface string *and* an equivalent spelling rule configuration. The latter condition is computationally expensive to test, and is probably not worth attempting, especially as words are typically short and hence not very much extra work needs to be done when this check is omitted.

If the string segmentation option (see Section 7.5.4 below) is taken then failing to collapse paths with the same string remainders and equivalent configurations could cause a lot of duplicate work. When either of the string segmentation options is selected the algorithm described in the previous section does not work, because it is directed by what the grammar is looking for, and in the string segmentation option there is no grammar rule that characterises the whole string. Hence, at word boundaries there may be no guidance from the chart to the segmenter. When one of these options is selected the initialisation of the chart requires that *all* segmentations must first be found and added to the agenda (much as in a conventional bottom-up parser).

7.5.4 Formats returned by the analyser

In most of the discussion so far, both in this chapter and earlier chapters, the assumption has been that the lexical look-up process consists of computing a syntactic category for a given word. In fact the implemented system allows the user to vary the information passed back by the look-up process, in two independent ways — a word can be labelled either with a syntactic category, or with a full morphological analysis representing the tree computed by the word grammar parser (see Section 7.5.1); also, the system can either analyse the input as a single word, or as a sequence of words. That is, the overall result can be in one of four possible formats. The choice of formats can be thought of in two dimensions: how a word is described (category or analysis tree); and single word form or string segmentation form.

During the analysis of words, a structure is built by the word parser which records all the lexical information about the component morphemes, together with the morphotactic rules which were used to combine them (see Section 7.5.1). The overall BNF for the data-structure, which is expressed as Lisp S-expressions, is:

```
<word-structure> ::=
        ( <category> <rule-name> <word-structure>* )
      | ( <category> ENTRY <lexical-entry> )
```

The result of looking up the word `applications` might be:

```
(((BAR 0) (PLU +) (INFL -) (N +) (V -))
 SUFFIXING
 ( ((BAR 0) (PLU -) (N +) (V -) (INFL +))
   SUFFIXING
   ( ((INFL +) (BAR 0) (V +) (N -))
     ENTRY
     (apply appli
        ((INFL +) (BAR 0) (V +) (N -))
        APPLY NIL))
   ( ((BAR -1) (FIX SUF) (INFL +) (PLU -) (N +)
              (V -) (STEM ((V +) (N -) (INFL +))))
      ENTRY
      (+ation ashon
         ((BAR -1) (FIX SUF) (INFL +) (PLU -) (N +)
          (V -) (STEM ((V +) (N -) (INFL +))))
         ATION NIL))
 )
 ( ((BAR -1) (FIX SUF) (INFL -) (PLU +) (V -)
            (N +) (STEM ((N +) (V -) (INFL +))))
    ENTRY
    (+s s
        ((BAR -1) (FIX SUF) (INFL -) (PLU +) (V -)
         (N +) (STEM ((N +) (V -) (INFL +)))) S NIL)))
```

The first choice that the user has is whether to receive this whole structure, or merely the overall category with all MorphologyOnly features removed, which in the above example would be:

```
((BAR 0) (PLU +) (N +) (V -))
```

The other dimension in the returned format is that the analyser can accept two forms of input, words or sequences of words (informally speaking).

Under the usual settings, the look-up function returns a simple list of word descriptions (categories or word structure trees respectively). That is, all analyses of the given string that span it and have a root category that matches the definition in the Top declaration in the word grammar (see Section 3.5.1). If the word cannot be analysed, an empty list of descriptions is returned.

However, if the user selects the *string segmentation* option, the input string is treated as a potential sequence of words, and a chart representation is returned — a set of *edges* representing all the possible partitions of the string into words (again, a word is defined by the `Top` category declaration). Such structures are intended to be used for segmenting sentences into a form that can easily be fed into a chart parser that deals with sentence level syntax. The BNF for these results is:

```
<chart representation> ::=
    (
       ( <chart start vertex> <chart end vertex> )
        <edge> *
    )
<edge> ::=
   (
    <edge start vertex>
    <edge end vertex>
    <edge label>
   )
```

where the vertex names are arbitrary Lisp symbols. The form of the edge label depends on which other option is selected — the edge label is either a syntactic category or an analysis tree. For example, applying the look-up to

```
john liked mary
```

might give the following (with suitable assumptions about the linguistic rules and entries being used):

```
((g00001 g00002)
   (g00001 g00003 ((BAR 2) (N +) (V -) (PLU -)))
   (g00003 g00004 ((BAR 0) (N -) (V +) (VFORM ED)))
   (g00003 g00004 ((BAR 0) (N -) (V +) (VFORM EN)))
   (g00004 g00002 ((BAR 2) (N +) (V -) (PLU -)))
)
```

This interface was included as it was felt that a sentence level parser might need such a structure, rather than calling the dictionary separately for each individual word. However, the sentence parser with which our software was tested made no use of this option, and thus this format cannot be regarded as properly validated.

7.6 Dictionary command interpreter

To make life easier when using the system for developing word grammars, spelling rules and lexical entries, a simple command interpreter (DCI) was written. This was not part of the actual analyser system but is an example of a program that uses the dictionary and analysis functions. The DCI allows easier interactive access to the various Lisp functions, without the user needing to be acquainted with Lisp. Once it is running, the user has access to simple commands which can initiate any of the following:

- The pre-processing (compiling) of any data files (i.e. a linguistic description).
- The loading of linguistic data files.
- The clearing out of currently loaded linguistic data.
- Altering the `Top` category used by the currently loaded word grammar.
- Looking up morphemes (without any analysis).
- Looking up words (with full morphological analysis).
- Segmenting surface strings (using spelling rules but *not* the word grammar).
- Using the spelling rules to generate a surface string from a given concatenation of lexical strings.
- Turning on debugging facilities.
- Stepping through the spelling rules with a given lexical string and surface string.

7.6.1 Spelling rule debugging

Writing spelling rules is not easy. Rules can accidently be written which have unintended interactions with other rules. To help the user in developing a set of rules, a spelling rule debugger was developed. It can take a lexical form and a surface form and compare them using the current set of spelling rules. It displays which rules are being used during a match and prints out the reason for any failure.

The user must supply strings of equal length — i.e. null symbols must be included explicitly. For example (using the spelling rules in Appendix D.1), the lexical and surface strings for `moved` would be

Lexical string: `move+ed`
Surface string: `mov00ed`

The spelling rule debugger has two modes of analysis, "`STEP`" (or "`s`", the default) and "`INFO`" (or "`i`"). "`STEP`" steps through each pair describing the current state of the matching rules, pausing at each stage; while "`INFO`" simply attempts to match the two strings and gives a summary of the results at the end. For example, an analysis of the word **`flies`** is shown below (the set of spelling rules used is a subset of those in Appendix D.1 having the same coverage as [Kart83b])

```
> spd
Enter Lexical string: fly+s
Enter Surface string: flies
Which mode ? s
Debug Mode is STEP

Lexical string :  f l y + s
                  ^
Surface string :  f l i e s
The pair (f f) was licensed by:  DEFAULT
Left hand side(s) active:
   I-Spelling Elision Elision Y-replacement

Lexical string :  f l y + s
                    ^
Surface string :  f l i e s
The pair (l l) was licensed by:  DEFAULT
Left hand side(s) active:
   I-Spelling Elision Elision Y-replacement

Lexical string :  f l y + s
                      ^
Surface string :  f l i e s
The pair (y i) was licensed by:  Y-replacement
Right hand side(s) pending for
   the rule(s) Y-replacement for the pair (y i)
Left hand side(s) active:
   I-Spelling Epenthesis

Lexical string :  f l y + s
                        ^
Surface string :  f l i e s
```

```
The pair (+ e) was licensed by:  Epenthesis
Right hand side(s) pending for
   the rule(s) Epenthesis for the pair (+ e)
   the rule(s) Y-replacement for the pair (y i)
Left hand side(s) active:
   I-Spelling

Lexical string :  f l y + s
                          ^

Surface string :  f l i e s
The pair (s s) was licensed by:  DEFAULT
The following rule(s) have terminated:
   Y-replacement Epenthesis
Left hand side(s) active:
   I-Spelling Elision Elision Y-replacement
   Epenthesis Epenthesis
```

At each stage the name of the rule licensing the current pair is displayed [2]. This is will usually be DEFAULT where they are the same character. Also the names of the rules currently active (both left and right hand contexts) are named. The left hand context of a spelling rule is said to be *active* when it matches some substring of the scanned forms up to the current point. Right hand sides of rules are *pending* when the rule has licensed a pair but the full right context has yet to be found. If there are two possible uses of a rule at the current point, then the rule name is displayed twice.

There are various ways a match can fail. Firstly the current pair may not be licensed by any of the rules or the defaults. The second reason for failure is rule blocking, which occurs when a left and right context of a surface coercion or a composite rule are found but the middle pair is not as stated in the rule. The final failure type is where a right hand side fails to match after the rule has licensed a pair. (There is also the problem of rule-interaction — see [Blac87].) Another possible direction to take when debugging the spelling rules is to use the `cm` (concatenate morphemes) command giving it the the sequence of lexical forms to be processed. This will show which surface strings can correspond to the lexical string.

---

2 Recall that a rule "licenses" a pair if the *left context* is satisfied — i.e. there is a provisional match.

7.6.2 Word grammar debugging

The word grammar is used to parse the segmented lexical string with a chart parser. The word parser debugger allows the user to investigate which sub-structures were successfully built during a word parse. The command `db` is effectively the same as the ordinary word look-up, but enters a debug loop after it has analysed the word. On entry into the debug loop the number of edges and vertices are displayed, with references to the edges and vertices being made as integers. Commands can then be given to display a particular edge or vertex.

7.7 Other implementation issues

7.7.1 Parsing unrestricted unification grammar

One major bottleneck in a chart parser is finding which grammar rules are applicable and should be added to the chart. This stage is often called *proposing* (see algorithm in Section 7.5.1 above). That is, when a complete constituent is found it is necessary to search the grammar for all rules that this constituent might expand (assuming the parser is running bottom-up). This can be an expensive process, since, if done naively, it requires a unification operation for each rule in the grammar. To get round this problem a different access method has been implemented for indexing the grammar. At compile time a special table of grammar rule names is built,[3] indexed by feature names and feature values, such that looking up a feature and then a value will give a list of grammar rules whose first daughter (i.e. the first category on the left hand side) *cannot* unify with a category that has that feature value pair.

For example given the two grammar rules

```
(VerbSuffix
   ((CAT Verb) (INFL ?INFL)) ->
      ((CAT Verb) (INFL -)),
      ((CAT VSuffix) (INFL ?INFL)) )

(NounSuffix
   ((CAT Noun) (INFL ?INFL)) ->
```

3 It is actually implemented as a discrimination list (as in [Char85, p. 153]).

```
((CAT Noun) (INFL -)),
((CAT NSuffix) (INFL ?INFL)) )
```

The following discrimination table is constructed from the left daughters (the left daughters are used because the chart parser is running bottom up — for running top-down the list should be created from the mother categories):

Features	**Feature Values**			
CAT	Verb	Noun	NSuffix	VSuffix
	NounSuffix	VerbSuffix	NounSuffix VerbSuffix	NounSuffix VerbSuffix
INFL	PLU	PAST	ING	
	NounSuffix VerbSuffix	NounSuffix VerbSuffix	NounSuffix VerbSuffix	

Each table entry contains the rule names which are *not* suitable for categories with that feature marking. For example, a category marked with `(CAT NOUN)` cannot be the left daughter of the rule `VerbSuffix`.

The matching process that happens during parsing is as follows. The proposing process starts with an initial *suitable rules* list of all the grammar rules, then for each feature value pair in the proposed category the table is used to find out what rules are unsuitable, thus reducing the list of suitable rules. This typically leaves about one full unification to complete the proposing stage.

Some points should also be mentioned at this time. Note in the above example there is no entry for the feature value combination `(INFL -)`. This is because if a proposed category has that feature and value there are no rules that are unsuitable, and combinations that can make no discrimination do not appear in the table. This emphasises the fact that in unrestricted unification *clashing* features are the distinguishing criterion.

Also it should be explained how this filtering process deals with variables in the rules and the proposing category. Variables are treated as if they range over the whole feature range (which may not be true) thus they cannot discriminate. This means that the discrimination provided by the table may be over-general and more rules may be found than are actually required. This is acceptable because a real unification operation will be done later in the parse so it will not change the number of parses, though it may slow the analysis down. Also the time required to make the discrimination table deal correctly with variables (and category valued features) is probably not worth the possible extra time that is lost when stray rules are added to the chart. Of course this does depend on the actual grammar and if the first daughters of the grammar rules are actually under-constrained then the analysis process will be slower — but this would also be true if unification were used at propose time instead.

7.7.2 Parsing term unification grammar

At a late stage in the project it was decided to experiment with term unification instead of just unrestricted unification. In term unification, for categories to unify they must have the *same* number of features (in addition to the normal condition of having non-clashing values). Thus the unification becomes like that used in the programming language Prolog, or in resolution theorem proving, where terms must have the same arity before they can successfully unify.

In our implementation of term unification we went a stage further in that category types (i.e. allowable feature combinations) must be explicitly declared; types would exist implicitly in any term unification system (in the sense that only certain combinations occur) but it seems desirable both for linguistic clarity and for computational efficiency to do this.

Category type definitions consist of an atomic name and a list of feature names, and all categories in the grammar (and lexicon) must be of one and only one of these category types (see Section 3.5). When categories are initially processed by the system, categories are converted (after alias expansion) into an internal form. To find the correct type definition, the feature names in the given category are checked against the feature names in the type definitions, and there should be a unique type definition whose features are a superset of those in the category. Then for each feature name listed in that type which does not appear in the user-specified category a variable value is inserted which ranges over the range of that feature. The actual internal form of a category consists of a simple list where the first element is the category type (the name of the category type from the category definition) and the rest of the list are the *values* of the features in the order the features were specified in the category definition. No feature names are necessary because the category type is sufficient to distinguish the feature names when necessary. (When categories are returned or printed by the system they are reconstructed using their feature names.)

Unification is now a simpler process in that there is no need to find the appropriate feature in each category as their positions are known. However there is now the problem that all categories are fully specified and (depending on the description) larger, even though most of the values are probably variables. This means that there is (possibly) more feature value unification to be done. The result of this is that for our GPSG description term unification is slower than unrestricted unification. This might change if a description more suitable for term unification was written, or a more efficient term unification procedure were implemented.

Apart from unification, the other major advantage is in *proposing* a morpheme in the grammar during analysis (cf. Section 7.5.1). Because all categories have an atomic type name the grammar can be treated as a form of (modified) context free grammar, thus opening the possibility of various optimisations commonly used for context free parsing. Given any category type proposed to the grammar it is possible to find out which grammar rules it may match by merely looking at the category types of the first daughter of each rule. This will of course not be very discriminating, but it will be very fast. In fact one can go further and calculate at grammar compile time for each category type which rules are appropriate, and then taking the category type of the mother of the rule find out which rules are appropriate and so on, thereby creating a table (*reachability matrix*) as described in [Aho72, p.300]. Using this relation we can replace the proposing stage of the parsing by only one call when a new lexical entry is added to the chart. Thus at that stage all relevant rules can be added to the chart (if not already there) and no other proposing is necessary at any other part of the algorithm.

7.7.3 Non-inflectable categories

In addition to the various linguistically motivated declarations which define the constructs in the linguistic description, a user may also optionally declare categories to be in a class called `NonInflect`. Each lexical entry whose syntactic category is an extension of one of these "non-inflectable" categories will be marked (internally) as valid *only* at the extreme right hand end of a word. This declaration allows the system to analyse words more efficiently and hence speed up look-up time. Possible categories for inclusion in this set are (in English) prepositions, determiners, irregular inflected forms, inflectional suffixes, etc.

An example declaration might be

```
NonInflect = { ((CAT prep)),
               ((CAT determiner)),
               ((INFL -)) }
```

Another way of indicating non-inflectable categories is by including in the list of lexical entries the *directive* (i.e. an instruction to the lexicon pre-processor) `noninflect`. Entries in the lexicon file between the directives

```
#noninflect on

#noninflect off
```

are treated as non-inflectable (irrespective of their syntactic field values). The restriction on the occurrence of such morphemes is imposed by the morpheme segmenter (Section 7.5.3), which will not include such morphemes in its results unless they correspond to the exhausting of the surface string.

Notice that if these options are used in conjunction with the string segmentation options (Section 7.5.4 above), the effect will be to prevent any "non-inflectable" items from occurring anywhere except at the end of a complete string (sentence), rather than at the end of a word. This is not a very helpful facility.

7.7.4 Keeping the lexicon in store

During the pre-processing (compilation) of the lexicon, each lexical entry is normally written out to a disk file and the byte position (within that file) of the start of the entry is held in the lexicon tree. (That is, only the citation form, as embodied in the lexicon tree, is held as a data structure inside the Lisp program.) It is, however, possible to direct the lexicon compiler to keep the entry as an ordinary Lisp structure rather than on disk. This is intended for common words (typically closed-class) which will be accessed often, as it will be faster to analyse entries in which no disk access is necessary (of course such issues depend on the underlying operating system the morphological system is running on). In fact, most of the other processes involved in lexical look-up (e.g. unification, two-level segmentation) are more computationally intensive, so the saving in time is rarely significant. However some Lisps do not support this file indexing method so that this mechanism has to be used for all lexical entries when running on those implementations.

7.7.5 Atomic forms

A large proportion of words that appear in normal text (in English) are in their base form and in fact require no morphological analysis at all. This suggests the possibility that before morphological analysis takes place any given word should be directly looked up in the lexicon (as a single entry) and only if that look-up is unsuccessful should a full analysis be carried out. This looks promising at first, but there is the problem that some words may be in the lexicon directly and also may be analysable as some other (non-atomic) form. This proposed short-cut would ignore the analysed form completely. It might be that such words are rare and could be treated specially, but even then it is not clear that there is much to be gained by this technique. Some informal experiments were carried out, but there was not much of an improvement in the speed of look-up, since words which consist of a single morpheme are already analysed very rapidly by the system. This is because the word grammar parser does not try to use grammar rules of more than one daughter for morphemes that end a word. Hence single morpheme words can usually be analysed without any use of the word grammar at all.

7.7.6 Caching

Another technique which was experimented with was the maintenance of a small table of words already looked up, so that a word need only be looked up once. This is quite successful for small demonstrations, etc. (and the Grammar Development Environment described in [Grov89] uses such a cache store along with our software) but if many words are going to be looked up the size of the cache will be such that it will take time to index it and it may then be slower than the full analyser system. One further development of this (which we did not explore) would be to create some very large list of words and their analyses, based on the information represented in linguistic form in our system, and then use conventional computer science techniques for efficient indexing to access this table. There is the problem that the word list would probably not be complete as it is likely that the lexical description will allow for an infinite set of words, but some way of avoiding this problem might be possible, e.g. considering only words of up to five morphemes, not using the same suffix twice or even resorting to full morphological analysis only when a word is not found in the generated list. Such an approach would be of practical utility if the lexicon was being used for the same set of words over a period of time (but would be of little linguistic interest).

7.8 Practical considerations

One of our problems throughout the project was the actual speed of the implementation, as each improvement in efficiency was usually overtaken by further complexity introduced by enhancements in the linguistic formalisms. Owing to the need to allow constant change and experimentation, the program was written with priority given to clarity and ease of change, rather than speed, and we did not have time to carry out serious instrumentation or complexity analysis. As mentioned earlier, another consideration was the ease of porting the software to other Lisp systems; in fact, the software has run successfully on a wide range of machines, including IBM PCs, Xerox Lisp Machines, Vax 11/750s, Suns, HPs, etc. (all under various implementations of Common Lisp). The program was essentially a prototype which tested the feasibility of the ideas involved, and which is suitable as a research tool; it was not intended to be a commercial product.

The final version of the system (summer 1987) took about 0.1 seconds per word for analysis, using a GPSG description (see Appendices) with around 7000 morphemes, with unrestricted unification, running on Franz Lisp (version 38.79) on a Sun 3/260 (4 MIPS) with 16 megabytes of memory. On the original development machine (Sun 2/120 with 4 megabytes, 1 MIP) the time was about 0.7 seconds. The system is also (and in later years, primarily) used in Common Lisp, which is unfortunately slower in spite of attempts to make the system more efficient in that language. The same test, in Allegro Common Lisp (version 3.1.4) running on a Sun 4/330 with 24 megabytes (12.5 MIPS) takes about 0.25 seconds per word. Using a simpler description (with similar morphological coverage but less complex feature structures) the Common Lisp version on a Sun 4/330 can analyse a word in 0.065 seconds.

These figures are very rough as carrying out accurate timing is very difficult. The test data used were the first 1000 word tokens in a project document, all of which were looked up several times and an average taken. It seems fair to say that a non-trivial lexicon and analyser can recognise words in around 0.1 to 0.2 seconds (on a reasonable sized workstation). As improvements in hardware are giving significant speed-ups each year (and as long as software does not always take all that advantage away), the analysis time can be expected to drop with newer technology, and a more efficient re-implementation (perhaps in some other programming language) could also provide a significant increase in the speed.

7.8.1 Size of lexicons

The size of lexicon which can be handled is not easy to characterise precisely. There is no limit built in to any of the algorithms or structures, but particular Lisp systems or operating systems impose space limitations. In exploratory work at the Centre for the New Oxford English Dictionary, University of Waterloo, some encouraging results were obtained. A Franz Lisp system with three times the normal amount of space was generated on a Sun 3/160 (2 MIPS) with 16 megabytes of memory. A small word grammar and the standard set of spelling rules (Appendix D.1) were used, and a lexicon constructed from letters A to F of the New OED. After removing various entries for practical reasons, a total of about 45,000 entries were left. These were compiled (as six separate lexicons, to avoid space overflow during compilation) and loaded together into the analyser. Look-up then took about three times as long as using the simpler description mentioned above with our own hand-crafted entries.

Boguraev and Briscoe [Bogu87] developed a lexicon for our system of around 62,000 morphemes based on the entries in the Longman Dictionary of Contemporary English [Proc78]. Using a set of morphological rules based on our description (Appendix D), the compilation of the lexicon took some time but the eventual lexicon and analyser ran in a reasonable time — looking up a word took about 1.5 seconds on average, on a Sun 4/330.

The actual speed of analysis of a word is very dependent on the set of morphological rules (both spelling and word grammar). Nevertheless, these informal experiments with large lexicons suggest that the implementation is suitable for use with serious linguistic descriptions, not just toy examples.

8 Limitations and Extensions

8.1 Spelling rules

The two-level model of morphographemics has been very successful, having been applied not only to English, but to languages such as Finnish, French, German, Japanese, Rumanian, French, Old Church Slavonic, Swedish (see [Gazd85a] for citations), and experimental descriptions of Swahili, Estonian, Cheremis, and Sanskrit have been devised (Koskenniemi, personal communication). There are certain difficulties in writing rule sets which are internally consistent and empirically adequate (see [Blac87] for some discussion), although some of the more straightforward of these obstacles can be overcome by using a more sophisticated rule compiler (as in [Kart87]). Nevertheless, there are still some notable deficiencies of the formalism, some of which we now briefly mention.

8.1.1 Symbols and features

As the historical survey in Chapter 2 explained, this strand of research originated in phonological work using distinctive feature matrices to represent phonetic segments. The Koskenniemi model that we adopted was concerned more narrowly with typewritten orthography, quite appropriately for a natural language system which was based on keyboard input. Consequently, the symbols manipulated by the transducers are atomic items representing single letters (or comparable abstract underlying entities). This limits the ability of the notation to express elegantly generalisations which would be very natural in a feature-based approach. Inspection of a typical two-level grammar reveals that the *sets* of characters which are declared in order to collapse rules are often phonologically-defined classes. For example, our description (see Appendix D.1) made use of the sets

```
{a e i o u y}
{s x z}
```

which seem to constitute phonologically "natural" classes, if we had distinctive features available to characterise them. If we were to return to the use of matrices of features to represent segments, such regularities might be stated more easily; moreover, it might also allow the possibility of handling phenomena such as assimilation.

Of course, we can continue to express many of these generalisations using the set-definition facility, but even then there is the complication that the phonologically "natural" class of entities is sometimes conventionally spelled using more than one character. For example, in the case of the second of the character sets shown above, the common property in question, that of "sibilance" (which triggers a modification in the attachment of the suffix `s`), is shared by the symbol sequences `sh` and `ch`. This would require that set-definitions can include *sequences* of symbols, demanding some revisions to the formalism. We have not explored this. (Notice that this is not the more prosaic issue of whether the *mnemonics* used for alphabetic symbols may contain more than one keyboard character.)

If the rule notation were to be applied to *phonological* material, the argument for re-introducing a feature mechanism would be even more compelling. We would need a suitable style of rule, and a processing mechanism able to match underspecified feature matrices. That is, the concepts of *unification grammar* (see Chapter 3) might well have to be introduced into the interpretation of morphophonemic rules. This would be quite reasonable, given the historical origins of feature-based representation. Of course, as the previous discussion showed, the existing two-level formalism would allow us to model distinctive features indirectly, via the definition of appropriate sets in terms of which the rules could be stated, but this is a rather inelegant and unperspicuous approach.

It would be possible to design a compiler which took distinctive feature descriptions and unpacked them into character and character set based descriptions of the type just sketched, but this approach would lose the economy of description that distinctive features were intended to achieve. Variable sharing, for example, could only be handled by expanding out to separate automata for each possible value of a variable. If this were merely a matter of execution, with no impact on efficiency, this might not matter, but the suspicion arises that compiling a feature-based description into a character-based one would result in a very large and unwieldy object indeed. However, extending the existing formalism and its associated interpreter to allow for, in effect, unification, would in itself require substantial further research, although [Cars88] describes some proposals for manipulating feature matrices using automata.

8.1.2 Interleaving

As is well known, the two-level formalism is not capable, in its pure form, of handling some types of "non-concatenative" morphological phenomena, such as those found in the Semitic languages like Arabic and Hebrew. In such languages, many words have consonantal roots such as `k-t-b` (*book/write*). Different verb inflections, or nominalising morphology, interleave a vocalic pattern governed by harmony with the consonantal root; different vocalic morphemes give rise to forms such as:[1]

kataba	to write/3ps
katabtu	I wrote
ektub	I write
kutub	books

While it is not certain that a two-level model cannot describe facts like these, it appears that it cannot do so with economy or elegance, since it involves several separate but corresponding changes. However, Kataja and Koskenniemi [Kata88] sketch a solution involving a set of lexicons which are to be intersected, and an arrangement for moving between lexicons within a string.

Another approach based on the intersection of lexicons is that of [Kay87], in which the system to account for the Arabic phenomena relies on the alphabet of the automata being composed of quadruples, rather than pairs. His approach may thus be thought of as involving a "four-tape acceptor", each of the tapes being annotated with a character string. As in the two-level model, one string comprises the surface form; the others contain information concerning:

1. the "root" (i.e. the "lexical item" — `ktb` for the example above)
2. the "vocalism" — the pattern of vowels within the word
3. the "prosodic template" — a sequence of vowel (`V`) and consonant (`C`) symbols whose purpose is to control the phenomena of vowel lengthening and consonant gemination

While this approach keeps Arabic morphology within the domain of finite state technology, it does so more in the letter than in the spirit,

1 See, for example, [Gold90, p.95ff.] for an account of the Arabic facts within the framework of "autosegmental" phonology. The work of Kay [Kay87] mentioned below is a reconstruction of this descriptive approach.

and it certainly goes beyond the more limited notion of two-level morphology defined in Chapter 2. As explained there, arbitrary parallel combinations of transducers provide a more powerful expressive device than the basic Koskenniemi rules; indeed, they virtually constitute an arbitrary programming language. It therefore seems to us that more powerful mechanisms really are needed here.

Similar remarks apply to the various types of reduplication phenomena that are found in many languages. [Ande88] discusses reduplication, and also describes several other morphophonological phenomena which appear to be difficult to cope with satisfactorily within the two-level framework.

While these examples, and our previous discussion, suggest that the application of two-level morphology to some areas of phonological description is rather clumsy, it is probably worth remarking that serious alternatives are very thin on the ground. There are remarkably few implemented systems for phonological description based on more theoretically fashionable notations.

Cahill [Cahi90b, Cahi90a] describes a highly general formalism (MOLUSC) for describing phonological (or morphographemic) phenomena using the *syllable* as the organisational structure (instead of describing uniform sequences of segments). This does appear to meet the methodological requirements we have set (computational feasibility and theoretical generality), particularly when coupled with the DATR system [Gazd89], but the fact that it works in a wholly different manner to our combination of two-level morphology and unification grammar means that a proper comparison is non-trivial, and is beyond the scope of this chapter.

8.1.3 Influencing rule application

Even within the domain of graphemic representations there is a further major disadvantage to the use of the two-level model, namely that there is no clean way for a rule to make reference to non-graphemic properties. For example, if some spelling rule is true only of items in some syntactic class, or some class specifiable only by non-graphemic means, there is no simple way of enforcing this restriction, other than by using special characters in the lexical form to trigger or inhibit the application of the rule(s) in question. This device was used extensively by Koskenniemi in his description of Finnish, and may be perfectly legitimate in many contexts. However, this seems an undesirable move, particularly if the resulting description is intended to be used with existing dictionaries or word lists, which would not contain the necessary special characters.

Two simple examples demonstrating the need for such a mechanism are the following:

1. The English description contains a spelling rule which has the effect of doubling a single stem-final consonant when a following suffix begins with a vowel, as in, for example, `bigger`. In polysyllabic stems, this "gemination" process is to some extent subject to the stress pattern of the stem — compare `forgetting` and `targeting`. With no indication in the lexical form of where the primary stress is located, it is not possible to analyse `forgetting` and `targeting` without also accepting `*forgeting` and `*targetting`.
2. French adjectives with stem final sequences of < vowel `s` > (e.g. `gros`, "big") double the `s` when followed by the feminine suffix `e` — `grosse`. Verbs with stem final `s` do not undergo this doubling when followed by orthographically identical but morphosyntactically distinct suffixes; the first person singular present subjunctive form of `lire` ("read" — appropriate stem `lis`) is `lise`, not `*lisse`. In effect, the lexical form of certain French adjectives and verbs must encode their syntactic category, in addition to their orthographic and perhaps phonological properties.

Bear [Bear88] suggests that a clearer mechanism for overcoming some of these problems would be to associate with morphemes *negative rule features* indicating that they do not undergo particular rules. Thus a morpheme like `target` would be marked `[-Gemination]`, or something appropriate. Analyses derived using these rules on these morphemes would be discarded.

The same mechanism could be used more extensively in the description of languages where phonological or graphemic changes are conditioned by membership of a particular declension or conjugational class, as is the case for Finnish. This mechanism would also remedy a descriptive inadequacy of the two-level formalism — whenever some change is optional for some morphemes but obligatory for others, there is no way of enforcing this without resort to special rule-triggering characters. Otherwise, the changes have to be optional or obligatory for all morphemes.

Trost [Tros90] describes an extension of the rule feature mechanism, whereby each rule is associated with a feature structure which must be unified with that of the morpheme recognised by the rule. His example is German umlaut; for example, in forming the plural of `man`, the combination `Mann+er` becomes `Männer`. It has often been observed that *phonological* phenomena may be influenced by morpho-syntactic properties of the items involved. The importance of this type of example is that it shows that *morphographemic* processing can also be influenced not just by the properties of the morpheme to which the spelling or sound change applies, but by the (morpho-)syntactic context in which that morpheme appears.

Trost's solution is to mark the rule mapping `a` to `ä` as `[umlaut +]`. The stem `Mann` will be marked with a feature `[umlaut X]` (since it can appear with or without umlaut). The affix `-er` will be marked `[umlaut +]`, and a morpho-syntax rule combining the two unifies these values in the obvious way:

```
N[agr plural] -> N[agr singular, umlaut X]
                 Affix[agr plural, umlaut X]
```

(This is not the actual rule given by Trost — his example is more complex in ways not relevant here.)

In an analysis process, negative rule features, or feature markings like Trost's, act as filters, informally speaking, in the sense that the graphemic rules produce all possibilities, some of which are discarded when the features are checked. In synthesising a word, the features guide which rules can be applied to produce the desired output.

Note that there are some unexplored formal subtleties in this extension to the formalism. In Koskenniemi's original notation it is possible to write conflicting Surface Coercion Rules:

```
A-to-B
   a:b <= x:x --- y:y
A-to-C
   a:c <= x:x --- y:y
```

These rules each disallow the sequence required by the other. The result is that the symbol-pair language generated (see Appendix F.4) will not include any sequences of the form `x:x a:Z y:y`, for any value of `Z`. If we have rule features, and a relevant morpheme is marked as not undergoing one of these rules, then the language will include such sequences, provided they are not disallowed by other rules. However, under such circumstances, it is not possible to interpret the process of analysis as one of free application of the rules, followed by filtering of morphemes bearing inappropriate rule features, for if the negative rule features are not taken into account at the rule application stage, there will never be anything to filter.

Trost is dealing with a variant of two-level morphology in which rules are classed into *optional* or *obligatory*, which is slightly different from our arrangement (see Chapter 2). One problem that would arise when trying to apply this approach to our version of two-level morphology is that the use of two-level rules could now have side-effects on feature-structures within the word grammar. We have defined a symbol pair as being allowed by the Context Restriction Rules (operator "=>") if *at least one* such rule matches it completely; if more than one rule matches, the symbol-pair is still valid, with no additional consequences. However, if different rules had different morphotactic features attached to them, and if some lexical items had variable (i.e. uninstantiated) values for those features, there might be several matching rules for a given symbol pair, with each rule causing a different instantiation of the features. A new definition of well-formedness (derivation) would be needed which took account of this.

Notice also that this mechanism allows for some very complicated interactions between rules. It will now be possible, for example, for one morphographemic rule to block the application of another. In cases where they have the same context, this happens automatically. However, the rule feature mechanism can allow non-local dependencies between rules via the setting of appropriate feature values. That is, one rule may set a feature which prevents another rule from applying. It may be that this device could be used to good effect in the treatment of vowel harmony in the Finno-Ugric and Semitic languages, and other similarly problematic phenomena, but it may also lead to descriptions which are difficult to understand and debug.

8.1.4 Other two-level formalisms

Black et al. [Blac87] produced various further criticisms of Koskenniemi's original types of rule:

1. They quickly become difficult to debug, although they are better than transducers in this respect.
2. It is possible to write sets of rules in which the context presupposed by one conflicts with the operation of another. One of the rules must then be extended to allow explicitly for this interaction.
3. Rules can affect only one symbol pair at a time.

Black et al. also suggested a different formalism which attempted to overcome all three of these problems. The rules envisaged were of the form:

```
SurfaceChars  --> LexicalChars    (S-to-L)

SurfaceChars  <-- LexicalChars    (L-to-S)
```

where `SurfaceChars` and `LexicalChars` are lists of characters from the appropriate vocabularies, each of the same length. The interpretation of the rules is given in terms of the constraints that a lexical and surface pairing must meet:

1. There must be a partitioning of the surface string such that each element in the partition matches the LHS of some S-to-L rule, and the lexical string is the concatenation of the corresponding RHSs.
2. in a lexical string, any substring that matches the RHS of an L-to-S rule must correspond to the surface string specified by the LHS of that rule.

As in two-level rules, there are also *composite rules*, written with the connective `<-->`, which conflate one S-to-L rule and one L-to-S rule. An example of an obligatory change involving more than one character which can now be easily described is

```
il0i <--> le+i
```

(for analyses such as `probability` as `probable+ity` and `stability` as `stable+ity`). An optional change might be that of the archaic plurals for words ending in `f`, as in `hooves` and `hoofs`:

```
ves --> f+s
```

Ruessink [Rues89] presents a development of this notation. Firstly, he adds an explicit context to the rules; in the Black et al. formalism the context is not distinguished explicitly (though it is usually obvious which characters are effectively acting as a context). Secondly, Ruessink proposes dropping the requirement that the LHS have the same number of characters as the RHS. This has certain consequences for the interpretation of the rules; it is now required that an L-to-S rule has a corresponding S-to-L rule in order that the relevant partitions of the lexical string can be determined at all. For practical purposes, then, there are two rule types — S-to-L, describing optional change, and composite rules, describing obligatory changes. Van Noord [Noor90] gives examples of rules for English within this formalism using a Prolog-based notation.

At the present time, it appears that this type of two-level rule offers some advantages of readability and descriptive flexibility, especially when combined with a rule feature mechanism like that described above (Section 8.1.3). It has already been used to produce descriptions of English, Dutch, and Spanish which are more compact than those written within the original two-level notation, and promises to bring similar advantages in the description of languages displaying more complex properties.

8.1.5 Iteration

Intuitively, what provides much of the power (and complexity) in the two-level mechanism is the facility for constraining symbol-pairs which are arbitrarily far apart, using the iteration symbols `*` (or `1+` in our implementation — see Chapter 7). This capacity is not used in our description of English (see Appendix D), since English morphographemic phenomena are largely local in nature (as observed in [Bart87]). The linguistic justification for this notation seems to come from phenomena such as vowel harmony, where the phonological characteristics of a particular segment are determined by the properties of another segment some distance to the left or right.

It is important here to distinguish between genuine iteration of the sort represented by iteration symbols in the rules, and the occasional use of loops to implement, in hand-constructed transducers, analyses of phenomena which are not inherently iterative. For example, some of the transducers in [Kart83b] or [Kosk83b] have loops as a convenient way to implement inherently local phenomena. This comes about because the rule interpreter is a fairly conventional transducer mechanism, which runs all the transducers all the time rather than "re-starting" a matching process whenever it is needed (see Section 7.3.2). These extra loops are therefore needed to allow the transducer to skip over material that is not pertinent to the class of matches which it can detect.

It is presumably an empirical question how far morphographemic dependencies stretch in a given language, and seems unlikely that there are genuine cases where segments can affect each other over very large distances (e.g. several hundred segments). (See [Kosk88] for some comments on the empirical lack of complexity of real linguistic data.) Unfortunately, this does not mean that there will be a clear limit to how far such processes can extend. An analogy can be made with the question of centre-embedding in the syntax of English sentences; it is clear that the process cannot occur to an indefinite level, but there is no well-defined cut-off point at which further embedding leads to unacceptability. Nevertheless, it might be worth exploring the complexity consequences of limiting the extent of morphographemic constraints in two-level rules. For the moment, let us once again focus just on the basic two-level mechanism, without nulls and without any further mappings to surface or lexical strings. Suppose we disallow the indefinite Kleene iteration symbols, but allow a superscript positive integer to be added to a subexpression in a context, meaning "up to this number of occurrences". This would mean that every rule would have an associated *maximum span* — an integer M representing the length of the longest possible sequence of symbol-pairs that it could ever match, and no instance of a rule could match symbol-pairs further apart than $M-1$ places. Suppose we have a two-level grammar with N rules (assuming for simplicity that these are all completely concrete rules, with no set or variable symbols in them), in which the maximum span of any rule does not exceed M. This would mean that, within a scan of a string, there could never be more than $N \times M$ potential matching rules at a given point in the string. That gives a bound (constant for a given grammar) on how many instances of rules could be relevant to any given symbol-pair.

Even if something of this sort could be made to work linguistically, it would reduce rather than eliminate the processing load involved in the process of matching a surface string to the lexicon via the rules.

8.2 Word grammar and feature conventions

The form of word grammar rules adopted (Chapter 3) is fairly general, so most phenomena which can be expressed in terms of hierarchical constituency can be covered.

As mentioned elsewhere, it would be highly satisfactory if the internal word structure assigned by rules could also be used for semantic interpretation, but we have not explored this aspect. Such an approach would have difficulty with any complex or compound item where the internal structure as determined by morphosyntactic criteria was different from that desirable for semantic purposes. It is sometimes argued that examples such as

```
nuclear physicist
transformational grammarian
criminal lawyer
```

present such a problem, but this is less clear-cut within our framework, since the combination of `physics` with `+ist` would occur at the lexical (morphological) level, whereas the combination of `nuclear` with `physicist` would occur at the sentence level. At the very least, it demands that the semantics concocted for words such as `physicist` allow some slot or parameter to be available for further modification at the sentence level.

There are various ways in which one might approach the description of phenomena like these. The `simplest` alternative is to regard affixes like `+ian` or `+ist` as forming separate morphemes in the sequence made available to the sentence grammar, as must be done with the possessive "`'s`". Then no word level syntax is involved and the sentence grammar will generate two analyses:

```
[[nuclear physics] ist]
[nuclear [physics ist]]
```

of which the first represents the most likely interpretation in neutral contexts. However, the affixes which should receive this treatment may be difficult to characterise, if we are to avoid also analysing sequences like "`unification parser`" in two different ways:

```
[unification [parse er]]
[[unification parse] er]
```

It is not clear that these analyses correspond to different interpretations.

An alternative would be to assign a special feature to the relevant affix, allowing it, when figuring in a compound nominal, to receive a "type-raised" interpretation so that the meaning of the nominal would be a function of the meaning of `physicist` and `nuclear`. This would require some adjustment to the syntax rules for nominals so as to trigger the appropriate semantic behaviour, but would be straightforward to implement. In fact, given the ability to assign interpretations of sufficiently high type to morphological affixes, our approach to word grammar will be compatible with almost any envisageable scheme of semantic analysis.

8.3 Lexical entries

Our notion of lexical entry, while very general, is also rather crude. As we have mentioned already, most of the fields of the entries were not exploited, and were regarded as containing "dummy" items in our analyses. While it should not be too difficult to devise phonetic/phonological symbols for insertion in the lexicon (given a theory of phonology — cf. Section 8.1), it would be more difficult if the phonetic field were to be used to look up the lexicon (see comments above on spelling rules). Some significant research would also be needed to devise suitable semantic structures for individual entries, particularly if these items were to be used in a compositional semantics within words (see Section 8.2).

Perhaps more problematic is the formal structure of lexical entries, which lack any notion of disjunction or listing of alternatives. It would not be sufficient to allow each entry simply to have a set of values in each field, as this would not allow one syntactic category within an entry to be paired with a particular semantic value and no other, as might often be the case. The definition of an atomic lexical entry should perhaps be redefined to allow a single citation form to be associated with more than one tuple of other fields (syntactic category, etc.). A more flexible scheme might be to have a very high-level notation for expressing lexical entries which expands into an internal form equivalent to the current basic notation. This idea was considered briefly at one stage of the research, but we did not have a ready answer to the question of representing the results returned by the lexical look-up component — if the value returned by this computation was phrased in terms of the low-level atomic entries, then the linguist who reads it (or the sentence grammar) has to deal with this supposedly internal representation; on the other hand, if the original high-level notation is a disjunctive schema representing several combinations of syntax-semantics, how can it be returned as a value when only one such combination is concerned? This issue is probably not insoluble, but we did not consider it important enough to devote time to it.

8.4 Lexical rules

Although the spelling rules, word structure rules, and perhaps the feature passing conventions, are fairly elegant linguistic formalisms with a precise declarative interpretation, which could be reasonably compared with current proposals in theoretical linguistics, the lexical rules are a little less clean. It was important for all our rules to be interpretable procedurally, but in the case of the lexical rules they are wholly procedural. To some extent their form and meaning is a by-product of the computational or practical aspects of our project, since the three-way distinction between the linguist-specified lexicon, the intermediate stored lexicon, and the lexicon made available by the morphological rules is crucial in an actual implementation, but not of central concern to a theoretical linguist (although it could be argued that some such conceptual distinctions are necessary if notations for lexical entries and rules which operate on them are to be given a precise interpretation). As can be seen from the discussion in Chapter 5, lexical rules were as much a practical tool as a linguistic mechanism.

It is tempting to draw an analogy between our devices and the various types of lexical rules employed or assumed in theoretical linguistics. In general, however, the kind of operation performed by the latter exceeds the power of our lexical rules. The obstacle to direct replication of such rules within our framework lies in the restricted nature of the pattern matching and variable binding facilities present. More specifically, any lexical operation which demands the analysis of fields other than the morphosyntactic category can be emulated only in a roundabout fashion, if at all.

The "Third Singular Lexical Rule" of Pollard and Sag [Poll87, p.213] for example, makes use of a *morphological operator* which is said to "...

return the (irregular) 3RDSNG value of the input if one is provided, and add *-s* to the input's PHONOLOGY otherwise", simultaneously specifying that syntactic information is to be inherited from the *3rdsng* type. Leaving aside the hierarchical aspects of lexical organisation employed here (which can in essence be reproduced), in order to meet the requirement of the morphological operation a rule would have to be able to modify the citation form of an entry, adding `s` or `es` according to its internal structure, or, if it is irregular, replacing it with an alternate form. In our (rather crude) form of lexical rules, citation and phonological forms are treated as unanalysable atoms, which may be copied or replaced only as units.

Little use is made in our description of English of the semantic field. One obvious item to place there would be an expression encoding the order in which a verb combines with its arguments. Thus, an entry for `give` might be:

```
(give
  give
  ((CAT V)
   (SUBCAT ((FIRST ((CAT NP)(CASE ACC)))
            (REST ((FIRST ((CAT PP)(PFORM TO)))
                   (REST ((FIRST ((CAT NP)(CASE NOM)))
                          (REST ()))))))))
  (lambda x (lambda y (lambda z (give (z)(x)(y)))))
  NIL)
```

where we assume that the sentence grammar treats the value of `SUBCAT` in this entry as a stack (see Section 5.8), and that it provides a means of combining the meaning of subject and object NPs with that of the verb. Also, the meaning of the verb is expressed as a function taking three arguments, which one could characterise as "source" (the giver), "theme" (the thing given), and "goal" (the recipient) respectively, so that the sentence "`Andrew gave beer to Charles`" receives, on appropriate assumptions about the interpretation of "case-marking" PPs representing indirect objects, the translation

```
(give (Andrew)(beer)(Charles))
```

Many such ditransitive verbs also appear with a double NP object; these might have entries such as

```
(give
  give
  ((CAT V)
   (SUBCAT ((FIRST ((CAT NP)(CASE ACC)))
            (REST ((FIRST ((CAT NP)(CASE ACC)))
                   (REST ((FIRST ((CAT NP)(CASE NOM)))
                          (REST ())))))))))
  (lambda x (lambda y (lambda z (give (z)(y)(x)))))
  NIL)
```

in which the SUBCAT value and semantic field together provide the sentence "Andrew gave Charles beer" with the same translation as the "unshifted" version, thus making the two sentences paraphrases.

In order to relate these two types of entry by means of a "Dative Alternation" lexical rule of the kind envisaged by [Bres82, p.25] one might wish to employ a Multiplication Rule that would produce an entry for the double-NP complement variant of this class of verbs from entries for the NP-PP complement variant.[2]

While the SUBCAT value can be manipulated as required, no pattern can be written for the semantic field that generalises properly across different entries. A semantics field pattern containing a variable:

```
(lambda x (lambda y (lambda z (_fn (z)(x)(y)))))
```

will not do, since it is only in the syntactic field that variables are recognised and available for use in a complex pattern. Nor is any general solution is to be found in abandoning the semantics field altogether, and incorporating semantic information into the syntax field; the necessity of declaring feature names and values means that this, too, would preclude generalising over entries.

Under these circumstances, the only available method is to define, for each relevant morphological rule, a semantic operator which, acting on the contents of the semantic field, would produce the desired effect, and which can be inserted by the rule without reference to the internal

2 As has been noted before many times, neither of these sets of verbs includes the other. That is to say, given the existence of e.g. donate (we can have "donate a sculpture to the museum" but not "donate the museum a sculpture") and fine ("fine transgressors fifty pounds" but not "fine fifty pounds to transgressors"), any lexical rule would have to be prevented from applying to certain exceptional entries.

structure of the semantic field. An appropriate operator in this case would be

```
(lambda entry
   (lambda x
      (lambda y
         (lambda z (entry (y) (x) (z))))))
```

which will, when all beta-reductions have been carried out, permute the arguments to the original verb in the desired way. This restriction on what can be carried out by such rules has the desirable side effect of forcing any semantic manipulations to be of a wholly compositional character. Semantically, a Multiplication Rule must be strictly a function from old entries to new ones.

Briefly, then, the lexical rules provided in our system cannot be used satisfactorily to replicate lexical processes which involve the manipulation of the internal structure of non-morphosyntactic information within entries. As a result, the user of the system is tied quite strongly to a particular conception of morphological and lexical behaviour; it is not possible, for example, to easily implement general non-concatenative or "word and process" accounts of word formation (e.g. [Ande88], [Cald89]) as an alternative to the segment-based accounts for which the word grammar is intended.

8.5 Idioms

We have not considered the difficult problem of idioms. Although we do allow arbitrary strings of text to occur in the citation forms of lexical entries (e.g. "`on the whole`"), this is far from being sufficient to cater for the syntactic and semantic richness of idioms. It is virtually impossible for us to allow inflection to occur inside such a fixed phrase, so although "`keep an eye on`" could have a lexical entry, it would not be systematically related to a phrases such as "`keep`*ing* `an eye on`".

To the extent that we had in mind a theory of idioms, it was that outlined in [Pulman] in which the lexical forms are used to prime access to specific idiom rules. However, in order to allow for the semi-compositional nature of some idioms, these rules operate not on surface but on logical forms resulting from semantic interpretation. This allows for idioms to have a fully compositional syntax, and thus for inflectional markings to occur within them. Thus the mechanism is separate from, though entirely consistent with, the lexical mechanisms developed here.

8.6 Compounds

Noun compounds are a notoriously difficult area, and it was not obvious how to tackle the problem of assigning multiple analyses to sequences of more than two nouns. From the purely syntactic point of view, compounding presents few problems; in the general case, the linguistically correct structure for a compound of arbitrary length is a binary tree. A simple treatment along lines like

```
N -> N N
```

will produce many parses for a complex compound, only one of which may correspond to a plausible interpretation. Which of the potentially many such trees is appropriate in some specific instance is an issue that can only be resolved by taking into account not only the semantics of the components themselves, but also contextual factors (see, for example, [Isab84], [Spar84]).

One conclusion that may be drawn from this is that the relation between syntax and semantics is not straightforward. It seems pointless to produce all possible parses if all but one are going to be filtered out by semantic interpretation. A more efficient strategy would be to produce a single canonical parse which is not intended to correspond directly to an interpretation, but which can be used as the basis for a semantic interpretation procedure to rearrange the components in a semantically appropriate way. The end result, in principle, is the same.

Our treatment takes one step towards this latter position by enforcing a left-recursive analysis on compound nominals. In these structures, the rightmost element is the "head", in the sense that it determines the overall category of the word. Thus a parse will have the shape

$[_N\ [_N\ [_N\ \text{n}]\ \text{n}]\ \text{n}]$

Assuming that the variable `?any` has been declared as taking the possible values `ANY` and `NOT`, and that non-compound words bear the specification `[COMPOUND NOT]`, the following possible rule would allow any sequence of words to be analysed as forming a word, assigning the type of structure indicated above:

```
( COMPOUNDS-ANY
    [COMPOUND ANY] ->
              [BAR 0, INFL +, COMPOUND ?any],
              [BAR 0, INFL +, COMPOUND NOT] )
```

Unfortunately, this is rather over-general, and would produce many unexpected results — `readable`, in addition to the desired analysis involving `read` and the adjectival suffix `+able`, is also analysed as a compound of the verb `read` and the adjective `able`.

Both nouns and adjectives are specified as `[N +]`, and so the following slightly more restricted version, in which `?na` ranges over `NA` and `NOT`, would allow sequences of noun-noun, adjective-noun, adjective-adjective, and noun-adjective, again with the first element either a compound or a simple word:

```
( COMPOUNDS-NA
   [COMPOUND NA] ->
              [BAR 0, N +, INFL +, COMPOUND ?na],
              [BAR 0, N +, INFL +, COMPOUND NOT] )
```

Either of these rules would give rise to spurious analyses, mainly because many apparently "possible" compound words coincide in form with non-compound words. Clearly, the rule `COMPOUNDS-NA` analyses a subset of the constructions analysed by `COMPOUNDS-ANY`. A second consequence of including a relatively general compounding rule is that the analyser considers many more lexical items as potential segments of the word being analysed, and this led to a deterioration in performance in the implemented system. We therefore settled for a still more restrictive version, which states that a compound noun may consist of either two simple nouns or a simple noun preceded by a compound noun. This rule permits both possibilities, the variable `?n` ranging over `N` and `NOT`.

```
( COMPOUNDS-N
   [COMPOUND N] ->
              [BAR 0, V -, N +, INFL +, COMPOUND ?n],
              [BAR 0, V -, N +, INFL +, COMPOUND NOT] )
```

While the left-recursive analysis adopted here solves the efficiency problem, it may still not be optimal from the point of view of semantic interpretation, given the assumption of rule-to-rule syntax/semantics.

The reason for this is the large contextual element in the interpretation of compound nominals (see [Spar84]). The appropriate relation even in simple cases can only be inferred on the basis of knowledge of the meanings of the individual words involved, and does not correspond to any structural property — compare "`sketch book`", "`law book`", "`cheque book`", etc. It is convenient to capture this fact by assigning to the nominal a meaning at the level of compositional semantics of the form $nn(N1, N2)$, where nn is a functor that, when evaluated, captures the non-compositional contextual element of meaning by operating on the meanings of the nominals supplied to it in an appropriate way. The recursive structure implied by our rule means that the semantic structure that would emerge for something like `modem carrier detect line` would be:

$$nn(nn(nn(\texttt{modem}, \texttt{carrier}), \texttt{detect}), \texttt{line})$$

Unfortunately, the meaning of this expression is not best described as a set of functions of that type (`carrier` and `detect` group together), at least, not without building into the nn functor a very complex piece of machinery. What is needed to give maximum flexibility in the interpretation of nn, given that virtually any possible semantic grouping is possible, is to make it a functor of all the nominals involved in the expression:

$$nn(\texttt{modem}, \texttt{carrier}, \texttt{detect}, \texttt{line})$$

Thus nn is really a family of functors. This structure is most easily achieved by introducing as little explicit syntactic structure as possible, most obviously by allowing an extension to the word grammar notation to allow the right-hand side of a rule to specify that *one or more* of a category should occur (the so-called "Kleene +" notation). A rule could then be written something like:

```
(FLAT-COMPOUND
  [CAT N, COMPOUND N]       ->
         [CAT N, COMPOUND NOT] +,
         [CAT N, COMPOUND NOT] )
```

8.7 Irregularity and blocking

Where inflectional affixation is concerned, our English description correctly prevents the acceptance of forms such as `mans` (as the plural of `man`) and `goed` (as the past of `go`). In the case of derivation, it is more difficult to decide whether a possible form is to be excluded; `expansion` is the preferred nominalisation of `expand`, but `expandment` seems a tolerable alternative. The existence of a (quite widely used) "irregularly derived" form produces the effect known in the theoretical literature as *blocking*, whereby more conventional forms are not used. In general, the attitude taken to this phenomenon depends on the objective of one's work — is the lexicon to characterise the words which are to be found in some well-defined corpus of text, or is it to characterise the notion of "possible word of some language"? If the former, then it is acceptable to exclude from consideration less preferred forms such as `expandment` which do not occur in the corpus. If the intention is to define the notion of "possible word", on the other hand, it is doubtful whether these apparently "blocked" forms can safely be excluded. This is also the case even if the aim is not to give a theoretical account, but merely to deal with words found in unrestricted texts. Motivated solutions have been offered to capture the phenomenon of blocking, but these usually involve hard-wiring some default mechanism. We regard this as a disadvantage for a system intended for practical use, since it is astonishing how many so-called irregular forms are encountered in their regular form in real-life texts and conversations. Readers who doubt this assertion are invited to examine the front page of their favourite quality newspaper to test its truth.

8.8 The implemented system

The implemented software has many limitations, ranging from minor oversights to more significant problems.

8.8.1 Notational restrictions

The implementation of two-level spelling rules has some omissions, as noted in Chapter 7. The Kleene star is not allowed in context expressions, nor are various characters such as brackets (unless quoted). In earlier versions, there was the further limitation that every concrete symbol in these rules (i.e. not set names or variables) must be a single keyboard character, and could not be an arbitrary mnemonic symbol composed of several letters or digits. This made it awkward to specify lexical entries which contain, within their citation forms, special characters representing "archiphonemes" or other abstract entities.

8.8.2 Efficiency

The time limits of the project allowed us to develop a fairly stable set of Lisp programs, but these have to be seen as *prototypes*, in the artificial intelligence tradition of experimental programming. We have demonstrated the feasibility of implementing the given behaviour (functionality) in a workable system, but we have not devoted much effort to maximising the efficiency of the processing, either in terms of time or space. In particular, the careful application of sound computer science techniques, and perhaps re-implementation in a different programming language, could speed up the processing times enormously (although with current hardware, response times are quite acceptable even with very large dictionaries).

One idea which we considered, but did not follow up (owing to its lack of significant linguistic interest), was that of using the various linguistic rules (including all the morphological ones), to create a vastly more expanded dictionary, which included inflectional and derivational forms explicitly, and then encoding this list for look-up using the most efficient scheme available (see Section 7.7.6).

8.8.3 Generation

Although we implemented a very limited form of morphographemic generation using the spelling rules, we did not have a full generator which could be used, for example, as a component of a text generator program. What would be required would be an algorithm which, starting from an underspecified syntactic category and some semantic information, would compute, using all the morphological rules, a suitable surface form. This would not be completely trivial to achieve, as the initial syntactic category for the computation might contain features which would arise from various affixation processes, including the application of the feature passing conventions, so that finding the correct morphemes to concatenate might require subtle use of linguistic information.

8.9 Conclusions

The study of morphological mechanisms which are both theoretically respectable and computationally feasible is a relatively new area of computational linguistics, and there is obviously much more that has to be explored. We have not been able, in the time and space available, to discuss all of the theoretical or implementational issues involved, but we hope that we have presented a clear definition of a coherent, general, and realistic (if imperfect) framework which allows theoretical questions to be posed, and practical lexicons to be constructed.

A Definition of the Linguistic Notation

This appendix defines the exact notation used by the implemented system described in Chapter 7. The presentation uses conventional BNF to define the various constructs, with Lisp-style comments added to some of the definitions for further explanation; such remarks are preceded by a semi-colon. The basic item **<symbol>** is a Lisp symbol and **<s-expression>** is a Lisp expression which does not contain macro-characters (i.e. parentheses, numbers and symbols only) *except* that upper-case and lower-case letters are treated as distinct in both these constructs. A **<variable>** is any symbol starting with an underscore. Optionality of an expression is not indicated using brackets, as in some BNFs, but by allowing some constructs to have an "empty" expansion. Indefinite repetition of an expression zero or more times is indicated by * following that expression, and one or more repetitions is indicated by *1. Options specific to unrestricted unification are commented with "UU only" and those specific to term unification are marked "TU only".

Comments could appear anywhere in the data files used by the various programs; they began with a semi-colon and continued to the end of the line (following the Lisp convention).

A.1 Spelling rules

```
<spelling rules> ::= SurfaceAlphabet <enumerated set>
                     SurfaceSets <set declaration> *
                     LexicalAlphabet <enumerated set>
                     LexicalSets <set declaration> *
                     DefaultPairs <pair> *
                     Rules <rule> *

<enumerated set> ::= { <alphabet char> * }

<alphabet char> ::= <surface character>
                  | <lexical character>
                  | 0            ;; null symbol

<surface character>
            <single non-special character>
          | <quoted character>
```

```
<lexical character> ::=
            <single non-special character>
          | <quoted character>

<quoted character>  ::=
            "<single non-special character>"
```

A <single non-special character> can be any normal typable character, and a <quoted character> is a <single non-special character> surrounded by double quotes. If any of the following characters is used, it *must* be surrounded by double quotes:

```
space, tab, newline, comma, ), (, #, ;, :,
}, {, >, <, ], [, !
```

For example, " " for space. Double quotes may be used by using a double double quote within quotes; i.e. """" for ".

```
<set declaration> ::=  <symbol> is <enumerated set>

<rule> ::=
    <name> <pair> <operator> <contexts> <where clause>

<operator> ::=    =>  |  <=  |  <=>

<contexts> ::=  <simple context>
             |  <simple context> or <contexts>

<simple context> ::= <context expr> --- <context expr>

<context expr> ::=  <pair>
       |  < <itemlist> >     ; sequential items
       |  { <itemlist> }     ; or choice of items
       |  ( <itemlist> )1+   ; one or more occurrences

<itemlist> ::= <context expr>
       | <context expr> <itemlist>
```

```
<where clause> ::=
        where <where variable name>
              in <enumerated set>
      |         ;; no where clause

<pair> ::= <lexical symbol> : <surface symbol>

<lexical symbol> ::= <lexical character>
                   | <lexical set name>
                   | <where variable name>
                   | 0                      ; null symbol

<surface symbol> ::= <surface character>
                   | <surface set name>
                   | <where variable name>
                   | 0                      ; null symbol
```

A.2 Lexical entries

```
<lexical-entry> ::=
     (  <citation-field>
        <phonological-field>
        <syntax-field>
        <semantics-field>
        <user-field>  )

<citation-field> ::= <lexical-alphabet symbol> *1
                   | "<lexical-alphabet symbol> *1"
```

Any normal typable characters may be used as a `<lexical-alphabet symbol>`, but if any of the following characters are used, the entire citation form must be surrounded by double quotes:

```
space, tab, newline, comma, ), (, #, ;, :,
}, {, >, <, ], [, !
```

Double quotes may be used within citations by using a double double quote within quotes. For example, `"hello""world"` will give the form `hello"world` in the lexicon. Notice that this set of characters requiring quotation is the same as those requiring quotation in spelling rules. Lower-case and upper-case are distinguished inside citation forms.

```
<syntax-field> ::= <category>

<semantics-field> ::= <s-expression>

<user-field> ::=  <s-expression>

<phonological-field> ::=  <s-expression>
```

A.3 Lexical rules

A.3.1 All types of lexical rule

```
<name> := <symbol>

< pre-condition > ::=
           < literal > and < pre-condition >
       |   < literal >

< literal > ::= ~ < lexical entry pattern >
              | < lexical entry pattern >

< lexical entry pattern > ::=
         ( < citation-field pattern >
           < phonological pattern >
           < syntactic pattern >
           < semantic pattern >
           < user-field pattern > )

< citation-field pattern > ::=
                     _            ; underscore
              | < citation-field >

< phonological pattern > ::=
                     _            ; underscore
```

```
            | < phonological-field>

< semantic pattern > ::=
                  _              ; underscore
            | < s-expression >

< user-field pattern > ::=
                  _              ; underscore
            | < s-expression >

< syntactic pattern > ::=
                  _              ; underscore
            | ( < feature patterns > < rest > )

< rest > ::=  < variable >
            |                    ; empty

< feature patterns > ::=
              < feature pattern >
              <  feature patterns >
            |                    ; empty

< feature pattern > ::=
        ~ ( < feature name >
            < feature value pattern > )
        | ( < feature name >
            < feature value pattern > )

< feature value pattern > ::=
              _              ; underscore
          |  < feature value >
          |  < variable >
```

A.3.2 Completion Rules

```
<completion rule> ::=
    <name> : <pre-condition> => <entry skeleton>

< entry skeleton > ::=
```

```
        ( < citation form >
          < phonological form>
          < syntactic form >
          < semantic form >
          < user field form > )

    < citation form > ::=  &
                |   < symbol >

    < phonological form > ::=  &
                |   < symbol >

    < semantic form > ::=  &
                |   < s-expression >

    < user field form > ::=  &
                |   < s-expression >

    < syntactic form > ::=  &
                | ( < feature forms > )

    < feature forms > ::=
                  < feature form > < feature forms >
                |                               ;; empty

    < feature form > ::= ( < feature name >
                           < feature value form > )
                |   < variable >

    < feature value form > ::=
                |  < variable>
                |  < atomic value >
                |  < syntactic form >
```

A.3.3 Multiplication Rules

```
<multiplication rule> ::=
   <name> : <pre-condition> =>> ( <entry skeleton> * )
```

The syntax of an entry skeleton is as defined earlier (Section A.3.2).

A.3.4 Consistency Checks

```
<consistency check> ::=
   <name> : <pre-condition> demands <post-condition>
```

The <post-condition> has the same syntax as the <pre-condition>.

A.4 Complete lexicon

```
<lexicon> ::= Declarations <decls> *
              Rules  <rule types>
              Entries <entry> *

<decls> ::=
      Alias <alias name> = <category>
    | Feature <feature name> <feature range>
    | Variable <variable name> = <variable range>
    | NonInflect = { <category list> }
    | CatDef <cat name> has <feature list>  ;; TU only

<variable range> ::=
      { <feature value list> } ;; atomic-valued
    | category | CAT           ;; category-valued

<category list> ::=
      <category> , <category list>
    | <category>

<feature range> ::=
      { <feature value list> }
    | category | CAT

<feature list> ::=
      { <feature name list> }

<feature name list> ::=
      <feature name> , <feature name list>
```

```
    | <feature name>

<feature value list> ::=
      <feature value> , <feature value list>
    | <feature value>

<feature name>, <feature value>, <alias name>,
      <variable name>, <cat name>  ::= <symbol>

<category> ::=
      <GPSG category form>
    | <simple category form>

<GPSG category form> ::=
    | <alias name>
    | <alias name> <feature bundle>
    | <feature bundle>

<feature bundle> ::=
      [ <GPSG feature pair list> ]

<GPSG feature pair list> ::=
      <GPSG feature pair> , <GPSG feature pair list>
    | <GPSG feature pair>

<GPSG feature pair> ::=
    | <feature name> <category>
    | <alias name>

<simple category form> ::=
      ( <feature pair> * )

<feature pair> ::=
      <alias name>
    | ( <feature name> <category> )
    | ( <feature name> <feature value> )

<rule types> ::=
```

```
        Completion Rules <completion rule> *
        Multiplication Rules <multiplication rule> *
        Consistency Checks <consistency check> *
      | Multiplication Rules <multiplication rule> *
        Completion Rules <completion rule> *
        Consistency Checks <consistency check> *
```

A.5 Word grammar

```
<word grammar> ::=
     Declarations <declaration> *
     Grammar <word-structure-rule> *1

<declaration> ::=
     Alias  <alias name>  =  <category>
   | Variable  <variable name>  =
                                 <grammar variable range>
   | Feature  <feature name> <feature range>
   | FeatureClass  <feature class name>  =
                                 <feature list>
   | Defaults  <default list>
   | LCategory  <lcategory definition>     ;; UU only
   | Top    =  <category>                  ;; UU only
   | CatDof <cat name> has <feature list>  ;; TU only
   | Top    =  <category type list>        ;; TU only

<grammar variable range> ::=
     { <alias list> }          ;; rule-category var
   | { <feature value list> }  ;; atomic-valued var
   | category  |  CAT          ;; category-valued var

<alias list> ::=
     <alias name>  ,  <alias list>
   | <alias name>

<feature class name> ::=
     WHead
   | WSister
   | MorphologyOnly
```

```
<category type list> ::=
     { <category type name list> }

<category type name list> ::=
     <cat name>  ,  <category type name list>
   | <cat name>

<cat name> ::=
     <symbol>

<default list> ::=
     <feature name> <feature value>  ,  <default list>
   | <feature name> <feature value>

<lcategory definition> ::=
     <category>  =>  <feature list>
   | <category-valued feature> <category>
            =>  <feature list>

<feature name> ::=  <symbol>

<feature value> ::=  <symbol>

<alias name> ::=  <symbol>

<variable name> ::=  <symbol>

<word-structure-rule> ::=
     ( <name> <node-spec>  ->  <node-spec list> )

<node-spec list> ::=
     <node-spec>  ,  <node-spec list>
   | <node-spec>

<node-spec> ::=  <rule category>

<rule category> ::=
    <GPSG rule category form>
  | <simple rule category form>
```

```
<GPSG rule category form> ::=
    <variable name>
  | <variable name> <rule feature bundle>
  | <alias name>
  | <alias name> <rule feature bundle>
  | <rule feature bundle>

<rule feature bundle> ::=
    [ <GPSG rule feature pair list> ]

<GPSG rule feature pair list> ::=
    <GPSG rule feature pair>  ,
    <GPSG feature pair list>
  | <GPSG rule feature pair>

<GPSG rule feature pair> ::=
    <feature name> <variable name>
  | <feature name> <category>
  | <alias name>

<simple rule category form> ::=
    ( <rule feature pair> * )

<rule feature pair> ::=
    <alias name>
  | <variable name>
  | ( <feature name> <variable name>  )
  | ( <feature name> <category>  )
  | ( <feature name> <feature value>  )
```

B Syntactic and Morphological Features

The features in lexical entries and in our word structure rules fulfil two purposes — to define valid morpheme combinations (and their syntactic markings), and to supply appropriate syntactic information for the sentence grammar.

B.1 Morphological features

These features are primarily motivated by morphological phenomena.

AT {-, +} Whether a stem takes any of the suffix class **+ation**, **+ative**, **+atory** or **+ion**, **+ive**, **+ory** — **invent** is [AT -], **present** is [AT +].

LAT {-, +} Whether an item is "latinate". Certain affixes (e.g. **+ize**, **ation**, etc.) attach to only latinate stems, such as **normal** or **combine**.

INFL {-, +} Whether an item is inflectable — **went** and **walked** are [INFL -], **walk** [INFL +].

REG {-, +} Whether a verb has regular past forms — **stand** (**stood**) is [REG -], **walk** (**walked**) [REG +].

FIX {PRE, SUF} Whether an affix is a prefix or a suffix — **pre-** is [FIX PRE], **+ize** [FIX SUF].

COMPOUND {N, NA, ANY, NOT} The category of a compound — **dog** is [COMPOUND NOT], **dog-house** [COMPOUND N]. See Section 8.6.

STEM category The type of stem to which an affix may attach — this feature is intimately connected with the Word-Sister Convention, discussed in Section 4.3.3.

B.2 Syntactic features

These features are primarily motivated by the needs of the sentence grammar.

AGR category Its value encodes the categories with which it agrees — **goes** has the AGR specification [AGR [N +, V -, BAR 2, PER 3, PLU -]], i.e. "agrees with a third person singular noun phrase".

BAR {-1, 0, 1, 2} Distinguishes the various phrasal "levels" important to the syntax/lexicon system. Affixes are [BAR -1], words [BAR 0], certain intermediate categories [BAR 1], and sentences and other phrasal constituents [BAR 2].

V {-, +} Distinguishes and cross-classifies (with N) the four major categories — verbal suffixes, verbs, verb phrases, sentences, adjectives, and adjectival suffixes and phrases are [V +]; nominal suffixes, nouns, nominal and noun phrases, prepositions and prepositional phrases are [V -].

N {-, +} Distinguishes and cross-classifies (with V) the four major categories — nominal suffixes, nouns, nominal and noun phrases, adjectives, and adjectival suffixes and phrases are [N +]; verbal suffixes, verbs, verb phrases, sentences, prepositions and prepositional phrases are [N -].

PRD {-, +} Whether an item is predicative. The distribution of adjectives within the sentence grammar is controlled by this feature — alike, ill, etc. are [PRD +], while chief, utter, etc. are [PRD -]. Others have a variable value. PRD also distinguishes passive ([PRD +]) from past participle ([PRD -]) verb forms.

QUA {-, +} Whether an item is "quantificatory" — determiners such as a, the, every, and few are marked as [QUA +], as are adjectives such as certain, possessives such as their, and numerals such as five and fifth.

ADV {-, +} Whether an item is adverbial. The suffix +ly is marked as [ADV +], and words such as cleverly, derived by attachment of +ly to an adjective, bear the same marking. Non-derived but similarly formed adverbs (e.g. gently), and many other adverbial elements (e.g. hitherto, meanwhile, well) are also [ADV +].

SUBJ {-, +} Distinguishes verb phrases, marked as [SUBJ -], from sentences, marked as [SUBJ +], both of which are instances of [V +,N -,BAR 2]. See [Bors83] for motivation for this analysis.

AUX {-, +} Whether a verb (phrase) is auxiliary — be, have and the modals (can, could, may, must, etc.) are [AUX +], other verbs [AUX -]

FIN {-, +} Distinguishes finite from non-finite verbal categories — for example going and gone are [FIN -], goes and went [FIN +].

PAST {-, +} Tense of a finite verb — goes is [PAST -], went [PAST +].

INV {-, +} In the syntax, INV distinguishes "inverted" sentences from others. Inverted sentences are those in which the subject follows the verb; in English such a verb must be a finite auxiliary, and the sentence is typically an interrogative. The feature is relevant to the lexicon because the negative auxiliary aren't must be specified as [INV +] when it agrees with a first person singular subject (i.e. to permit "Aren't I lucky" but not "I aren't lucky").

NEG {-, +} Whether an auxiliary verb is negative — must is [NEG -], while mustn't is [NEG +]. N't is not treated as an affix in this description.

PLU {-, +} The number of a noun or pronoun — they and men are [PLU +], he and man [PLU -]. You and sheep are not lexically specified for PLU, and receive a variable value from an LCategory statement which allows them to behave as if they were both [PLU +] and [PLU -].

DEF {-, +} Definiteness of determiners — the, both, etc. are [DEF +], and a, some, etc. [DEF -].

COUNT {-, +} Whether a noun is "countable" — for example hunger, coherence, and mathematics are [COUNT -], while ant and way are [COUNT +].

PART {-, +} Whether a determiner can appear in partitive constructions — all, both, and which are [PART +], and every and no [PART -].

PN {-, +} Whether a nominal entry is for a proper name — Cambridge, Italy, etc. are [PN +], other nouns [PN -].

POSS {-, +} Whether an item is a possessive determiner — her, my, whose, etc. are [POSS +], as is the possessive clitic 's.

TITLE {-, +} Whether an entry is for a form of address — count, sir, miss, etc. are assigned the value +.

PER {1, 2, 3} Person — nouns are [PER 3]; personal pronouns are [PER 1] (I, me, we, us), [PER 2] (you) or [PER 3] (he, her, they, etc.). Reflexive pronouns are given values for the feature REFL (q.v.) which contain appropriate PER specifications.

`CASE {NOM, ACC}` Case — only distinctive in pronoun entries, where `me`, `him`, `us`, etc. are `[CASE ACC]` and `I`, `he`, `we`, etc. `[CASE NOM]`. Ordinary noun entries contain no `CASE` specification; a variable value for this feature is inserted by an `LCategory` statement.

`AFORM {ER, EST, NONE}` Specifies the inflectional form of an adjective — `better` and `bigger` are `[AFORM ER]`, `best` and `biggest [AFORM EST]`, and `good` and `big [AFORM NONE]`.

`NFORM {IT, THERE, NORM}` The type of a noun phrase. The dummy subjects `it` and `there` (e.g. `it's raining again` and `there were three pigs`) are specified as `[NFORM IT]` and as `[NFORM THERE]` respectively. Other noun phrases and the nouns which are their heads are `[NFORM NORM]`. The value of `AGR` (q.v.) in a verb's entry determines which type of subject it requires.

`PFORM {AT,BY,FOR,OF,TO}` Encodes the form of a preposition for the purpose of prepositional phrase subcategorisation. `To` is marked as `[PFORM TO]`, and this specification is passed by the sentence grammar mechanisms to the phrasal category of which it is the head, where it is available as a means of restricting the distribution of such phrases — `give`, for example, requiring an indirect object PP headed by `to`.

`SLASH category` This feature encodes information on unbounded dependencies. In the sentence grammar, a category with a specification `[SLASH` *X*`]` is the root of a tree from which a category of the type *X* is missing. No lexical categories are directly specified for `SLASH`, as none may contain an unbounded dependency gap. Nor is the gap itself treated as a lexical item by the sentence grammar; "traces" are inserted by the parser rather than the lexicon.

`REFL category` `REFL` is the feature encoding information on agreement for reflexive constructions — `themselves` has `[REFL [BAR 2,N +, V -,PLU +,PER 3]]`, and is placed by the sentence grammar in positions where it is controlled by a third person plural NP. `Herself`, `ourselves`, etc. have `REFL` specifications which differ in the expected ways.

`WH {-, +}` This feature distinguishes the "wh-pronouns" `what`, `which`, etc. (`[WH +]` from others.

UB {R, Q} Distinguishes those pronouns that may appear in relative clause constructions from those that may appear in constituent questions — **that** is [UB R], **what**, **why** and **how** are [UB Q], and **where**, **which**, **who**, etc., which may appear in either type of construction, are given variable values by an LCategory statement.

EVER {-, +} Used to distinguish relative pronouns from free relatives — **which**, **where**, and **who** are [EVER -], **whichever**, **wherever**, and **whoever** [EVER +].

NUM {ORD, CARD} Distinguishes the ordinal numerals (**first**, **second**, etc.) from cardinals (**one**, **two**, etc.).

VFORM {BSE, EN, ING, TO, NOT} The inflectional form of a verb — the uninflected "base" form (**go**) is [VFORM BSE], the past/passive participle (**gone**) [VFORM EN], present participle/gerund (**going**) [VFORM ING], and the infinitive (**to go**) [VFORM TO]. The treatment of verbal inflection and auxiliary constructions adopted in the sentence grammar is derived from [Warn85].

SUBCAT {NULL, NP, VPINF, ...} The subcategorisation class of a lexical item (i.e. the type of complement it takes) is encoded in its SUBCAT specification. Intransitive verbs, nouns, and adjectives are specified as [SUBCAT NULL], transitive verbs as [SUBCAT NP], and so on. The value is an atom, rather than a list of atoms or categories as in some frameworks. The particular atoms used as the value of SUBCAT are chosen for purely mnemonic reasons, as the correct association of lexical item and syntactic environment is achieved by referring to their SUBCAT specifications in the syntactic rules which introduce them. Minor categories (complementisers, conjunctions, etc.) also have SUBCAT specifications, e.g. [SUBCAT THAT], [SUBCAT AND], and are thus in effect treated as single-member subcategories. It is the presence of a SUBCAT specification which distinguishes lexical items from other constituents.

PRT {AS, IN, OFF, ON, UP} This feature is used to mark particles that are involved in phrasal verb constructions (e.g. **treat as** and **turn off**).

PRO {-, +} Whether a nominal entry is for a pronoun — **dog** is [PRO -], **they** [PRO +]. Certain prepositional items (**abroad**, **forever**, **outside**, etc.) are also treated as "pro-PPs"; the intention is to express their ability to appear alone as a complete prepositional phrase for the purpose of the sentence grammar, much as pronouns are able to function syntactically as complete noun phrases.

C Some Sample Lexical Entries

This appendix contains a representative set of lexical entries for use with the description in Appendix D. The necessary declarations for these entries are given in Section D.2 and the lexical rules used to expand these entries are given in Section D.4. These entries have been chosen primarily in order to illustrate a variety of lexical and affixational behaviour. See Section C.2 later for a sample of entries resulting from the application of lexical rules, and Appendix E for a sample of results of lexical look-up.

C.1 Basic Entries

C.1.1 Suffixes

The possessive is treated as a word rather than suffix — the sentence-level grammar is responsible for the correct attachments:

```
("'s" "" ((N +)(POSS +)(V -)) S NIL)
```

As in `readable`, etc.

```
("+able" "" ((AFORM NONE)(FIX SUF)(N +)(V +)(SUBCAT NULL)
             (STEM ((INFL +)(N -)(V +)))) ABLE NIL)
```

`national`, etc.

```
("+al" "" ((AFORM NONE)(FIX SUF)(LAT +)(N +)
           (STEM (N (LAT +)(INFL +)))(V +)) AL NIL)
```

`inflationary`, etc.

```
("+ary" "" ((FIX SUF)(N +)(STEM ((INFL +)(N +)(V -)))(V +))
            ARY NIL)
```

`presentation`, etc.

```
("+ation" "" ((FIX SUF)(LAT +)(N +)(SUBCAT NULL)(V -)
              (STEM ((INFL +)(AT +) V)))
             ATION NIL)
```

Three regular past tense suffixes are needed for three different subject-types (see entries for `+s`) — only one is shown here

```
("+ed" "" ((AGR NPNORM)(FIN +)(FIX SUF)(N -)(PAST +)
           (STEM ((AGR NPNORM)(INFL +)(REG +) V))(V +))
          ED NIL)
```

A single suffix for regular past participles

```
("+ed" "" ((FIX SUF)(N -)
           (STEM ((INFL +)(REG +) V))(V +)(VFORM EN))
          ED NIL)
```

`blacken`, etc. — phonological constraints on attachment are not accounted for

```
("+en" "" ((AGR ((BAR 2)(N +)(NFORM NORM)(V -)))
           (INFL +)(N -)(SUBCAT NP)(V +)(FIX SUF)
           (STEM (A (INFL +))))
          EN NIL)
```

For comparative adjectives,

```
("+er" "" ((AFORM ER)(FIX SUF)(N +)(QUA -)
           (STEM (A (INFL +)))(V +)) ER NIL)
```

Superlative adjectives,

```
("+est" "" ((AFORM EST)(FIX SUF)(N +)(QUA -)
            (STEM (A (INFL +)))(V +)) EST NIL)
```

Nouns as in `spoonful`, etc,

```
("+ful" "" ((FIX SUF)(LAT -)(N +)(V -)
            (STEM ((INFL +) N)))
           FUL NIL)
```

Present participles and gerunds

```
("+ing" "" ((FIX SUF)(N -)(V +) (VFORM ING)
            (STEM ((INFL +) V)))
           ING NIL)
```

`(AT -)` counterpart of `+ation`

```
("+ion" "" ((FIX SUF)(N +)((V -)
            (STEM ((AT -)(INFL +) V))) ION NIL)
```

`nationalism`, etc.

```
("+ism" "" ((FIX SUF)(N +)(V -)
            (STEM ((LAT +)(N +)))) ISM NIL)
```

`ability`, etc.

```
("+ity" "" ((FIX SUF)(LAT +)(N +)(V -)
            (STEM ((AFORM NONE)(LAT +)))) ITY NIL)
```

`nationalize`, etc.

```
("+ize" "" ((AGR ((BAR 2)(N +)(NFORM NORM)(V -)))
            (AUX -)(FIX SUF)(N -)(SUBCAT NP)(V +)
            (STEM ((ADV -)(AFORM NONE)(LAT +))))
           IZE NIL)
```

`faultless`, etc.

```
("+less" "" ((AFORM NONE)(FIX SUF)(LAT -)(N +)(V +)
             (STEM ((INFL +) N))) LESS NIL)
```

For adverbs derived from adjectives — `cleverly`, etc.

```
("+ly" "" ((ADV +)(FIX SUF)(INFL -)(N +)(V +)
           (STEM ((ADV -)(AFORM NONE)))) LY NIL)
```

`announcement`, etc.

```
("+ment" "" ((FIX SUF)(LAT -)(N +)(V -)
             (STEM ((INFL +) V))) MENT NIL)
```

`coarseness`, etc.

```
("+ness" "" ((FIX SUF)(LAT -)(N +)(V -)
             (STEM ((AFORM NONE)))) NESS NIL)
```

For verbs like `waterproof`, etc. that are derived from nouns

```
("+proof" "" ((FIX SUF)(LAT -)(N -)(V +)(SUBCAT NP)
              (STEM ((INFL +) N))) PROOF NIL)
```

There are three third person singular present tense suffixes, one for each subject-type (see Section 6.12)

```
("+s" "" ((AGR IT)(FIN +)(FIX SUF)(N -)(PAST -)
          (STEM ((AGR IT)(INFL +) V))(V +)) S NIL)
("+s" "" ((AGR S)(FIN +)(FIX SUF)(N -)(PAST -)
          (STEM ((AGR S)(INFL +) V))(V +)) S NIL)
("+s" "" ((AGR SING3)(FIN +)(FIX SUF)(N -)(PAST -)
          (STEM ((AGR NPNORM)(INFL +) V))(V +)) S NIL)
```

For regular plural nouns

```
("+s" "" ((FIX SUF)(N +)(PLU +)(POSS -)(V -)
          (STEM ((COUNT +)(INFL +) N)) S NIL)
```

C.1.2 Stems/words and prefixes

Comments are given for some entries, others are simply stated. `Alike` is predicative only

```
("alike" "" ((AFORM NONE)(LAT -)(N +)(PRD +)(V +))
            ALIKE NIL)
```

The aliases `SING1` etc. are defined in the feature declarations in Section D.2

```
("am" "" ((AGR SING1)(AUX +)(FIN +)(N -)
          (PAST -)(SUBCAT PRED)(V +))
         BE NIL)
```

The plural form of `analyses` is specifically listed. The singular form is specifically marked `(PLU -)` which causes `(INFL -)` to be added and hence stops inflections.

```
("analyses" "" ((N +)(PLU +)(V -)) ANALYSIS NIL)
("analysis" "" ((N +)(PLU -)(V -)) ANALYSIS NIL)
```

Conjunctions are minor categories

```
("and" "" ((SUBCAT AND)) AND NIL)
("announce" "" ((N -)(SUBCAT STHAT)(V +)) ANNOUNCE NIL)
("anti-" "" ((FIX PRE)(STEM ((INFL +)(N +)))) ANTI- NIL)
("appear" "" ((V +)(N -)(SUBCAT SR2)) APPEAR NIL)
("appropriate" "" ((AFORM NONE)(N +)(V +)) APPROPRIATE NIL)
("arch-" "" ((FIX PRE)(STEM ((INFL +) N))) ARCH- NIL)
```

```
("are" "" ((AGR PLUR)(AUX +)(FIN +)(N -)(PAST -)
           (SUBCAT PRED)(V +))
          BE NIL)
("aren't" "" ((AGR PLUR)(AUX +)(FIN +)(N -)(NEG +)(PAST -)
           (SUBCAT PRED)(V +))
          BE NIL)
```

As **bad** has no regular comparative or superlative, it is marked `(AFORM NONE)`

```
("bad" "" ((AFORM NONE)(N +)(V +)) BAD NIL)
("be" "" ((AUX +)(N -)(SUBCAT PRED)(V +)(VFORM BSE))
         BE NIL)
("been" "" ((AUX +)(N -)(SUBCAT PRED)(V +)(VFORM EN))
         BE NIL)
("being" "" ((AUX +)(N -)(SUBCAT PRED)(V +)(VFORM ING))
         BE NIL)
```

bend has irregular past forms, which have to be explicitly listed

```
("bend" "" ((LAT -)(N -)(REG -)(SUBCAT NP)(V +)) BEND NIL)
("bent" "" ((FIN -)(N -)(PAST +)(SUBCAT NP)(V +)) BEND NIL)
("bent" "" ((N -)(SUBCAT NP)(V +)(VFORM EN)) BEND NIL)
("big" "" ((LAT -)(N +)(V +)) BIG NIL)
("black" "" ((LAT -)(N +)(V +)) BLACK NIL)
("child" "" ((LAT -)(N +)(PLU -)(V -)) CHILD NIL)
("children" "" ((LAT -)(N +)(PLU +)(V -)) CHILD NIL)
("coarse" "" ((N +)(V +)) COARSE NIL)
("danger" "" ((LAT +)(N +)(V -)) DANGER NIL)
("dog" "" ((N +)(V -)) DOG NIL)
("eligible" "" ((AFORM NONE)(N +)(SUBCAT PPFOR)(V +))
               ELIGIBLE NIL)
("he" "" ((CASE NOM)(N +)(PER 3)(PLU -)(PRO +)(V -))
         HE NIL)
("him" "" ((CASE ACC)(N +)(PER 3)(PLU -)(PRO +)(V -))
         HE NIL)
("himself" "" ((N +)(V -)
              (REFL ((BAR 2)(N +)(PER 3)(PLU -)(V -))))
          HIMSELF NIL)
("house" "" ((N +)(V -)) HOUSE NIL)
```

```
("is" "" ((AGR SING3)(AUX +)(FIN +)(N -)(PAST -)
          (SUBCAT PRED)(V +))
         BE NIL)
```

The dummy subject `it`

```
("it" "" ((N +)(NFORM IT)(PRO +)(V -)) IT NIL)
("lock" "" ((N -)(V +)) LOCK NIL)
```

`Molasses` is a singular mass noun that looks like a plural

```
("molasses" "" ((COUNT -)(INFL -)(N +)(V -)) MOLASSES NIL)
("nation" "" ((N +)(V -)) NATION NIL)
("navigate" "" ((AT -)(N -)(V +)) NAVIGATE NIL)
("on" "" ((PRT ON)) ON NIL)
("present" "" ((N -)(V +)(SUBCAT NP_PPWITH)) PRESENT NIL)
```

`Rain` can take the dummy subject `it`

```
("rain" "" ((AGR IT)(N -)(V +)) RAIN NIL)
("read" "" ((N -)(REG -)(V +)) READ NIL)
("read" "" ((FIN +)(N -)(PAST +)(V +)) READ NIL)
("read" "" ((N -)(V +)(VFORM EN)) READ NIL)
("reptile" "" ((N +)(V -)) REPTILE NIL)
("since" "" ((N -)(V -)) SINCE NIL)
("something" "" ((N +)(PRO +)(V -)) SOMETHING NIL)
("super-" "" ((FIX PRE)(STEM ((INFL +)(N +)))) SUPER- NIL)
("to" "" ((AUX +)(FIN -)(N -)(SUBCAT INF)(V +)
          (VFORM TO)) TO NIL)
("to" "" ((N -)(PFORM TO)(V -)) TO NIL)
```

For `unreadable`, etc.

```
("un-" "" ((FIX PRE)(STEM ((V +)))) UN- NIL)
("underneath" "" ((N -)(PRO +)(V -)) UNDERNEATH NIL)
```

`Utter` as adjective is prenominal only

```
("utter" "" ((AFORM NONE)(N +)(PRD -)(V +)) UTTER NIL)
("was" "" ((AGR SING1)(AUX +)(FIN +)(N -)(PAST +)
           (SUBCAT PRED)(V +))
          BE NIL)
```

```
("wasn't" "" ((AGR SING3)(AUX +)(FIN +)(N -)(NEG +)
              (PAST +)(SUBCAT PRED)(V +))
          BE NIL)
("well" "" ((ADV +)(AFORM NONE)(N +)(V +)) WELL NIL)
("were" "" ((AGR PLUR)(AUX +)(FIN +)(N -)(PAST +)
            (SUBCAT PRED)(V +))
          BE NIL)
("weren't" "" ((AGR PLUR)(AUX +)(FIN +)(N -)(NEG +)
               (PAST +)(SUBCAT PRED)(V +))
          BE NIL)
```

The entry what for questions, the entry for use in relatives is different.

```
("what" "" ((N +)(PRO +)(UB Q)(V -)(WH +)) WHAT NIL)
```

Explicit listing of suppletive comparative and superlative forms of bad

```
("worse" "" ((AFORM ER)(N +)(V +)) BAD NIL)
("worst" "" ((AFORM EST)(N +)(V +)) BAD NIL)
```

C.2 Sample output from lexical rules

This section contains expanded entries illustrating the effect of the lexical rules in Section D.4 on the entries shown in Section C.1 above.

```
(+able "" ((V +)(N +)(NUM -)(ADV -)(QUA -)(INFL -)
           (AFORM NONE)(AT +)(LAT +)(FIX SUF)
           (BAR -1)(SUBCAT NULL)
           (STEM ((V +)(N -)(INFL +))))
      ABLE NIL)
(+est "" ((V +)(N +)(NUM -)(ADV -)(INFL -)(AFORM EST)
          (AT +)(LAT +)(FIX SUF)(BAR -1)(QUA -)
          (STEM ((INFL +)(N +)(V +)(BAR 0))))
      EST NIL)
(+ing "" ((V +)(N -)(AUX -)(INV -)(NEG -)(INFL -)
          (VFORM ING)(AT +)(LAT +)(FIX SUF)(BAR -1)(FIN -)
          (STEM ((N -)(V +)(BAR 0)(INFL +))))
      ING NIL)
(+proof "" ((V +)(N -)(INFL +)(REG +)(PRD -)(AUX -)(INV -)
            (NEG -)(FIX SUF)(BAR -1)(FIN -)(VFORM BSE)
```

```
          (SUBCAT NP)
          (STEM ((N +)(V -)(BAR 0)(INFL +)))(LAT -))
     PROOF NIL)
(and "" ((FIX NOT)(SUBCAT AND)) AND NIL)
(appear "" ((FIX NOT)(V +)(N -)(INFL +)(REG +)(BAR 0)
          (AGR ((BAR 2)(V -)(N +)(NFORM NORM)))
          (PRD -)(COMPOUND NOT)(AUX -)(INV -)(NEG -)
          (AT +)(LAT +)(FIN -)(VFORM BSE)(SUBCAT SR2))
     APPEAR NIL)
(appear "" ((V +)(N -)(VFORM BSE)(FIN -)(INFL +)(AUX -)
          (SUBCAT SR2)(FIX NOT)(REG +)(BAR 0)(PRD -)
          (AGR ((V -)(N +)(BAR 2)(CASE NOM)(NFORM IT)))
          (COMPOUND NOT)(INV -)(NEG -)(AT +)(LAT +))
     APPEAR NIL)
(appear "" ((V +)(N -)(VFORM BSE)(FIN -)(INFL +)(AUX -)
          (SUBCAT SR2)(FIX NOT)(REG +)(BAR 0)(AUX -)
          (AGR ((V +)(N -)(BAR 2)(SUBJ +)))(PRD -)
          (COMPOUND NOT)(INV -)(NEG -)(AT +)(LAT +))
     APPEAR NIL)
(appear "" ((V +)(N -)(VFORM NOT)(FIN +)(INFL -)(PAST -)
          (AGR ((N +)(V -)(BAR 2)(NFORM NORM)
               (CASE NOM)(PER 2)(PLU -)))
          (SUBCAT SR2)(FIX NOT)(REG +)(BAR 0)(PRD -)
          (COMPOUND NOT)(AUX -)(INV -)(NEG -)(AT +)
          (LAT +))
     APPEAR NIL)
(appear "" ((V +)(N -)(VFORM NOT)(FIN +)(INFL -)(PAST -)
          (AGR ((N +)(V -)(BAR 2)(NFORM NORM)
               (CASE NOM)(PER 1)(PLU -)))
          (SUBCAT SR2)(FIX NOT)(REG +)(BAR 0)(PRD -)
          (COMPOUND NOT)(AUX -)(INV -)(NEG -)(AT +)
          (LAT +))
     APPEAR NIL)
(appear "" ((V +)(N -)(VFORM NOT)(FIN +)(INFL -)(PAST -)
          (AGR ((N +)(V -)(BAR 2)(CASE NOM)
               (NFORM NORM)(PLU +)))
          (SUBCAT SR2)(FIX NOT)(REG +)(BAR 0)(PRD -)
          (COMPOUND NOT)(AUX -)(INV -)(NEG -)(AT +)
```

```
          (LAT +))
      APPEAR NIL)
(are "" ((V +)(N -)(VFORM NOT)(FIX NOT)(PRD -)
         (COMPOUND NOT)(AUX +)(NEG -)(BAR 0)(INFL -)
         (FIN +)(AT +)(LAT +)(SUBCAT PRED)(PAST -)
         (AGR ((PLU +)(CASE NOM)(NFORM NORM)
               (N +)(V -)(BAR 2))))
      BE NIL)
(arch- "" ((INFL +)(BAR -1)(FIX PRE)
           (STEM ((N +)(V -)(BAR 0)(INFL +))))
      ARCH- NIL)
(bad "" ((FIX NOT)(V +)(N +)(NUM -)(ADV -)(COMPOUND NOT)
         (BAR 0)(SUBCAT NULL)(QUA -)(INFL -)(AFORM NONE)
         (AT +)(LAT +))
      BAD NIL)
(be "" ((FIX NOT)(V +)(N -)(PRD -)(COMPOUND NOT)(AUX +)
        (NEG -)(BAR 0)(INFL -)(VFORM BSE)(AT +)(LAT +)
        (FIN -)(SUBCAT PRED))
      BE NIL)
(big "" ((FIX NOT)(V +)(N +)(AFORM NONE)(NUM -)(ADV -)
         (COMPOUND NOT)(BAR 0)(SUBCAT NULL)(QUA -)
         (INFL +)(LAT -))
      BIG NIL)
(black "" ((FIX NOT)(V +)(N +)(AFORM NONE)(NUM -)(ADV -)
           (COMPOUND NOT)(BAR 0)(SUBCAT NULL)(QUA -)
           (INFL +)(LAT -))
      BLACK NIL)
(child "" ((FIX NOT)(N +)(V -)(POSS -)(PRO -)(PN -)(PER 3)
           (PART -)(COMPOUND NOT)(BAR 0)(SUBCAT NULL)
           (NFORM NORM)(COUNT +)(INFL -)(PLU -)(LAT -))
      CHILD NIL)
(children "" ((FIX NOT)(N +)(V -)(POSS -)(PRO -)(PN -)
              (PER 3)(PART -)(COMPOUND NOT)(BAR 0)
              (SUBCAT NULL)(NFORM NORM)(COUNT +)(INFL -)
              (PLU +)(LAT -))
      CHILD NIL)
(he "" ((FIX NOT)(N +)(V -)(POSS -)(PN -)(PART -)(BAR 0)
        (SUBCAT NULL)(NFORM NORM)(COUNT +)(INFL -)(PLU -)
```

```
        (AT +)(LAT +)(PRO +)(PER 3)(CASE NOM))
      HE NIL)
(house "" ((FIX NOT)(N +)(V -)(POSS -)(PRO -)(PN -)(PER 3)
           (PART -)(COMPOUND NOT)(BAR 0)(SUBCAT NULL)
           (INFL +)(PLU -)(NFORM NORM)(COUNT +)(AT +)
           (LAT +))
      HOUSE NIL)
(lock "" ((FIX NOT)(V +)(N -)(INFL +)(REG +)(BAR 0)
          (AGR ((BAR 2)(V -)(N +)(NFORM NORM)))
          (PRD -)(COMPOUND NOT)(SUBCAT NULL)(AUX -)(INV -)
          (NEG -)(AT +)(LAT +)(FIN -)(VFORM BSE))
      LOCK NIL)
(lock "" ((VFORM NOT)(FIN +)(INFL -)(PAST -)
          (AGR ((N +)(V -)(BAR 2)(NFORM NORM)
                (CASE NOM)(PER 2)(PLU -)))
          (FIX NOT)(V +)(N -)(REG +)(BAR 0)(PRD -)
          (COMPOUND NOT)(SUBCAT NULL)(AUX -)(INV -)(NEG -)
          (AT +)(LAT +))
      LOCK NIL)
(lock "" ((VFORM NOT)(FIN +)(INFL -)(PAST -)
          (AGR ((N +)(V -)(BAR 2)(NFORM NORM)
                (CASE NOM)(PER 1)(PLU -)))
          (FIX NOT)(V +)(N -)(REG +)(BAR 0)(PRD -)
          (COMPOUND NOT)(SUBCAT NULL)(AUX -)(INV -)(NEG -)
          (AT +)(LAT +))
      LOCK NIL)
(lock "" ((VFORM NOT)(FIN +)(INFL -)(PAST -)
          (AGR ((N +)(V -)(BAR 2)(CASE NOM)
                (NFORM NORM)(PLU +)))
          (FIX NOT)(V +)(N -)(REG +)(BAR 0)(PRD -)
          (COMPOUND NOT)(SUBCAT NULL)(AUX -)(INV -)(NEG -)
          (AT +)(LAT +))
      LOCK NIL)
(molasses "" ((FIX NOT)(N +)(V -)(POSS -)(PRO -)(PN -)
              (PER 3)(PART -)(COMPOUND NOT)(BAR 0)
              (SUBCAT NULL)(NFORM NORM)(AT +)
              (LAT +)(INFL -)(COUNT -))
      MOLASSES NIL)
```

```
(on "" ((FIX NOT)(PRT ON)(V -)(N -)) ON NIL)
(rain "" ((FIX NOT)(V +)(N -)(INFL +)(REG +)
          (AGR ((N +)(V -)(BAR 2)(NFORM IT)(PLU -)(PER 3)))
          (PRD -)(COMPOUND NOT)(BAR 0)(SUBCAT NULL)(AUX -)
          (INV -)(NEG -)(AT +)(LAT +)(FIN -)(VFORM BSE))
      RAIN NIL)
(un- "" ((INFL +)(BAR -1)(FIX PRE)(STEM ((V +)))) UN- NIL)
```

D A Description of English Morphology

This appendix presents the linguistic description of a non-trivial subset of English morphology, in the implemented notation. As our implementation is a general tool for building morphological analysers, this description is only one of many possible ones. It was developed as part of the Alvey Natural Language Tools projects and hence has been written to be compatible with the corresponding grammar, a GPSG-based description [Bris87] (but see remarks in Section 6.14).

D.1 Spelling Rules

This section contains the basic spelling rules described in Chapter 2, in the format defined in Appendix A.

```
SurfaceAlphabet
    { a b c d e f g h i j k l m n o p q r s t u v w x y z
      - " " "’" }
SurfaceSets
    C is { b c d f g h j k l m n p r s t v w z }
    V is { a e i o u y }
    V2 is { e i o u y }          ;  for gemination
    NLR is { n l r }
    S is { s x z }
    C2 is { b d f k l m n p r s t v w z }
    NB is { l n r t u }
    NN is { b c f l o r s t v z }
    =  is { a b c d e f g h i j k l m n o p q r s t u v
            w x y z - " " "’" 0 }

LexicalAlphabet
    { a b c d e f g h i j k l m n o p q r s t u v w x y z
      - + " " "’" }
LexicalSets
    C is { b c d f g h j k l m n p r s t v w z }
    V is { a e i o u y }
    NLR is { n l r }
    S is { s x z }
    C2 is { b d f k l m n p r s t v w z }
```

```
    NC is { a b d e f g h j k l m n o p s t u v x z }
    NI is { a d e f h l m n o p s w y }
    = is { a b c d e f g h i j k l m n o p q r s t u v
           w x y z - + " " "'" }

DefaultPairs
    +:0   ;; boundary symbol matches null by default
    -:0   ;; hyphens are optional - i.e. match null
    0:" " ;; multiple spaces are contracted to one space
    " ":- ;; hyphens may be used instead of spaces

Rules
```

Add e at + boundary following sibilants or a surface i matching a lexical y — horses, churches, dishes, boxes, tries, etc.

```
Epenthesis
   +:e  <=>  { < s:s h:h > S:S y:i } --- s:s
        or   < c:c h:h > --- s:s
        or   < =:C { =:o =:u } > --- s:s
```

Double the final consonant of a word when the suffix begins with a vowel — bigger, tapped, etc.

```
Gemination-1
   +:X  => < { < q:q u:u > C:C } V:V =:X > --- { =:V2 =:a }
       where X in { b d f g m p s t z }
```

As for Gemination-1, but if the suffix starts with a the next character can not be n — travelled, etc.

```
Gemination-2
   +:Y  =>  < C:C V:V =:Y > --- =:V2
        or   < C:C V:V =:Y > --- < =:a =:NN >
         where Y in { n l r }
```

Lexical y corresponds to surface i — tried, presidential, sunnier, heaviness, multiplication, etc.

```
Y-to-I
   y:i  <=> { C:C c:t } --- < +:= a:a =:NB >
        or  { +:= C:C < q:q u:u > } --- < +:= NI:= >
        or  =:= --- < +:c a:a { t:t l:l } >  ;; c-insertion
```

Lexical e corresponds to no surface character in a variety of contexts.

```
Elision
   e:0  <=>  C2:C2 --- < +:0 V:= >             ; larg00er
        or   < C:C =:u >                       ; continu00ing
                             --- < +:0 { a:a i:i } >
        or   { < C:C V:V > g:g c:c }           ; rac00ed
                             --- < +:0 { e:e i:i } >
        or   l:0 --- +:0                       ; possib000ly
        or   c:c --- < +:0 a:0 t:t >           ; reduc000tion
        or   i:y --- +:0                       ; ty00ing
        or   =:= --- +:i                       ; reptil0ian
```

Lexical i corresponds to surface y when followed by a deleted e and a suffix starting with i — tying, etc.

```
I-to-Y
   i:y  <=>  =:= --- < e:0 +:0 i:i >
```

The lexical boundary symbol corresponds to surface c — application, meteorological, etc.

```
C-insertion
   +:c  <=>  < NC:= y:i >  --- < a:a { t:t l:l } >
```

A final c is not doubled in gemination contexts, but followed by k — trafficker, panicky, picnicking, etc.

```
K-insertion
   +:k  <=>  < V:V c:c > --- { e:e y:y }
        or   < V:V c:c > --- < i:i { n:n o:o f:f} >
```

Lexical a corresponds to no surface character when starting a suffix such as +ation — reduction, intervention, etc.

```
A-deletion
   a:0  <=>  < u:u c:c e:= +:0 > --- t:t
        or   < e:e n:n e:0 +:0 > --- t:t
```

Lexical e corresponds to surface i before +ous and suffixes starting with a except +able — gracious, preferential, etc.

```
E-to-I
   e:i  <=>  c:= --- < +:0 { =:a =:o } =:NB >
```

The lexical boundary symbol corresponds to surface `i` before the suffixes `+al` and `+an` — **`managerial`**, **`electrician`**, etc.

```
I-insertion
   +:i  <=>  < { +:0 C:C } V:V NLR:NLR >
                                   --- < a:a { n:n l:l } >
        or   < { +:0 C:C } V:V c:c > --- < a:a n:n >
        or   < { +:0 C:C } V:V l:l e:0 >
                                   --- < a:a { n:n l:l } >
```

Lexical `c` corresponds to surface `t` — **`preferential`** **`presidential`**, etc.

```
C-to-T
   c:t  <=>  n:n --- < =:i +:0 a:a =:NB >
```

Lexical `y` corresponds to no surface character when followed by a suffix starting with `i`, unless the suffix is `+ing` — **`harmonic`**, **`strategic`**, **`theorist`**, etc.

```
Y-deletion
   y:0  <=>  { <q:= u:= > C:= } --- < +:0 i:i =:NN >
```

Lexical `l` corresponds to no surface character when that would lead to double or triple `l`s — **`possibly`**, **`fully`**, etc.

```
L-deletion
   l:0  <=>  { < V:V b:b > p:p } --- < e:= +:0 l:l >
        or   < l:l l:l +:0 > --- =:=
```

Surface `i` corresponds to lexical `l` before surface `l` corresponding to lexical `e` — **`possibility`**, **`stabilize`**, etc.

```
L-to-I
   l:i  <=>  < V:V b:b > --- < e:= +:0 i:i { t:t z:z } >
```

Surface `l` corresponds to lexical `e` — see `L-to-I`

```
E-to-L
   e:l  <=>  l:i --- +:0
```

D.2 Feature Declarations

These basic feature, variable, and alias declarations are shared between the word grammar and the lexical entries. The features are described in greater detail in Appendix B.

The first group of features to be declared are relevant only to the operation of the word grammar. They are mostly members of the feature set `MorphologyOnly`, and are thus removed from the category returned on look-up.

```
Feature    AT         {-, +} ; item takes +ion or +ation?
Feature    LAT        {-, +} ; item is "latinate"?
Feature    INFL       {-, +} ; item is "inflectable"?
Feature    REG        {-, +} ; verb has regular past?
Feature    FIX        {PRE, SUF, NOT}    ; affix type
Feature    COMPOUND   {N, NA, ANY, NOT} ; compound class
Feature    STEM       CAT    ; If declared, STEM *must*
                             ; be category-valued
```

The remaining features are present in lexical entries in order to supply the sentence grammar with the categorial information it requires.

```
Feature AGR      CAT              ; category-valued
Feature BAR      {-1, 0, 1, 2}    ; "size" of item
Feature V        {-, +}           ; V & A are +, N & P are -
Feature N        {-, +}           ; N & A are +, V & P are -
Feature NULL     {-, +}           ; gaps are +
Feature PRD      {-, +}           ; predicative phrases +
Feature QUA      {-, +}           ; determiners
Feature ADV      {-, +}           ; adverbials and others
Feature SUBJ     {-, +}           ; VP is - and S is +
Feature AUX      {-, +}           ; auxiliary verb
Feature FIN      {-, +}           ; finite and non-finite
Feature PAST     {-, +}           ; Verb tense
Feature INV      {-, +}           ; V as head of inverted S
Feature NEG      {-, +}           ; negative verb
Feature PLU      {-, +}           ; plural or singular noun
Feature DEF      {-, +}           ; definite NPs
Feature COUNT    {-, +}           ; countable nouns
```

```
Feature PART      {-, +}            ; Ns in partitive phrases
Feature LOC       {-, +}            ; locative Ps and PPs
Feature POSS      {-, +}            ; possessive NPs
Feature PN        {-, +}            ; proper names
Feature PRO       {-, +}            ; pronoun/pro-P, or not
Feature TITLE     {-, +}            ; title a kind of N
Feature PER       {1, 2, 3}         ; 1st, 2nd, 3rd person Ns
Feature CASE      {NOM, ACC}        ; case of nouns
Feature AFORM     {ER, EST, NONE}   ; adjective morphology
Feature NFORM     {IT, THERE,       ; type of subject NP
                   NORM}            ;
Feature PFORM     {WITH, OF, TO,    ; Ps that are
                   AT, ABOUT, ON,   ; subcategorised for
                   IN, FOR, BY,     ; by other items
                   AGAINST, FROM,   ; ("case-marking")
                   NORM}            ;
Feature SLASH     CAT               ; unbounded dependencies
Feature REFL      CAT               ; reflexive dependencies
Feature WH        {+, -}            ; WH pros & other
Feature UB        {R, Q}            ; UDC type: Rel or Ques
Feature EVER      {+, -}            ; "which"/"whichever"
Feature NUM       {ORD, CARD, -}    ; types of number
Feature PRT       {AS,IN,OFF,       ; particles for
                   ON,UP}           ; phrasal verbs
Feature VFORM     {BSE, EN, ING, TO, NOT} ; verb morphology

Feature SUBCAT    {A1, AND, AP, BARE_S, BASE_VP, BOTH, BUT,
                   DETA, DETN, DO_COMPL, EITHER, ELSE, N1,
                   FOR, IF, INF, ING, IT_SUBJ, LOC, FIN_S,
                   NEITHER, NOPASS, NOR, NOT, NP, NP_AP,
                   NP_AS_PRED, NP_BASE_VP, NP_IN, NP_NP,
                   NP_OFF, NP_ON, NP_PPBY, NP_PPFOR,
                   NP_PPFROM, NP_PPIN, NP_PPINTO, NP_PPLOC,
                   NP_PPOF, NP_PPON, NP_PPTO, NP_PPWITH,
                   NP_PRED, NP_Q_S, NP_S, NP_UP, NULL,
                   OBJ_GAP, OE, ONE, OR, OR2, ORCONJ,
                   OTHERWISE, PLUR, PP, PPABOUT, PPAGAINST,
                   PPAT, PPBY, PPFOR, PPFROM, PPIN, PPOF,
```

```
                    PPOF_PPWITH, PPON, PPOVER, PPS_WITHABOUT,
                    PPTO, PPTO_THAT_S, PPWITH, PP_SBSE, PRED,
                    PSP, Q, Q_S, REFL, SBSE, SE1, SE2, SE3,
                    SFIN, SINF, SR1, SR2, STHAT, S_SUBJ,
                    THAN, THAT, TWONP, WHETHER}
```

In this portion of the description we only have one variable, ?sub. It has the same range as the feature SUBCAT.

```
Variable ?sub  = {A1, AND, AP, BARE_S, BASE_VP, BOTH, BUT,
                  DETA, DETN, DO_COMPL, EITHER, ELSE, N1,
                  FOR, IF, INF, ING, IT_SUBJ, LOC, FIN_S,
                  NEITHER, NOPASS, NOR, NOT, NP, NP_AP,
                  NP_AS_PRED, NP_BASE_VP, NP_IN, NP_NP,
                  NP_OFF, NP_ON, NP_PPBY, NP_PPFOR,
                  NP_PPFROM, NP_PPIN, NP_PPINTO, NP_PPLOC,
                  NP_PPOF, NP_PPON, NP_PPTO, NP_PPWITH,
                  NP_PRED, NP_Q_S, NP_S, NP_UP, NULL,
                  OBJ_GAP, OE, ONE, OR, OR2, ORCONJ,
                  OTHERWISE, PLUR, PP, PPABOUT, PPAGAINST,
                  PPAT, PPBY, PPFOR, PPFROM, PPIN, PPOF,
                  PPOF_PPWITH, PPON, PPOVER, PPS_WITHABOUT,
                  PPTO, PPTO_THAT_S, PPWITH, PP_SBSE, PRED,
                  PSP, Q, Q_S, REFL, SBSE, SE1, SE2, SE3,
                  SFIN, SINF, SR1, SR2, STHAT, S_SUBJ,
                  THAN, THAT, TWONP, WHETHER}
```

For ease of writing we defined a number of aliases.

```
Alias  N     =  ((BAR 0)(V -)(N +))
Alias  V     =  ((BAR 0)(V +)(N -))
Alias  P     =  ((BAR 0)(V -)(N -))
Alias  A     =  ((BAR 0)(V +)(N +))
Alias  NP    =  ((BAR 2)(V -)(N +))
Alias  PP    =  ((BAR 2)(V -)(N -))
Alias  S     =  ((BAR 2)(V +) (N -)(SUBJ +))
Alias  SING3  =  ((BAR 2)(V -)(N +)(NFORM NORM)
                             (CASE NOM)(PER 3)(PLU -))
Alias  SING2  =  ((BAR 2)(V -)(N +)(NFORM NORM)
                             (CASE NOM)(PER 2)(PLU -))
```

```
Alias  SING1  =  ((BAR 2)(V -)(N +)(NFORM NORM)
                                   (CASE NOM)(PER 1)(PLU -))
Alias  SING   =  ((BAR 2)(V -)(N +)(PLU -)(COUNT +))
Alias  PLUR   =  ((BAR 2)(V -)(N +)(NFORM NORM)
                  (CASE NOM)(PLU +))
Alias  N1SING =  ((BAR 1)(V -)(N +)(PLU -))
Alias  N1PLUR =  ((BAR 1)(V -)(N +)(PLU +))
Alias  IT     =  ((BAR 2)(V -)(N +)(NFORM IT))
Alias  NPNORM =  ((BAR 2)(V -)(N +)(NFORM NORM))
```

The `NonInflect` class has the effect of marking entries in the compiled lexicon which are to appear only at the end of (i.e. or as the whole of) a word. This will happen to any entry whose syntax field is an extension of a member of the `NonInflect` category set. In many cases, items whose entries are thus marked will be unable to appear within complex words for the independent reason that the word grammar does not allow them to. This class is partly motivated by efficiency, partly theoretical.

```
NonInflect = { ((V -)(N -)),         ; prepositions
               ((VFORM TO)),         ; 'to'
               ((PAST +)),           ; finite V past
               ((PAST -)),           ; finite V present
               ((AUX +)),            ; auxiliaries
               ((AFORM ER)),         ; comparative Adjs
               ((AFORM EST)),        ; superlative Adjs
               ((PLU +)),            ; plural nouns
               ((PLU -)(INFL -)),    ; irregular singulars
               ((PRO +)),            ; pronouns
               ((PN +)),             ; proper names
               ((ADV +))             ; adverbs
             }
```

D.3 Word Grammar

This is the basic word grammar in the formalism as described in Chapter 3. The feature and alias declarations are shared with the lexicon. There is an "include" mechanism which allows the declaration in the previous section to be included in the word grammar definition.

In addition we wish to declare some more variables.

```
Variable  ?agr  =  category
Variable  ?n    =  {N, NOT}
Variable  ?na   =  {NA, NOT}
Variable  ?any  =  {ANY, NOT}
```

The following feature classes declare which features are affected by the feature conventions (see Section 4.3).

```
FeatureClass WHead   =
           {N, V, INFL, PAST, AFORM, VFORM, ADV, PLU,
            AT, NUM, REG, LAT, PRD, FIN, COUNT, QUA,
            PART, PRO, PN, PER, NFORM, POSS}
FeatureClass WDaughter  =  {SUBCAT, AGR, INV, NEG, AUX}
```

The next class of features are deleted from the resulting word category before returning it to the sentence-level parser. Features in this class are those which are specific to the morphological analysis and not of interest to a sentence grammar.

```
FeatureClass MorphologyOnly  =
                     {AT, LAT, INFL, REG, COMPOUND, FIX}
```

In this description we have three feature defaults. All categories in a word syntax tree will be given these defaults if no other value is assigned.

```
Defaults          BAR 0, COMPOUND NOT, FIX NOT
```

The following `LCategory` statements are used to add default values to the top category of an analysis before passing it to the sentence-level parser.

```
LCategory  ((QUA +) (SUBCAT DETN))  =>  {DEF, POSS}
LCategory  ((N +) (V -) (PRO +))  =>  {DEF}
LCategory  ((N +) (V -))  =>
     {PLU, POSS, CASE, PRD, PN, PRO,
      COUNT, PART, NFORM, PER}
LCategory  ((N -) (V -))  =>  {LOC, PFORM, PRD}
LCategory  ((N +) (V +))  =>
     {AFORM, QUA, ADV, NUM, PART, NEG, DEF}
LCategory  ((V +))  =>  {PRD, AGR}
LCategory  ((V +) (N -))  =>
```

```
     {FIN, AUX, VFORM, NEG, INV, PAST}
LCategory  AGR ((N +)(V -)) =>
     {PLU, PER, COUNT, NFORM, CASE}
LCategory  SLASH ((N +)(V -)(BAR 2)) =>
     {PLU, PER, COUNT, NFORM, CASE}
LCategory  SLASH ((N -)(V -)(BAR 2)) => {PFORM, LOC}
LCategory  ((PRO +)(WH +)) => {UB}
LCategory  ((VFORM ING)) => {PRD}
```

This defines the type of the distinguished category for the grammar, i.e. any category that is not an affix.

```
Top  =  [FIX NOT]
```

That is the end of the declaration section of the word grammar. Now we can defined the actual word grammar rules. The feature passing conventions allow very general rules to be written for affixation. The first rules deals with attachment of prefixes to stems.

```
     ( PREFIXES
        [] ->
             [FIX PRE, BAR -1],
             [BAR 0] )
```

Also we have only one rule to deal with suffixing.

```
     ( SUFFIXES
        [] ->
             [BAR 0],
             [FIX SUF, BAR -1] )
```

Compounds are assigned a uniformly left-branching structure, with the rightmost element being the head. Three rules for the analysis of compounds are given here; they are progressively less restrictive in the categories they permit to appear as elements of a compound, and progressively more likely to give rise to apparently spurious parses. The reason for these is that many "possible" compounds coincide in form with non-compound words. A second consequence of including a relatively general compounding rule is that the parser will consider many more lexical items as potential segments of the word being analysed, and this leads to a deterioration in performance.

No more than one of these rules should be used at a time, as duplicate parses will otherwise arise. That is, only one of the following three compound rules should be included in the actual description.

A compound noun may consist of either two simple nouns or a simple noun preceded by a compound noun. This rule permits both possibilities, as the variable `?n` ranges over `N` and `NOT`. Its effects are duplicated by the more general rules that follow.

```
( COMPOUNDS-N
   [COMPOUND N] ->
            [BAR 0, N +, V -, INFL +, COMPOUND ?n],
            [BAR 0, N +, V -, INFL +, COMPOUND NOT] )
```

This second rule allows sequences of N-N, A-N, A-A, N-A, with, as before, the first element either a compound or a simple word.

```
( COMPOUNDS-NA
   [COMPOUND NA] ->
            [BAR 0, N +, INFL +, COMPOUND ?na],
            [BAR 0, N +, INFL +, COMPOUND NOT] )
```

This third rule allows any sequence of words to be parsed as a word. It is the most general compounding rules and produces many analyses.

```
( COMPOUNDS-ANY
    [COMPOUND ANY] ->
            [BAR 0, INFL +, COMPOUND ?any],
            [BAR 0, INFL +, COMPOUND NOT] )
```

The last two rules handle "zero-derivations". Note that all feature specifications desired to be present on the mother category must be stipulated in the rule, as the feature passing conventions and defaults do not apply to single daughtered trees. The first rule creates adjectives from passive verbs.

```
( PAS-TO-ADJ
    [N +, V +, AFORM NONE, QUA -, ADV -, INFL -,
     AGR ?agr, SUBCAT ?sub] ->
            [N -, V +, VFORM EN, PRD +, AUX -,
             AGR ?agr, SUBCAT ?sub, BAR 0] )
```

The final rule creates adjectives from present participles.

```
( ING-TO-ADJ
    [N +, V +, AFORM NONE, INFL -, QUA -, ADV -,
     AGR ?agr, SUBCAT ?sub] ->
                [N -, V +, VFORM ING, PRD -, AUX -,
                 AGR ?agr, SUBCAT ?sub, BAR 0] )
```

D.4 Lexical Rules

The system allows the user to present the Completion Rules either before or after the Multiplication Rules, and the rules are then applied in that order. Here we have decided to specify the Completion Rules first. Completion Rules are used to expand the basic form of the lexical entries, and the order in which they are specified is significant.

D.4.1 Completion Rules

The first completion rule adds `(VFORM BSE)`, `(INFL +)` and `(FIN -)` to verb entries — uninflected stem and bare infinitive forms are generally identical.

```
Completion Rules

Add_BSE:
   (_ _ ((V +) (N -) ~(INFL _) ~(FIN _) ~(VFORM _)
         _rest) _ _) =>
     (& & ((V +) (N -) (INFL +) (FIN -) (VFORM BSE)
           _rest) & &)
```

The next adds `(PRD -)` as default to verb entries with `(VFORM EN)` — creates entries for past participles.

```
Add_PRD_MINUS:
   (_ _ ((VFORM EN) ~(PRD _) ~(FIN _) _rest) _ _) =>
     (& & ((VFORM EN) (PRD -) (FIN -) _rest) & &)
```

Add `(FIN -)` as default to entries with `VFORM` specifications — these are non-finite.

```
Add_FIN:
   (_ _ ((VFORM _vf) ~(FIN _) _rest) _ _) =>
     (& & ((VFORM _vf) (FIN -) _rest) & &)
```

Add (BAR -1) as default to entries with FIX specifications — affixes are lower level units than complete words.

```
Add_BAR_MINUS_ONE:
   (_ _ ((FIX _fix) ~(BAR _) _rest) _ _) =>
      (& & ((FIX _fix) (BAR -1) _rest) & &)
```

Add (LAT +) to entries with V specifications — major categories are "latinate" by default.

```
Add_LAT_PLUS:
   (_ _ ((V _v) ~(LAT _) _rest) _ _) =>
      (& & ((V _v) (LAT +) _rest) & &)
```

Add (AT +) to entries with (LAT +) specifications — "latinate" stems can take the suffixes +ation, +ative, +ion, +ive. The latter pair require the specification (AT -) in their stem, and therefore may not attach to those having the default (AT +).

```
Add_AT_PLUS:
   (_ _ ((LAT +) ~(AT _) _rest) _ _) =>
      (& & ((AT +) (LAT +) _rest) & &)
```

Add (INFL -) as default to entries with AFORM specifications; this prevents inflection of irregular adjectives and those already inflected:

```
Add_INFL_MINUS_AFORM:
   (_ _ ((AFORM _af) ~(INFL _) _rest) _ _) =>
      (& & ((INFL -) (AFORM _af) _rest) & &)
```

Add (INFL -) as default to entries with VFORM specifications — past participles, gerunds, etc. cannot be inflected.

```
Add_INFL_MINUS_VFORM:
   (_ _ ((VFORM _vf) ~(INFL _) _rest) _ _) =>
      (& & ((INFL -) (VFORM _vf) _rest) & &)
```

Add (INFL -) as default to entries with FIN specifications — finite verbs cannot be further inflected.

```
Add_INFL_MINUS_FIN:
   (_ _ ((FIN _fin) ~(INFL _) _rest) _ _) =>
      (& & ((INFL -) (FIN _fin) _rest) & &)
```

Add (INFL -) as default to entries which have PLU specifications — either they are plural already or have irregular plurals.

```
Add_INFL_MINUS_PLU:
   (_ _ ((PLU _plu) ~(INFL _) _rest) _ _) =>
      (& & ((INFL -) (PLU _plu) _rest) & &)
```

Add (INFL -) as default to entries marked with (PRO +) — pronominals lack regular plural forms.

```
Add_INFL_MINUS_PRO:
   (_ _ ((PRO +) ~(INFL _) _rest) _ _) =>
      (& & ((PRO +) (INFL -) _rest) & &)
```

Add (INFL -) as default to (QUA +) adjective entries.

```
Add_INFL_MINUS_DETN:
   (_ _ ((V +) (N +) (QUA +) ~(INFL _) _rest) _ _) =>
      (& & ((V +) (N +) (QUA +) (INFL -) _rest) & &)
```

Add (BAR 0) as default to entries with V and N specifications

```
Add_BAR_ZERO:
   (_ _ ((N _n) (V _v) ~(BAR _) _rest) _ _) =>
      (& & ((BAR 0) (N _n) (V _v) _rest) & &)
```

Add (COUNT +) as default to noun entries — typical nouns are countable.

```
Add_COUNT:
   (_ _ ((N +) (V -) ~(PN +) ~(COUNT _) _rest) _ _) =>
      (& & ((N +) (V -) (COUNT +) _rest) & &)
```

Add (NFORM NORM) as default to noun entries — only the dummy subjects it and there have different specifications for NFORM.

```
Add_NFORM:
   (_ _ ((N +) (V -) ~(NFORM _) _rest) _ _) =>
      (& & ((N +) (V -) (NFORM NORM) _rest) & &)
```

Add (PLU -) as default to noun entries — most nouns are entered in their singular form, as the plural may be obtained by regular suffixation.

```
Add_PLU_MINUS:
   (_ _ ((V -) (N +) ~(INFL -) ~(PLU _) _rest) _ _) =>
      (& & ((N +) (V -) (PLU -) _rest) & &)
```

Add (INFL +) as default to entries with (BAR -1) specifications — typical affixes permit further suffixation. Inflectional suffixes are a special case, and have already had their entries augmented with (INFL -) by this stage.

```
Add_INFL_PLUS_BAR_MINUS_ONE:
   (_ _ ((BAR -1) ~(INFL _) _rest) _ _) =>
      (& & ((INFL +) (BAR -1) _rest) & &)
```

Add (INFL +) as default to entries with (BAR 0) specifications — typical words are inflectable, and exceptions are specified as (INFL -) either by hand or by a previous completion rule.

```
Add_INFL_PLUS_BAR_ZERO:
   (_ _ ((BAR 0) ~(INFL _) _rest) _ _) =>
      (& & ((INFL +) (BAR 0) _rest) & &)
```

Add (QUA -) as default to adjective entries — most adjectives cannot be used as determiners.

```
Add_QUA:
   (_ _ ((V +) (N +) ~(QUA _) _rest) _ _) =>
      (& & ((V +) (N +) (QUA -) _rest) & &)
```

Add (DEF -) as default to entries with (SUBCAT DETN) specifications — most of these determiners are indefinites.

```
Add_DEF_DETN:
   (_ _ ((N +) (V +) (SUBCAT DETN) ~(DEF _) _rest) _ _) =>
      (& & ((N +) (V +) (DEF -) (SUNCAT DETN) _rest) & &)
```

Add default AGR specification to entries with (SUBCAT DETN) — most determiners appear with NPs.

```
Add_AGR_DETN:
   (_ _ ((SUBCAT DETN) ~(AGR _) _rest) _ _) =>
      (& & ((SUBCAT DETN) (AGR ((N +) (V -) (BAR 2)))
            _rest) & &)
```

Add (AUX -) as default to verb entries — most verbs are not auxiliaries, and those which are, have been explicitly marked as such. Only auxiliary verbs can bear the specifications (INV +) or (NEG +), so this rule also adds suitable negative specifications.

```
Add_AUX_INV_NEG:
   (_ _ ((V + ) (N -) ~(AUX _) ~(INV _) ~(NEG _)
         _rest) _ _)
      =>
      (& & ((V + ) (N -) (AUX -) (INV -) (NEG -)
            _rest) & &)
```

Add (NEG -) to auxiliaries.

```
Add_AUX_NEG_MINUS:
   (_ _ ((V +) (N -) (AUX +) ~(NEG _) _rest) _ _) =>
      (& & ((V +) (N -) (AUX +) (NEG -) _rest) & &)
```

Add (PART +) as default to adjective entries with (SUBCAT DETN) specifications — determiner adjectives typically appear in partitive "*Det* of the *N*s" constructions.

```
Add_PART_DETN:
   (_ _ ((V +) (N +) (SUNCAT DETN) ~(PART _) _rest) _ _) =>
      (& & ((V +) (N +) (SUBCAT DETN) (PART +) _rest) & &)
```

Add (SUBCAT NP) as default to non-(PRO +) preposition entries — typically, prepositions take a NP complement.

```
Add_SUBCAT_NP_PREP:
   (_ _ ((V -) (N -) ~(PRO +) ~(SUBCAT _) _rest) _ _) =>
       (& & ((V -) (N -) (SUBCAT NP) _rest) & &)
```

Add (SUBCAT NULL) as default to (BAR 0) entries — words are intransitive unless they have been specified otherwise.

```
Add_SUBCAT_NULL_BAR_ZERO:
   (_ _ ((BAR 0) ~(SUBCAT _) _rest) _ _) =>
      (& & ((BAR 0) (SUBCAT NULL) _rest) & &)
```

Add (EVER -) as default to entries with (WH +) specifications — (EVER +) appears only in entries for free relative pronouns whatever, etc.

```
Add_EVER:
   (_ _ ((WH +) ~(EVER _) _rest) _ _) =>
      (& & ((WH +) (EVER -) _rest) & &)
```

Add (COMPOUND NOT) to major category entries — the word grammar uses this specification to enforce a single structure for compounds of arbitrary length.

```
Add_COMPOUND_NOT:
   (_ _ ((N _n) (V _v) ~(FIX _) ~(PN +) ~(PRO +)
         _rest) _ _)
      =>
      (& & ((N _n) (V _v) (COMPOUND NOT) _rest) & &)
```

Add (PRD -) as default to verb entries — verbs in general are not predicative.

```
Add_PRD:
   (_ _ ((V +) (N -) ~(VFORM ING) ~(PRD _) _rest) _ _) =>
      (& & ((V +) (N -) (PRD -) _rest) & &)
```

Add more to the value of AGR — the dummy subject it behaves like a third person singular pronoun.

```
Add_More_to_AGR:
   (_ _ ((V +) (N -) (AGR ((N +) (V -) (BAR 2)
         (NFORM IT) ~(PLU _) ~(PER _))) _rest) _ _)
      =>
      (& & ((V +) (N -) (AGR ((N +) (V -) (BAR 2)
            (NFORM IT) (PLU -) (PER 3))) _rest) & &)
```

Add (AGR NPNORM) as default to verb entries — most verbs do not appear with dummy or sentential subjects, but auxiliary verbs must be allowed to have any type of subject.

```
Add_AGR_NPNORM:
   (_ _ ((BAR 0) (V +) (N -) ~(AGR _) ~(AUX +)
         _rest) _ _)
      =>
      (& & ((BAR 0) (V +) (N -) (AGR ((BAR 2) (V -) (N +)
            (NFORM NORM))) _rest) & &)
```

Add (CASE NOM) to AGR value of finite verbs.

```
Add_AGR_CASE_NOM:
   (_ _ ((V +) (N -) (FIN +)
```

```
        (AGR ((BAR 2) (V -) (N +) ~(CASE _case)
              _agrrest)) _rest) _ _) =>
     (& & ((V +) (N -) (FIN +)
           (AGR ((BAR 2)(V -)(N +)(CASE NOM)
                 _agrrest)) _rest) & &)
```

Add (DEF +) as default to determiner entries.

```
Add_DEF_non_WH:
   (_ _ ((SUBCAT DETN) ~(DEF _) _rest) _ _) =>
      (& & ((SUBCAT DETN) (DEF +) _rest) & &)
```

Add (POSS -) as default to determiner entries — determiners are not possessive in general.

```
Add_POSS_DETN:
   (_ _ ((SUBCAT DETN) ~(POSS _) _rest) _ _) =>
      (& & ((SUBCAT DETN) (POSS -) _rest) & &)
```

Add (PART -) as default to noun entries.

```
Add_PART_PRO:
   (_ _ ((N +) (V -) ~(PART _) _rest) _ _) =>
      (& & ((N +) (V -) (PART -) _rest) & &)
```

Add (PER 3) as default to noun entries — they must induce third person singular agreement on present tense verbs.

```
Add_PER_3:
   (_ _ ((N +) (V -) ~(PER _) _rest) _ _) =>
      (& & ((N +) (V -) (PER 3) _rest) & &)
```

Add (ADV -) as default to adjective entries — adverbs derived from adjectives (e.g. quickly) will have (ADV +).

```
Add_ADV_ADJ:
   (_ _ ((V +) (N +) ~(ADV _) _rest) _ _) =>
      (& & ((V +) (N +) (ADV -) _rest) & &)
```

Add (NUM -) as default to adjective entries — only numerals are explicitly specified as (NUM +).

```
Add_NUM_ADJ:
   (_ _ ((V +) (N +) ~(NUM _) _rest) _ _) =>
      (& & ((V +) (N +) (NUM -) _rest) & &)
```

Add (AFORM NONE) as default to adjective entries.

```
Add_AFORM_NONE:
   (_ _ ((V +) (N +) ~(AFORM _) _rest) _ _) =>
      (& & ((V +) (N +) (AFORM NONE) _rest) & &)
```

Add a suitable AGR entry to cardinals.

```
Add_AGR_CARD:
   (_ _ ((NUM CARD) ~(AGR _) _rest) _ _) =>
      (& & ((NUM CARD) (AGR ((V -) (N +) (BAR 1)
            (COUNT +) (PLU +))) _rest) & &)
```

Add a suitable AGR entry to ordinals.

```
Add_AGR_ORD:
   ~(first _ _ _ _) and
   (_ _ ((NUM ORD) ~(AGR _) _rest) _ _) =>
      (& & ((NUM ORD) (AGR ((V -) (N +) (BAR 1)
           (COUNT +) (PLU -))) _rest) & &)
```

Add (PN -) as default to noun entries — typical nouns are not proper names, and those which are have already been specified as such.

```
Add_PN_MINUS:
   (_ _ ((N +) (V -) ~(PN _) _rest) _ _) =>
      (& & ((N +) (V -) (PN -) _rest) & &)
```

Add (PRO -) as default to noun entries — typical nouns are not pronouns, and those which are have already been specified as such.

```
Add_PRO_MINUS:
   (_ _ ((N +) (V -) ~(PRO _) _rest) _ _) =>
      (& & ((N +) (V -) (PRO -) _rest) & &)
```

Add (POSS -) as default to noun entries — bare nouns are not possessive, and pronouns that are have already been marked as such.

```
Add_POSS_MINUS:
   (_ _ ((N +) (V -) ~(POSS _) _rest) _ _) =>
      (& & ((N +) (V -) (POSS -) _rest) & &)
```

Add (REG +) as default to verb entries — i.e. verb entries that have regular past tense and past participle forms. Irregular verbs have already been marked as such in the lexicon.

```
Add_REG_MINUS:
   (_ _ ((V +) (N -) (INFL +) ~(REG _reg) _rest) _ _) =>
      (& & ((V +) (N -) (INFL +) (REG +) _rest) & &)
```

Add category features to entries for phrasal-verb particles. These are, in general, prepositions.

```
Add_P_PRT:
   (_ _ ((PRT _prt) _rest) _ _) =>
      (& & ((PRT _prt) (V -) (N -) _rest) & &)
```

Add (FIX NOT) to non-suffix entries.

```
Add_FIX_NOT:
   (_ _ ( ~(FIX _fix) _rest) _ _) =>
      (& & ((FIX NOT) _rest) & &)
```

Add (VFORM NOT) to verb entries that have no VFORM specification.

```
Add_VFORM_NOT:
   (_ _ ((V +) (N -) ~(VFORM _vform) _rest) _ _) =>
      (& & ((V +) (N -) (VFORM NOT) _rest) & &)
```

D.4.2 Multiplication Rules

Unlike Completion Rules which modify existing entries, Multiplication Rules construct new entries from existing ones.

The first rule adds an entry with (PRD +) for each transitive verb marked with (PRD -) and (VFORM EN)

```
Multiplication Rules

Multi_PASSIVES:
   (_ _ ((VFORM EN) (PRD -) _rest) _ _)
```

```
=>>
(
   (& & ((VFORM EN) (PRD +) _rest) & &)
)
```

Add "intransitive" entries for nouns taking complements — any noun can be "intransitive".

```
Multi_Intransitives:
   (_ _ ((N +) (V -) (SUBCAT _) _rest) _ _)
   and ~(_ _ ((SUBCAT NULL) _) _ _)
   and ~(_ _ ((SUBCAT ONE) _) _ _)
   =>>
   (
      (& & ((N +) (V -) (SUBCAT NULL) _rest) & &)
   )
```

Add entries allowing plural, first person, and second person agreement for all verbs. Two cases need to be taken into account — this first rule handles all non-auxiliary verbs which do not have sentential subjects alternating with `it` and subject extraposition.

```
Multi_Person_Agreement1:
   (_ _ ((VFORM BSE) (FIN -) (INFL +) ~(SUBCAT SR2)
         ~(AUX +) (AGR ((N +)(V -)(BAR 2)(NFORM NORM)))
         _rest) _ _)
   =>>
   (
      (& & ((VFORM NOT) (FIN +) (INFL -) (PAST -)
            (AGR ((N +)(V -)(BAR 2)(CASE NOM)
                  (NFORM NORM)(PLU +)))
            _rest) & &)
      (& & ((VFORM NOT) (FIN +) (INFL -) (PAST -)
            (AGR ((N +)(V -)(BAR 2)(NFORM NORM)(CASE NOM)
                  (PER 1)(PLU -)))
            _rest) & &)
      (& & ((VFORM NOT) (FIN +) (INFL -) (PAST -)
            (AGR ((N +)(V -)(BAR 2)(NFORM NORM)(CASE NOM)
                  (PER 2)(PLU -)))
            _rest) & &)   )
```

Verbs subcategorised as **SR2** (e.g. `seem`, `appear`) permit sentential subjects, both initial and extraposed in combination with the dummy `it`.

```
Multi_Person_Agreement2:
   (_ _ ((V +) (N -) (VFORM BSE) (FIN -) (INFL +)
         (SUBCAT SR2)
         (AGR ((N +)(V -)(BAR 2)(NFORM NORM)))
         _rest) _ _)
   =>>
   (
      (& & ((V +) (N -) (VFORM NOT) (FIN +) (INFL -)
            (PAST -) (SUBCAT SR2)
            (AGR ((N +)(V -)(BAR 2)(CASE NOM)(NFORM NORM)
                  (PLU +)))
            _rest) & &)
      (& & ((V +) (N -) (VFORM NOT) (FIN +) (INFL -)
            (PAST -) (SUBCAT SR2)
            (AGR ((N +)(V -)(BAR 2)(NFORM NORM)(CASE NOM)
                  (PER 1)(PLU -)))
            _rest) & &)
      (& & ((V +) (N -) (VFORM NOT) (FIN +) (INFL -)
            (PAST -) (SUBCAT SR2)
            (AGR ((N +)(V -)(BAR 2)(NFORM NORM)(CASE NOM)
                  (PER 2)(PLU -)))
            _rest) & &)
      (& & ((V +) (N -) (VFORM BSE) (FIN -) (INFL +)
            (SUBCAT SR2) (AGR ((V +)(N -)(BAR 2)(SUBJ +)))
           _rest) & &)
      ;; dummy it subject, base & present tense:
      (& & ((V +) (N -) (VFORM BSE) (FIN -) (INFL +)
            (SUBCAT SR2)
            (AGR ((V -)(N +)(BAR 2)(CASE NOM)(NFORM IT)))
            _rest) & &)
   )
```

D.4.3 Consistency Checks

The final set of lexical rules is the Consistency Checks. These allow entries to be fully checked to ensure they are correctly specified after all the other rules have applied. This is a useful feature which can be used to check that rules have produced the desired effects.

However, none are specified in this description.

E Sample Results of Lexical Look-up

This appendix contains examples illustrating the process of lexical look-up. The first, for the plural noun **houses**, is given in **CATEGORYFORM** format, in which the result is the root of the analysis tree with any feature specifications declared as being in the **MorphologyOnly** set removed. The remainder are given in the **WORDSTRUCTURE** format, the analysis tree annotated with the names of the rules which have applied. In both cases, feature specifications with variable values (indicated by @Dn) have been added by **LCategory** rules.

```
> w houses
Analysis : 1
((PRD @D65)(CASE @D64)(BAR 0)(SUBCAT NULL)(N +)(V -)
 (PRO -)(PN -)(PER 3)(PART -)(NFORM NORM)(COUNT +)
 (PLU +)(POSS -))

> f 2
Format is now WORDSTRUCTURE
> w houses
Analysis : 1
(((PRD @D8)(CASE @D7)(BAR 0)(COMPOUND NOT)(FIX NOT)
  (SUBCAT NULL)(N +)(V -)(PRO -)(PN -)(PER 3)(PART -)
  (NFORM NORM)(COUNT +)(INFL -)(PLU +)(AT +)(LAT +)
  (POSS -))
SUFFIXES
   (((LAT +)(AT +)(COUNT +)(NFORM NORM)(PLU -)(INFL +)
     (SUBCAT NULL)(COMPOUND NOT)(PART -)(PER 3)(PN -)
     (PRO -)(POSS -)(V -)(N +)(FIX NOT)(BAR 0))
   ENTRY
      (house "" ((FIX NOT)(N +)(V -)(POSS -)(PRO -)
               (PN -)(PER 3)(PART -)(COMPOUND NOT)
               (BAR 0)(SUBCAT NULL)(INFL +)(PLU -)
               (NFORM NORM)(COUNT +)(AT +)(LAT +))
              HOUSE NIL))
   (((POSS -)(STEM ((N +)(V -)(BAR 0)(INFL +)(COUNT +)))
     (LAT +)(AT +)(PLU +)(INFL -)(COUNT +)(NFORM NORM)
     (PART -)(PER 3)(PN -)(PRO -)(V -)(N +)(FIX SUF)
     (BAR -1))
   ENTRY
```

```
        (+s "" ((N +)(V -)(PRO -)(PN -)(PER 3)(PART -)
               (NFORM NORM)(COUNT +)(INFL -)(PLU +)(AT +)
               (LAT +)(FIX SUF)(BAR -1)
               (STEM ((N +)(V -)(BAR 0)(INFL +)(COUNT +)))
               (POSS -))
              S NIL)))
> w bigger
Analysis : 1
(((DEF @D17)(NEG @D16)(PART @D15)(AGR @D14)(PRD @D13)
  (BAR 0)(COMPOUND NOT)(FIX NOT)(SUBCAT NULL)(V +)
  (N +)(NUM -)(ADV -)(INFL -)(AFORM ER)(AT +)(LAT +)
  (QUA -))
SUFFIXES
   (((LAT -)(INFL +)(QUA -)(SUBCAT NULL)(COMPOUND NOT)
     (ADV -)(NUM -)(AFORM NONE)(N +)(V +)(FIX NOT)
     (BAR 0))
   ENTRY
      (big "" ((FIX NOT)(V +)(N +)(AFORM NONE)(NUM -)
                (ADV -)(COMPOUND NOT)(BAR 0)(SUBCAT NULL)
               (QUA -)(INFL +)(LAT -)) BIG NIL))
   (((QUA -)(STEM ((INFL +)(N +)(V +)(BAR 0)))(LAT +)
     (AT +)(AFORM ER)(INFL -)(ADV -)(NUM -)(N +)(V +)
     (FIX SUF)(BAR -1))
   ENTRY
      (+er "" ((V +)(N +)(NUM -)(ADV -)(INFL -)
                (AFORM ER)(AT +)(LAT +)(FIX SUF)(BAR -1)
                (STEM ((INFL +)(N +)(V +)(BAR 0)))
                (QUA -))
             ER NIL)))
```

The word `unlockable` receives two analyses within this description; in the first, the prefix `un-` attaches to the deverbal adjective `lockable`, while, in the second, the adjectival suffix `+able` attaches to the prefixed verb `unlock`. The structural ambiguity is intended to reflect the two readings of this word — "`not able to be locked`" vs. "`able to be unlocked`".

```
> w unlockable
2 analyses found
Analysis : 1
(((DEF @D52)(PART @D51)(PRD @D50)(AGR ((CASE @D49)
  (COUNT @D48)(PER @D47)(PLU @D46)(BAR 2)(V -)(N +)
  (NFORM NORM)))(BAR 0)(COMPOUND NOT)(FIX NOT)(AUX -)
  (INV -)(NEG -)(SUBCAT NULL)(V +)(N +)(NUM -)(ADV -)
  (QUA -)(INFL -)(AFORM NONE)(AT +)(LAT +))
PREFIXES
   (((STEM ((V +)))(INFL +)(FIX PRE)(BAR -1))
   ENTRY (un- "" ((INFL +)(BAR -1)(FIX PRE)
                (STEM ((V +)))) UN- NIL))
   (((LAT +)(AT +)(AFORM NONE)(INFL -)(QUA -)(ADV -)
     (NUM -)(N +)(V +)(SUBCAT NULL)(NEG -)(INV -)
     (AUX -)(FIX NOT)(COMPOUND NOT)
     (AGR ((BAR 2)(V -)(N +)(NFORM NORM)))(BAR 0))
   SUFFIXES
      (((REG -)(VFORM BSE)(FIN -)(INFL +)(LAT +)(AT +)
        (NEG -)(INV -)(AUX -)(SUBCAT NP)(COMPOUND NOT)
        (PRD -)(FIX NOT)
        (AGR ((BAR 2)(V -)(N +)(NFORM NORM)))
        (N -)(V +)(BAR 0))
      ENTRY
         (lock "" ((FIX NOT)(BAR 0)(V +)(N -)(AUX -)
                   (INV -)(NEG -)
                   (AGR ((BAR 2)(V -)(N +)(NFORM NORM)))
                   (PRD -)(COMPOUND NOT)(SUBCAT NP)
                   (AT +)(LAT +)(INFL +)(FIN -)
                   (VFORM BSE)(REG -)) LOCK NIL))
      (((STEM ((V +)(N -)(INFL +)))(SUBCAT NULL)(LAT +)
               (AT +)(AFORM NONE)(INFL -)(QUA -)(ADV -)
               (NUM -)(N +)(V +)(FIX SUF)(BAR -1))
      ENTRY
         (+ABLE "" ((V +)(N +)(NUM -)(ADV -)(QUA -)
                    (INFL -)(BAR -1)(AFORM NONE)(AT +)
                    (LAT +)(FIX SUF)(SUBCAT NULL)
                    (STEM ((V +)(N -)(INFL +))))
                   ABLE NIL)))
```

```
Analysis : 2
(((DEF @D45)(PART @D44)(PRD @D43)
  (AGR ((CASE @D42)(COUNT @D41)(PER @D40)(PLU @D39)
        (BAR 2)(V -)(N +)(NFORM NORM)))
  (BAR 0)(COMPOUND NOT)(FIX NOT)(AUX -)(INV -)(NEG -)
  (SUBCAT NULL)(V +)(N +)(NUM -)(ADV -)(QUA -)(INFL -)
  (AFORM NONE)(AT +)(LAT +))
SUFFIXES
   (((REG -)(VFORM BSE)(FIN -)(INFL +)(LAT +)(AT +)
     (PRD -)(N -)(V +)(NEG -)(INV -)(AUX -)(SUBCAT NULL)
     (FIX NOT)(COMPOUND NOT)
     (AGR ((BAR 2)(V -)(N +)(NFORM NORM)))(BAR 0))
   PREFIXES
      (((STEM ((V +)))(INFL +)(FIX PRE)(BAR -1))
      ENTRY
         (un- "" ((INFL +)(BAR -1)(FIX PRE)(STEM ((V +))))
                 UN- NIL))
      (((REG -)(VFORM BSE)(FIN -)(INFL +)(LAT +)(AT +)
        (NEG -)(INV -)(AUX -)(SUBCAT NULL)(COMPOUND NOT)
        (PRD -)(N -)(V +)(FIX NOT)
        (AGR ((BAR 2)(V -)(N +)(NFORM NORM)))(BAR 0))
      ENTRY
         (lock "" ((FIX NOT)(BAR 0)(V +)(N -)(AT +)(LAT +)
                   (INFL +)
                   (AGR ((BAR 2)(V -)(N +)(NFORM NORM)))
                   (PRD -)(COMPOUND NOT)(SUBCAT NULL)
                   (AUX -)(INV -)(NEG -)(FIN -)(VFORM BSE)
                   (REG -))
                 LOCK NIL)))
  (((STEM ((V +)(N -)(INFL +)))(SUBCAT NULL)(LAT +)
    (AT +)(FIX SUF)(AFORM NONE)(INFL -)(QUA -)(ADV -)
    (NUM -)(N +)(V +)(BAR -1))
  ENTRY
     (+able "" ((V +)(N +)(NUM -)(ADV -)(QUA -)(INFL -)
                (AFORM NONE)(AT +)(LAT +)(FIX SUF)
                (BAR -1)(SUBCAT NULL)
                (STEM ((V +)(N -)(INFL +)))) ABLE NIL))
```

F Formal Definitions

F.1 Features and categories

Notation: For any set A, by $\mathcal{P}(A)$ we mean the power set of A.

A *feature-system* is a tuple ($Names$, $Values$, $Variables$, $Range$, $Type$) such that:

1. $Names$ is a finite set, the *features*, or *feature names*.
2. $Values$ is a finite set, the (atomic) *feature values*.
3. $Variables$ is a set, possibly infinite, disjoint from $Values$.
4. $Range$ is a function from $Names$ to $\mathcal{P}(Values) \cup \{CAT\}$.
5. $Type$ is a function from $Variables$ to $\mathcal{P}(Values) \cup \{CAT\}$.

where CAT is an item which is not in $Values$ (and which is not a set).

Let F = ($Names$, $Values$, $Variables$, $Range$, $Type$) be a feature-system. The set of *categories based on* F (written $Cat(F)$ for convenience) is the set of all sets C of pairs (f, v) such that:

1. Every $f \in Names$.
2. for every $(f, v) \in C$, *either*
   (a) $v \in Range(f)$, *or*
   (b) $Range(f) = CAT$ and $v \in Cat(F)$, *or*
   (c) $v \in Variables$ and $Range(f) \cap Type(v) \neq \emptyset$.
3. There are no pairs (f, v), $(f, v') \in C$ with $v \neq v'$ (i.e. no feature name occurs more than once).

A category C' is said to be an *extension* of a category C (written "$C \sqsubseteq C'$") iff

1. For every $(f, v) \in C$, there is a pair $(f, v') \in C'$, such that *either*
   (a) $v \in Values$ and $v = v'$, *or*
   (b) $v \in Variables$ and $v' \in Variables$ and $Type(v) \supseteq Type(v')$, *or*
   (c) $v \in Variables$ and $v' \in Type(v)$, *or*

(d) $v \in Variables, Type(v) = CAT$, and $v' \in Cat(F)$, *or*

(e) $v \in Cat(F)$ and v' is an extension of v.

2. If (f_1, v), $(f_2, v) \in C$, and $v \in Variables$, then C' must contain values (f_1, v'), (f_2, v'), for some v'.

It is convenient, for use in defining well-formedness of trees, to generalise this traditional definition to *tuples* of categories:

A tuple of categories $(C'_1, \ldots, C'_n)$ is said to be an *extension* of a tuple of categories $(C_1, \ldots, C_n)$ iff

1. For $1 \leq i \leq n$, $C_i \sqsubseteq C'_i$.
2. If $(f_1, v) \in C_i$, and $(f_2, v) \in C_j$ (for any i, j), and $v \in Variables$, then C'_i, C'_j must contain values (f_1, v'), (f_2, v') respectively, for some v'.

For the purposes of the rest of our formal definitions, we do not need to define "unification", but for completeness it is useful to include the following definition.

The *unification* of two categories C_1 and C_2 (written "$C_1 \sqcup C_2$") is any category C' which meets the following conditions:

1. $C_1 \sqsubseteq C'$.
2. $C_2 \sqsubseteq C'$.
3. If C'' is a category such that $C_1 \sqsubseteq C''$, and $C_2 \sqsubseteq C''$ then $C' \sqsubseteq C''$.

It is also useful to explain the remark made in Chapter 3 about categories being equivalent "up to the renaming of variables". This notion can be made precise in the following way.

Given a feature-system, notated as above, let ϕ be any injection from $Variables$ to $Variables$ such that $Type(\phi(x)) = Type(x)$ for any variable x. Define ϕ_{cat}, *the generalisation of* ϕ *to categories* as follows:

1. If $x \in Variables$, then $\phi_{cat}(x) = \phi(x)$.
2. If $x \in Values$, then $\phi_{cat}(x) = x$.
3. If $x \in Cat(F)$, then $\phi_{cat}(x) = \{(f, \phi_{cat}(v)) \mid (f, v) \in Cat(F)\}$.

Two categories C and C' are defined to be *equivalent*, written "$C \equiv C'$", iff there is an injection $\phi : Variables \rightarrow Variables$ such that $\phi_{cat}(C) = C'$.

The relation "≡" can be shown to be an equivalence relation. Also, the unification of two categories is unique, up to this definition of equivalence.

These definitions are perhaps excessively concrete, and would perhaps be better defined using more abstract notions of "variable" and "subsumption", but at least this presentation connects directly with the implementation.

F.2 Grammars, conventions, and defaults

Let $F = (Names,\ Values,\ Variables,\ Range,\ Type)$ be a feature-system. A *feature-rule* based on F is a n-tuple $(c_0, \ldots, c_n)$ (where $n \geq 1$) where each $c_i \in Cat(F)$. A *feature-grammar* (based on F) is a pair (F, R) where R is a set of feature-rules based on F.

Let $F = (Names,\ Values,\ Variables,\ Range,\ Type)$ be a feature-system. A *local tree condition based on F* is a mapping from $Cat(F)^+$ to $\{0, 1\}$ (i.e. a classification of tuples of categories).

Let $F = (Names,\ Values,\ Variables,\ Range,\ Type)$ be a feature-system. A set of *default definitions for F* is a set D of pairs (f, v) such that:

1. Every $f \in Names$.
2. For every (f, v), *either* $v \in Range(f)$, *or* $Range(f) = CAT$ and $v \in Cat(F)$
3. There are no pairs (f, v), $(f, v') \in D$ with $v \neq v'$ (i.c. no feature-name occurs more than once).

Formally, a set of default definitions is like a category without variables in it, but it would be confusing to define it thus.

Let F be a feature-system, D a set of default definitions for F, and let C, $C' \in Cat(F)$. C' is said to be a *default extension of C using D* iff

1. C' is an extension of C.
2. For every feature-specification $(f, v') \in C'$, either $(f, v) \in C$ (for some value v), or $(f, v') \in D$.

C' is also a *full* default extension of C (using D) if for every $(f, v) \in D$, there is an element $(f, v') \in C'$ (i.e. there are no default definitions unused).

A *word structure grammar* is a tuple $((F, R), S, D, P)$ where (F, R) is a feature-grammar, $S \in Cat(F)$, D is a set of default definitions for F, and P is a set of local tree conditions based on F.

F.3 Trees and well-formedness

We take as basic the notion of a *rooted, ordered, labelled tree.* The *fringe* of a tree is the tuple formed by its terminal nodes in order.

Let $((F, R), S, D, P)$ be a word structure grammar as above. A rooted, ordered tree whose nodes are labelled with elements of $Cat(F)$, is said to be *well-formed with respect to* $((F, R), S, D, P)$ iff for every non-terminal node with label C and daughters $C_1, \ldots, C_n$,

1. There is a rule $(D_0, \ldots, D_n) \in R$ and a category $C_0 \in Cat(F)$ such that $(C_0, \ldots, C_n)$ is an extension of $(D_0, \ldots, D_n)$.
2. For every $p \in P$, $p((C_0, \ldots, C_n)) = 1$.
3. C is a full default extension (using D) of C_0.

With $((F, R), S, D, P)$ as above, a rooted ordered tree T whose nodes are labelled with elements of $Cat(F)$ is said to be *generated by* $((F,R)$, S, D, $P)$ iff T is well-formed with respect to $((F, R), S, D, P)$, *and* the root label of T is an extension of S.

F.4 Two-Level rules

Given any two finite symbolic alphabets, A and A', a *symbol-pair* from A and A' is a pair (a, a') where $a \in A$ and $a' \in A'$. Such symbol-pairs will normally be written as $a : a'$. A *symbol-pair sequence from* A and A' is a sequence (possibly empty) of symbol-pairs from A and A', and a *symbol-pair language over* A *and* A' is a set of symbol-pair sequences (i.e. a subset of $(A \times A')^*$).

Given two alphabets A and A', and a symbol-pair sequence S from A and A', a sequence $(P_1, \ldots, P_n)$ of symbol-pair sequences from A and A' is said to be a *partition* of S iff $S = P_1, \ldots, P_n$ (i.e. the concatenation of the P_i).

Given two symbol sets A and A', a *context-expression from* A *and* A' is a regular expression over $A \times A'$. (That is, a context-expression characterises a regular set of sequences of symbol-pairs.)

Given two alphabets A and A', a *two-level morphological rule* over A and A' consists of a pair (P, C) where P is a symbol-pair from A and A', and C is a non-empty set of pairs (LC, RC) where LC and RC are context-expressions from A and A'. The reason for including a *set* of pairs of contexts, is that we must cater, in the general case, for there being a disjunction of pairs of contexts. In the case where the set is a singleton, this reduces to the simple (non-disjunctive) case.

A context-expression σ is said to *match at the right-end* a symbol-pair sequence S iff there is a partition (P_1, P_2) of S such that P_2 is an element of the set characterised by σ.

A context-expression σ is said to *match at the left-end* a symbol-pair sequence S iff there is a partition (P_1, P_2) of S such that P_1 is an element of the set characterised by σ.

A set R of two-level morphological rules *contextually allows* a symbol-pair sequence S iff, for every partition $(P_1, a : a', P_2)$ of S, *either* there is no rule of the form $(a : a', C) \in R$, *or* there is at least one rule $(a : a', C) \in R$ such that C contains a context pair (LC, RC) such that LC matches P_1 at the right end and RC matches P_2 at the left end.

A two-level morphological rule $R = ((a, a'), C)$ *coercively allows* a symbol-pair sequence S iff for every possible partition $(P_1, b : b', P_2)$ of S and every element $(LC, RC) \in C$ such that LC matches P_1 at the right end, and RC matches P_2 at the left end, if $b = a$, then $b' = a'$.

Given two alphabets A and A', a *two-level morphological grammar* based on A and A' consists of a pair (CR, SC) where CR and SC are finite sets of two level morphological rules over A and A'. The two sets of rules are the Context Restriction and Surface Coercion rules respectively.

A symbol-pair $a : a'$ is said to *occur* in a rule $(b : b', C)$ iff *either* $a : a' = b : b'$ *or* for at least one element (LC, RC) of C, $a : a'$ occurs in at least one of LC and RC. Given a two-level morphological grammar $R = (CR, SC)$, the *set of feasible pairs in* R is the set of symbol-pairs:

$$\{a : a' \mid a : a' \text{ occurs in an element of } CR \cup SC\} \ \cup$$
$$\{a : a \mid a \in A \cap A'\}$$

In an implemented system, the user may be allowed to declare certain pairs as feasible, but at this level of abstraction we do not need to include this in our definition of a two-level morphological grammar, since such an effect could be represented by including rather vacuous context-restriction rules of the form

$(a : b, \{(\epsilon, \epsilon)\})$

where ϵ is the empty regular expression.

F.4.1 Generation

Given a two-level morphological grammar $R = (CR, SC)$, a symbol-pair sequence S is *generated* by R iff all the following hold:

1. All the symbol-pairs in S are feasible pairs in R.
2. Each rule in SC coercively allows S.
3. The set CR of rules contextually allows S.

Suppose we have some symbolic alphabet A. We define the function *delete* from $A \times A^*$ to A^* as follows, where ϵ denotes the empty string and the dot "." indicates concatenation of strings:

$$delete(a, \epsilon) = \epsilon$$
$$delete(a, a.S) = delete(a, S)$$
$$delete(a, b.S) = b.delete(a, S) \text{ for any } b \neq a.$$

The other minor formal definition we need is to allow us to move from equal-length sequences of symbol-pairs to pairs of equal-length symbol-sequences in the obvious way. Suppose S_1 and S_2 are two sequences of symbols, of equal length, with $S_1 = a_1, \ldots, a_n$ and $S_2 = b_1, \ldots, b_n$. Then the *symbol-pair sequence associated with S_1 and S_2* is the sequence

$$a_1 : b_1, \ldots, a_n : b_n$$

We can then define a two-level morphological grammar as *accepting* a pair of strings of equal length, iff their associated symbol-pair sequence is generated by the grammar.

F.4.2 Lexical segmentation

A *lexical segmentation system* consists of a tuple $(AL, AS, 0, L, R)$ where AL is a finite set (the *lexical alphabet*), AS is a finite set (the *surface alphabet*), 0 is a symbol which is not an element of $AL \cup AS$, L is a set (the set of *lexical forms*) of non-null elements of AL^*, and R is a two-level morphological grammar based on $AL \cup \{0\}$ and $AS \cup \{0\}$.

A lexical segmentation system $(AL, AS, 0, L, R)$, *segments* a string $S \in AS^*$ *as* $(l_1, \ldots, l_n)$ where $l_i \in L$ for all i, if there are strings $S_1 \in AL^*$, $S_2 \in AS^*$ such that the following all hold:

1. $delete(0, S_1) = l_1 \, l_2 \ldots l_n$.
2. $delete(0, S_2) = S$.
3. R accepts (S_1, S_2).

F.5 Spelling and word structure

Let $G = ((F, R), S, D, P)$ be a word structure grammar as above. Let $G' = (AL, AS, 0, L, R')$ be a lexical segmentation system, and let Lex be a mapping from L to $\mathcal{P}(Cat(F))$ (i.e. Lex maps each lexical string to a *set* of categories). Then (G, G', Lex) *assigns* string $s \in AS^+$ the category $C \in Cat(F)$ iff

1. There is a rooted ordered tree T labelled with elements of $Cat(F)$ which is well-formed with respect to G, whose root is labelled C, and whose fringe nodes are labelled $(d_1, \ldots, d_n)$.
2. G' segments s as the sequence $(l_1, \ldots, l_n)$.
3. There is a sequence of categories $(c_1, \ldots, c_n)$ such that for $1 \leq i \leq n$, $c_i \in Lex(l_i)$, and d_i is an extension of c_i.

Also, (G, G', Lex) *generates* s iff (G, G', Lex) assigns s a category C such that $S \sqsubseteq C$.

G Complexity of Two-Level Morphology

In Chapter 2, we stated that Barton et al.'s proof of NP-hardness for the transducer representation of two-level rules [Bart87] could be modified to cover the more restricted definition of two-level rules given in Appendix F. Here we sketch that revised version of the complexity proof.

The model we are considering here comprises not only the actual two-level rules, but the mappings between the rules and the surface string and lexical forms, as outlined in Chapter 2. That is, we are not here considering the simple matching of equal length strings (cf. the generative power argument in [Ritc89, Ritc90]) — we are making use of the whole mechanism, although we do not need to use nulls (in these respects, the analysis follows that of Barton et al.). We will not use the set theoretic definitions directly, but will use our Koskenniemi-style notation (see Chapter 2) to present the rules. We shall also make use of variable symbols in rules as an abbreviatory convention (as happens in practical implementations) but the effect of this will be allowed for in the analysis.

Barton's proof consists of showing that, given a formula of propositional logic in conjunctive normal form (CNF), with exactly 3 terms in each conjunct, it is straightforward to devise a representation of this formula, and a two-level grammar and lexicon which together will accept the formula if and only if the formula is satisfiable. That is, he shows that the solution of an arbitrary instance of the 3-SAT problem, [Gare79, pp. 48-50], can be transformed (in polynomial time) into the recognition problem for two-level rules. This reduction of a known NP-complete problem (3-SAT) to the two-level recognition problem shows that two-level recognition is NP-hard; i.e. of a very high (exponential) level of complexity. Barton also observes that the two-level recognition problem is actually NP-complete — that is, a non-deterministic polynomial algorithm does exist — but this is still an undesirably high level of computational complexity.

Suppose we are given an arbitrary propositional logic formula of the sort described above — in conjunctive normal form, with exactly three disjuncts in each conjunct. To transform this into a two-level recognition problem, we require a lexicon which has one entry for each configuration of truth values which could satisfy a disjunction of three literals of propositional logic, phrased as "templates" for such disjunctions, in the sense that the symbols `T` and `F` are written where atomic propositional symbols could occur, optionally preceded by negation signs, and separated by the disjunction symbol `v`. That is, the lexicon contains sequences such as:

```
TvTvT
FvTvT
FvFvT
-Fv-Fv-F
Fv-Fv-F
FvFv-F
```

Since there are four possible values (`T,F,-T, -F`) in each of three positions, there are 64 different combinations, two of which (`F v F v F, -T v -T v -T`) have to be left out as they do not represent overall satisfaction of a disjunction. This part of the lexicon is required no matter what the content of the formula is.

For reasons which will be explained below, we also need to be able to include in each formula a sequence of all the propositional symbols being used, so for each propositional symbol there will be a single entry consisting of that symbol. There will also be an entry for the left-bracket "`[`" and the right-bracket "`]`".

The actual formula to be checked (recognised) will be expressed as a sequence of disjunctions, separated by no punctuation (i.e. the conjunction is implicit). At the front of the formula there will be a sequence of symbols, one for each atomic propositional symbol being used. And finally the whole encoding is enclosed in brackets — "`[`" and "`]`". That is, a formula which might traditionally be written as

```
(x v -y v z) & (w v -z v x) & (-x v y v z)
```

would be expressed as

```
[wxyzxv-yvzwv-zvx-xvyvz]
```

Matching such strings against the lexicon described above entails matching the initial sequence of symbols with the single-symbol lexical entries, and also pairing up atomic symbols with `T` or `F` values, in such a way that an exact match of an individual disjunct corresponds to finding a truth-assignment for the symbols in it which satisfies that disjunct.

We then need to construct two-level rules which will carry out this match and, crucially, ensure that any pairings of propositional symbols to `T` and `F` are consistent throughout the whole formula.

The technique consists of writing a rule which ensures that the *binding* of a variable is consistent throughout the match, the satisfaction of a formula (i.e. that it is true) being dealt with by the fact that the lexicon contains only templates which make conjuncts true.

The following lexical set is needed:

`= is { T, F, -, v }`

and several surface sets:

`= is {-, v, x, y, z,.....}` (i.e. all the atomic propositional symbols, and two connectives)

`NOTX is {-, v, y,z,....}` (i.e. all the symbols except `x`)

`NOTY is {-, v, x,z,....}` (i.e. all the symbols except `y`)

etc. (i.e. one set for the complement of each surface symbol)

For each atomic propositional symbol we need a rule which ensures the consistency of the "binding". If we have three variables `x`, `y`, `z` the required rules would be as follows (where angle brackets enclose sequences of expressions, braces enclose set of a disjunctive alternatives, and * indicates zero or more occurrences of the preceding expression; there is no need to declare any feasible pairs explicitly — all the pairings needed will emerge automatically from the rules):

```
x:x => [:[ --- < y:y z:z ( { T:x =:NOTX } )* ]:] >
    or [:[ --- < y:y z:z ( { F:x =:NOTX } )* ]:] >

y:y => < [:[ x:x > --- < z:z ( { T:y =:NOTY } )* ]:] >
    or < [:[ x:x > --- < z:z ( { F:y =:NOTY } )* ]:] >

z:z => < [:[ x:x y:y > --- < ( { T:z =:NOTZ } )* ]:] >
    or < [:[ x:x y:y > --- < ( { F:z =:NOTZ } )* ]:] >
```

The reason for the brackets is to ensure that the contexts in the rule are forced to match the entire formula; without this portion of the contextual patterns, a match could occur in some local portion of the formula, which would not impose constraints on all the occurrences of a given letter. The above "grammar" also accepts the empty formula, and concatenations of independently satisfiable formulae, but that is not a problem — all that is necessary is that the formula we started with is accepted by the grammar and lexicon if and only if it is satisfiable.

For example the surface representation of a formula:

```
( x v y v -z ) & (x v -y v z)
```

would be

```
[xyzxvyv-zxv-yvz]
```

which would validly match the sequence of lexical forms

```
[
x
y
z
TvFv-F
Tv-FvF
]
```

The real intent of each rule is to impose on the context the constraint that each propositional symbol is paired consistently with a particular truth value; the main symbol-pair in each rule is used just as a convenience. It might seem that it is not essential to have the initial sequence of atomic symbols. The reason for this is that all the rules defining the context of a particular symbol-pair are treated as a disjunction. Hence, if we chose a single symbol-pair (e.g. `[:[`) as the target symbol-pair, it would stipulate that the context for a left-bracket was either that `x` be consistent throughout, or that `y` be consistent throughout, etc. By having a rule for each propositional symbol, the disjunctions range over only the possible values for *other* symbols.

This reduction (from 3-SAT to two-level recognition) is fairly straightforward — the size of the lexicon varies linearly with the number of propositional symbols (though not with the size of the formulae), and for N propositional symbols there is a requirement for N rules, each abbreviating of the order of N rules; that is, there are $O(N^2)$ concrete (unabbreviated) rules. Hence the reduction from 3-SAT is polynomial, as required.

Bibliography

[Aho72] A. Aho and J. Ullman. *The Theory of Parsing, Translation, and Compiling. Volume 1: Parsing.* Prentice-Hall, Englewood Cliffs, NJ, 1972.

[Alle78] M. Allen. *Morphological Investigations.* PhD thesis, University of Connecticut, Storrs, Connecticut, 1978.

[Ande88] S. Anderson. Morphological theory. In F. Newmeyer, editor, *Linguistics: The Cambridge Survey. Vol 1: Linguistic Theory: Foundations*, pages 146–191, Cambridge University Press, 1988.

[Antw90] E.L. Antworth. *PC-KIMMO : a two-level processor for morphological analysis. Occasional Publications in Academic Computing No. 16*, Summer Institute of Linguistics, Dallas, Texas, 1990.

[Aron76] M. Aronoff. *Word Formation in Generative Grammar. Linguistic Inquiry Monograph 1*, MIT Press, Cambridge, Mass., 1976.

[Bart86] E. Barton. Computational complexity in two-level morphology. In *Proceedings of 24th Conference of the Association for Computational Linguistics*, pages 53–59, 1986.

[Bart87] E. Barton, R. Berwick, and E. Ristad. *Computational Complexity and Natural Language.* The MIT Press, 1987.

[Bear85] J. Bear. Interpreting two-level phonological rules directly. 1985. SRI, International, Menlo Park, CA.

[Bear86] J. Bear. A morphological recogniser with syntactic and phonological rules. In *Proceedings of 11th International Conference on Computational Linguistics*, pages 272–276, Bonn, West Germany, 1986.

[Bear88] J. Bear. Morphology with two-level rules and negative rule features. In *Proceedings of 12th International Conference on Computational Linguistics*, pages 28–31, Budapest, Hungary, 1988.

[Beck75] J. Becker. The phrasal lexicon. In R. Schank and B.L. Nash-Webber, editors, *Theoretical Issues in Natural Language Processing*, pages 60–63, Cambridge, Ma., 1975.

[Blac87] A. Black, G. Ritchie, S. Pulman, and G. Russell. Formalisms for morphographemic description. In *Proceedings of 3rd Conference of the European Chapter of the Association for Computational Linguistics*, pages 11–18, 1987.

[Bogu87] B. Boguraev and T. Briscoe. Large lexicons for natural language processing utilising the grammar coding system of LDOCE. *Computational Linguistics*, 13(3-4):203–218, 1987.

[Bors83] R. Borsley. A Welsh agreement process and the status of VP and S. In G. Gazdar, E. Klein, and G. Pullum, editors, *Order, Concord and Constituency*, pages 57–74, Foris Publications, Dordrecht, 1983.

[Bres82] J. Bresnan. The passive in lexical theory. In *The Mental Representation of Grammatical Relations*, pages 3–86, MIT Press, 1982.

[Bris87] T. Briscoe, C. Grover, B. Boguraev, and J. Carroll. A formalism and environment for the development of a large grammar of English. In *Proceedings of 10th International Joint Conference on Artificial Intelligence*, pages 703–708, Milano, Italy, 1987.

[Bund83] A. Bundy. *The Computer Modelling of Mathematical Reasoning.* Academic Press, London, 1983.

[Cahi90a] L. Cahill and G. Gazdar. The semantics of MOLUSC. In *Proceedings of 9th European Conference on Artificial Intelligence*, pages 126–131, Stockholm, 1990.

[Cahi90b] L.J. Cahill. Syllable-based morphology. In *Proceedings of 13th International Conference on Computational Linguistics*, pages 48–53, 1990.

[Cald89] J. Calder. Paradigmatic morphology. In *Proceedings of 4th Conference of European Chapter of the Association for Computational Linguistics*, pages 58–65, Manchester, 1989.

[Cars88] J. Carson. Unification and transduction in computational phonology. In *Proceedings of 12th International Conference on Computational Linguistics*, pages 106–111, 1988.

[Char85] E. Charniak and D. McDermott. *Introduction to Artificial Intelligence.* Addison-Wesley, Reading, Mass., 1985.

[Chom65] N. Chomsky. *Aspects of the Theory of Syntax.* MIT Press, Cambridge, Mass., 1965.

[Chom68] N. Chomsky and M. Halle. *The Sound Pattern of English.* Harper and Row, New York, 1968.

[Chom81] N. Chomsky. *Lectures on Government and Binding.* Foris, Dordrecht, 1981.

[Dalr83] M. Dalrymple, E. Doron, J. Goggin, B. Goodman, and J. McCarthy, editors. *Texas Linguistic Forum 22.* Department of Linguistics, University of Texas, 1983.

[Di S87] A. Di Sciullo and E. Williams. *On the Definition of Word.* MIT Press, Cambridge, Mass., 1987.

[Fabb88] N. Fabb. English suffixation is constrained only by selection restrictions. *Natural Language and Linguistic Theory*, 6(4):527–539, 1988.

[Gare79] M. Garey and D. Johnson. *Computers and Intractability.* Freeman and Co., San Francisco, Ca., 1979.

[Gazd85a] G. Gazdar. Finite state morphology: a review of Koskenniemi (1983). *Linguistics*, 23(4):597–607, 1985.

[Gazd85b] G. Gazdar, E. Klein, G. Pullum, and I. Sag. *Generalized Phrase Structure Grammar.* Blackwell, Oxford, 1985.

[Gazd88] G. Gazdar, G. Pullum, R. Carpenter, E. Klein, T. Hukari, and R. Levine. Category structures. *Computational Linguistics*, 14, 1:1–19, 1988.

[Gazd89] G. Gazdar and R. Evans. Inference in DATR. In *Proceedings of 4th Conference of European Chapter of the Association for Computational Linguistics*, pages 66–71, 1989.

[Gold90] J. Goldsmith. *Autosegmental and Metrical Phonology.* Basil Blackwell Ltd., Oxford, England, 1990.

[Grov89] C. Grover, T. Briscoe, J. Carroll, and B. Boguraev. *The Alvey Natural Language Tools Project Grammar (Second Release).* Technical Report 162, Computing Laboratory, Cambridge University, UK, 1989.

[Hall62] M. Halle. Phonology in a generative grammar. *Word*, 18:54–72, 1962.

[Hopc79] J. Hopcroft and J. Ullman. *Introduction to automata theory, languages, and computation.* Addison-Wesley, Reading, Mass., 1979.

[Isab84] P. Isabelle. Another look at nominal compounds. In *Proceedings of the 10th International Conference on Computational Linguistics/22nd Annual Conference of the Association for Computational Linguistics*, pages 509–516, Stanford University, California, 1984.

[Jack77] R. Jackendoff. *$\bar{X}$ Syntax: A Study in Phrase Structure. Linguistic Inquiry Monograph 2*, MIT Press, 1977.

[Jaeg80] O. Jaeggli. Spanish diminutives. In F. H. Nuessel, Jr., editor, *Contemporary Studies in Romance Languages*, pages 125–148, Indiana University Linguistics Club, Bloomingdale, Indiana, 1980.

[John72] D. Johnson. *Formal Aspects of Phonological Description.* Mouton, The Hague, 1972.

[Kapl88] R. Kaplan. Finite-state transducers. Invited talk, April 1988. Alvey Workshop on Parsing and Pattern Recognition, Oxford.

[Kart83a] L. Karttunen. KIMMO: a general morphological processor. *Texas Linguistics Forum*, 22:165–186, 1983.

[Kart83b] L. Karttunen and K. Wittenburg. A two-level morphological analysis of English. *Texas Linguistics Forum*, 22:217–228, 1983.

[Kart87] L. Karttunen, K. Koskenniemi, and R. Kaplan. A compiler for two-level phonological rules. June 1987. Unpublished, CSLI, Stanford University, Ca.

[Kata88] L. Kataja and K. Koskenniemi. Finite-state description of Semitic morphology: a case-study of ancient Akkadian. In *Proceedings of 12th International Conference on Computational Linguistics*, pages 313–315, 1988.

[Kay84] M. Kay. Functional unification grammar – a formalism for machine translation. In *Proceedings of the 10th International Conference on Computational Linguistics*, pages 75–78, Stanford University, California, 1984.

[Kay85] M. Kay. Parsing in functional unification grammar. In D. Dowty, L. Karttunen, and A Zwicky, editors, *Natural Language Parsing*, pages 251–278, Cambridge University Press, London, 1985.

[Kay87] M. Kay. Nonconcatenative finite-state morphology. In *Proceedings of 3rd Conference of the European Chapter of the Association for Computational Linguistics*, pages 2–10, 1987.

[Knut73] D. Knuth. *The Art of Computer Programming. Volume 3: Sorting and Searching.* Addison-Wesley, Reading, Mass., 1973.

[Kosk83a] K. Koskenniemi. Two-level model for morphological analysis. In *Proceedings of the 8th International Joint Conference on Artificial Intelligence*, pages 683–685, Karlsruhe, 1983.

[Kosk83b] K. Koskenniemi. *Two-level Morphology: a general computational model for word-form recognition and production.* Publication 11, University of Helsinki, Department of General Linguistics, Finland, 1983.

[Kosk84] K. Koskenniemi. A general computational model for word-form recognition and production. In *Proceedings of the 10th International Conference on Computational Linguistics/22nd Annual Conference of the Association for Computational Linguistics*, pages 178–181, Stanford University, California, 1984.

[Kosk85] K. Koskenniemi. Compilation of automata from morphological two-level rules. In *Papers from the Fifth Scandinavian Conference of Computational Linguistics*, pages 143–149, University of Helsinki, Helsinki, December 1985. Publication 15.

[Kosk88] K. Koskenniemi and K. W. Church. Complexity, two-level morphology and Finnish. In *Proceedings of 12th International Conference on Computational Linguistics*, pages 335–340, 1988.

[Lieb80] R. Lieber. *On the Organization of the Lexicon.* PhD thesis, MIT, 1980. (Also published by the Indiana University Linguistics Club, 1981).

[Macl67] S. Maclane and G. Birkhoff. *Algebra.* Macmillan, London, 1967.

[Noor90] G. van Noord. *Morphology in MiMo2.* Working Paper, University of Utrecht, 1990.

[Part90] B.H. Partee, A. ter Meulen, and R.E. Wall. *Mathematical Methods in Linguistics.* Kluwer Academic, Dordrecht, 1990.

[Pere80] F. Pereira and D. H. D. Warren. Definite clause grammars for language analysis – a survey of the formalism and a comparison with augmented transition networks. *Artificial Intelligence*, 13:231–278, 1980.

[Poll87] C. Pollard and I Sag. *Information-based Syntax and Semantics: Volume 1: Fundamentals. CSLI Lecture Notes Number 13*, Center for the Study of Language and Information, 1987.

[Proc78] P. Procter. *Longman Dictionary of Contemporary English.* Longman Group Ltd., Harlow and London, England, 1978.

[Pulman] S. G. Pulman. A computational theory of idioms. In P. Tabossi and C. Cacciari, editors, *On Idioms*, Laurence Erlbaum, New York, forthcoming.

[Reap88] M. Reape and H. Thompson. Parallel intersection and serial composition of finite state transducers. In *Proceedings of 12th International Conference on Computational Linguistics*, pages 535–539, Budapest, Hungary, 1988.

[Ritc85] G. Ritchie. Simulating a Turing machine using functional unification grammar. In T. O'Shea, editor, *Advances in Artificial Intelligence*, pages 285–294, North Holland, 1985.

[Ritc87a] G. Ritchie, A. Black, S. Pulman, and G. Russell. *The Edinburgh/ Cambridge Morphological Analyser and Dictionary System: System Description.* Software Paper 11, Department of Artificial Intelligence, University of Edinburgh, Edinburgh, 1987.

[Ritc87b] G. Ritchie, A. Black, S. Pulman, and G. Russell. *The Edinburgh/ Cambridge Morphological Analyser and Dictionary System: User Manual.* Software Paper 10, Department of Artificial Intelligence, University of Edinburgh, Edinburgh, 1987.

[Ritc87c] G.D. Ritchie, S.G. Pulman, A.W. Black, and G.J. Russell. A computational framework for lexical description. *Computational Linguistics*, 13, 3-4:290–307, 1987.

[Ritc89] G. Ritchie. On the generative power of two-level morphological rules. In *Proceedings of the 4th Conference of the European Chapter of the Association for Computational Linguistics*, pages 51–57, 1989.

[Ritc90] G. Ritchie. *Languages Generated by Two-level Morphological Rules.* Research Paper 496, Department of Artificial Intelligence, University of Edinburgh, 1990. To appear in *Computational Linguistics.*

[Robi65] J. Robinson. A machine oriented logic based on the resolution principle. *Journal of the Association of Computing Machinery*, 12:23–41, 1965.

[Rues89] H. Ruessink. *Two Level Formalisms.* Working Paper 5, Rijksuniversiteit Utrecht, 1989.

[Schu61] M. Schutzenberger. A remark on finite transducers. *Information and Control*, 4:185–196, 1961.

[Seig74] D. Seigel. *Topics in English Morphology.* PhD thesis, MIT, Cambridge, Mass., 1974.

[Selk82] E. Selkirk. *The Syntax of Words.* MIT Press, 1982.

[Shei84] S. Sheiber. The design of a computer language for linguistic information. In *Proceedings of the 10th International Conference on Computational Linguistics/22nd Annual Conference of the Association for Computational Linguistics*, pages 362–366, Stanford University, California, 1984.

[Shie86] S. Shieber. *An Introduction to Unification Approaches to Grammar. CSLI Lecture Notes Number 4*, Center for the Study of Language and Information, 1986.

[Spar84] K. Sparck Jones. So what about parsing compound nouns? In K. Sparck Jones and Y. Wilks, editors, *Automatic Natural Language Parsing*, pages 164–168, Ellis Horwood, 1984.

[Thom84] H. Thompson and G. Ritchie. Implementing natural language parsers. In T. O'Shea and M. Eisenstadt, editors, *Artificial Intelligence: Tools, Techniques and Applications*, chapter 9, pages 245–300, Harper and Row, New York, 1984.

[Thor68] J. Thorne, P. Bratley, and H. Dewar. The syntactic analysis of English by machine. In D. Michie, editor, *Machine Intelligence 3*, pages 281–309, Edinburgh University Press, Edinburgh, 1968.

[Tros90] H. Trost. The application of two level morphology to non-concatenative German morphology. In *Proceedings of 13th International Conference on Computational Linguistics*, pages 371–376, 1990.

[Warn85] A. R. Warner. *The Structuring of the English Auxiliaries: A Phrase Structure Grammar.* Technical Report, Indiana University Linguistics Club, Bloomington, Indiana, 1985.

[Will81] E. Williams. On the notions 'lexically related' and 'head of a word'. *Linguistic Inquiry*, 12:245–274, 1981.

[Wino83] T. Winograd. *Language as a Cognitive Process. Volume 1: Syntax.* Addison-Wesley, Reading, Mass., 1983.

Name Index

Subject Index

D

E

F

O

P

Q

R

S

T

X

Z

The MIT Press, with Peter Denning as general consulting editor, publishes computer science books in the following series:

ACL-MIT Press Series in Natural Language Processing
Aravind K. Joshi, Karen Sparck Jones, and Mark Y. Liberman, editors

ACM Doctoral Dissertation Award and Distinguished Dissertation Series

Artificial Intelligence
Patrick Winston, founding editor
J. Michael Brady, Daniel G. Bobrow, and Randall Davis, editors

Charles Babbage Institute Reprint Series for the History of Computing
Martin Campbell-Kelly, editor

Computer Systems
Herb Schwetman, editor

Explorations with Logo
E. Paul Goldenberg, editor

Foundations of Computing
Michael Garey and Albert Meyer, editors

History of Computing
I. Bernard Cohen and William Aspray, editors

Logic Programming
Ehud Shapiro, editor; Fernando Pereira, Koichi Furukawa, Jean-Louis Lassez, and David H. D. Warren, associate editors

The MIT Press Electrical Engineering and Computer Science Series

Research Monographs in Parallel and Distributed Processing
Christopher Jesshope and David Klappholz, editors

Scientific and Engineering Computation
Janusz Kowalik, editor

Technical Communication and Information Systems
Ed Barrett, editor